THE NATURE OF
INTERNATIONAL SOCIETY

THE NATURE OF INTERNATIONAL SOCIETY

BY
C. A. W. MANNING

*Montague Burton Professor of International Relations
in the University of London*

JOHN WILEY & SONS, INC.
NEW YORK

Copyright © 1962 by C. A. W. Manning

This book was first published in Great Britain for
The London School of Economics and Political
Science (*University of London*)

*Printed in Great Britain by Richard Clay and Company, Ltd.,
Bungay, Suffolk*

To
THE INQUIRING GENERATION
AND
TO THE MEMORY
OF
SIR MONTAGUE
WHO SAW THE NEED

CONTENTS

CHAP.		PAGE
I	Social Maps	1
II	The Nation and the Imagination	11
III	Ploys of the Mind	28
IV	The Projected Pseudo-will	45
V	Phantom Alibi	54
VI	Eiconics and Eirenics	64
VII	Pond-bottom Purview	77
VIII	Conventional 'Convictions'	88
IX	The Mystique of the Law	101
X	Some Moral Niceties	114
XI	Theories and their Uses	128
XII	*Securus Judicat . . . ?*	140
XIII	Sorts of Games	151
XIV	Where, from Here?	165
XV	Influence and Immunity	182
XVI	Social Cosmology—its Problems, Procedures and Place	200
	Index	217

PREFACE

To tell the world about the world. That, the world might suspect, must presumably be the purpose of such a book as this, on such a subject. The very suspicion of it might be enough to repel the serious reader, even if he himself would make no claim to have known it all before. To those with sufficient understanding already of the universal social complex this introductory essay (and that is all it is) can have little to offer.

But among the newer, still inquiring, generation there may perhaps be those who can find in it some food for timely thought. It is for them that, with a blend of arrogance and apprehension, its message is meant.

The apprehension and the arrogance go together. For the topics to be touched upon lie not along the frontiers of knowledge but among the very fundamentals of everyday life. It is not an XYZ book, but an ABC. Who indeed, without an overplus of self-assurance, could license himself for the attempting of such a book? And who, without a shudder of self-distrust, could then present his product to the shrugs or the inattention of the wise and the others who know?

When the new-born duckling discards its shell, it is as with an adult awareness of what water will be like, and aptitudes adequate to its adventurings in the river. With the human infant it is conspicuously different. For meeting the challenge of its environment it begins but imperfectly endowed. Only with experience and education are its insufficiencies abated; and then to no more than a certain extent. Yet man in the Free World is from a fairly early age faced fairly often with issues a proper grasp of which is sensibly to be looked for only in such as have a certain understanding of the field where the issues arise. For such an understanding he may consequently feel the need.

There is a sense in which education is something supplied, by those who have for longer been finding their way around, to assist the explorations of others who have been at it less long.

What to one must come as a discovery may long since have been familiar to another. Some in London, for instance, may have yet to identify the Nelson Column. In doing so, whether independently or with the help of a guide, it is their Topography that they will be improving. And, as there is a local urban, so is there also a global social Topography, in which all may have their gaps to fill. Instruction at school and university might in this regard do more than a little for the maturing individual, though doubtless never enough. And a type of teaching implies a type of relevant reading-matter. Hence these chapters.

A word must yet be said about the proper classing for such a book. It is plainly not History, or Politics, or Law. It is neither conventional Psychology nor standard-pattern Sociology. Not even from the philosophers will it be sure of recognition as coming within their professional purview. Yet there, one must dare submit, is where even so elementary-level a study must, if anywhere, essentially belong. For do not they, the philosophers, concern themselves, characteristically, with the presuppositions, and the place in the master-plan of systematic inquiry, of the various other subjects of sophisticated concern? Are not 'meta-history', for example, and 'meta-linguistics'—to name only two of the type—intrinsically philosophical, rather than restrictively scientific, in their approach? In so far as such subjects as these may be presentable as propaedeutics to the taking up of others whose names we know, it is to them that the new one here developed might claim to be closest akin. But in that case as propaedeutic to what? To International Law? To Government? To Civics? Perhaps it may best be assumed that, while for others too it might aspire to be of value, for the student of the setting in which diplomacy happens it would hope to be accepted as a *sine qua non*. 'Meta-diplomatics', then, this débutant discipline might logically, if with a smile, expect to be called!

An essay, then, for beginners, and for those on whose advice these depend. Yet not, after all, for them alone. Candour compels the admission that there have also been often in mind those sometimes conservative people, the architects of college curricula, without whose endorsement the would-be wise appreciater of the overall social process might never, in a given milieu, with given hurdles ahead, have effectively the opportunity to become a beginner, officially, at all. What in the relevant situations those academic legislators will pertinently consider is whether the subject here in question is either too formidable to be tackled, too trivial to be accommodated, or too simple and self-explanatory to merit recognition, even as an optional 'subsidiary', in the syllabus for a first degree.

C. A. W. M.

CHAPTER I

SOCIAL MAPS

The Universities and the Universe

The earth is large, but it is at the same time small. Seen in relation to the totality of the physical cosmos it is as less than a speck in the sky. But seen as in the proportions of our common day it is the habitat of all mankind. Mankind taken as a whole is a cosmos, a social universe, in itself. And it is into membership of this universal society that every one of us is born.

Like any other living organism, man in growing up needs sufficiently to accommodate himself to his environment as given. To this there are the two aspects, the physical and the social. In so far as he sets out to improve his awareness of his environment he may be said to study cosmology; and, corresponding to the two aspects of it, he thus becomes physically, and socially, cosmology-conscious.

Awareness of the physical cosmos is in some measure fostered by almost any form of education. Who is not taught something about the atom at the one extreme and the nebula at the other? Of the social cosmos, by contrast, less systematic provision has in general been made for rendering the future citizen better aware. Indeed the very suggestion of seeing the social environment in its global dimension as the subject-matter for a kind of cosmology will be a novelty to not a few. Yet that, surely, is just what it is. And, if there is a case for acquainting the young man with the perhaps expanding physical universe on the one hand, there surely is at least a comparable case for helping him to find his bearings in the notoriously contracting social universe on the other. For there are aspects of the social universe which, though obvious when pointed out and important when perceived, may escape the notice even of the generally well-educated man. The acceptance of elementary social cosmology in universities, if not also in schools, might go far toward correcting this traditional state of affairs.

Public World and Private Visions

Viewed successively through red, blue and yellow lenses the same scene will appear respectively green, orange and purple; and within it different objects, and different features of the same objects, will in turn more readily catch the eye. This metaphor of the lenses is helpful in discussion of the social cosmos. For according to the light in which we observe it we may see it as made up of human individuals; of movements, groups, collectivities, organisations and so on; or, of sovereign states.

To say of the average adolescent that he knows less than with advantage he might do of the global milieu within which it is for him to live is not to say that he necessarily knows nothing of it at all. Nobody's mind can ever in this respect have been a *tabula rasa*. Some image of social reality, each his private image of it, every one of us may be assumed to have. One's conception of what, in its social dimension, the world is like and of the processes that take place within it, is a part of one's very personality, a product of one's upbringing and experience and a basis from which in future to move forward toward the enjoyment of a better view. One's picture of the social cosmos can never be re-begun *de novo*. It can only be taken as presently it is, with all its flaws, and modified, broadened, developed perhaps, in the light of new insights and discoveries; but never simply displaced.

And, as one's picture is an ever-changing one, so one's very capacity for appreciating what, stage by stage, one may further come to see is itself likewise subject to change. 'When I was a child, I thought as a child. But now . . .' Not only does each of us, in presence of today's events, reappraise, as if unconsciously, the situation as it stands throughout the planet, but his equipment for the making of his reappraisals may well be better now than formerly, and by tomorrow may well have become better still. To his mental stature it is simply not true to say that man cannot add by taking thought. This is why the study of the social cosmos should presumably be of benefit to almost anyone who is privileged to include it within the pattern of his university programme. For this is one of those matters in which self-help can give quicker results if supplemented by the help of those others who know from their own greater experience something more of what is required.

Let Him that Thinketh he Knoweth . . .!

It has been remarked by Sorel and others that men live on the whole by their illusions. Certain it is that we all of us do have to base our behaviour upon assumptions as to whose validity we can by no means always be sure. We have perforce to rely on our impressions 'as of now', even though in retrospect we can see that some of those on which we similarly relied in the past were mistaken. The best that we can do is to use as we go along whatever opportunities we may be given for rendering our ever-fallible impressions less unrealistic and less irrelevant to our need. When, disembarking with his car, an American in England for the first time proceeds at a good speed to Stratford-on-Avon, he does not rely on instinct only to guide him on his way. The roads are well sign-posted, and he has excellent maps. Almost one might say that he not merely believes, but positively knows, that he is on the right road. But the landscape of life across which man has, as best he can, to find his path is not merely physical. More importantly, of course, for the purpose of our present discussion, that landscape is social also. No equally reliable maps are available of our total social environment.

Give Us the Tool and . . .

Whether we actually think in them or not, words must surely be a great help to all of us in our thinking. It is curious to consider how recently some of our most convenient terms first became available for our use, in getting a purchase, so to say, on our experience. The concept of 'mind' is an interesting example. Nothing seems easier than to credit oneself with a mind. Whether this is simply because we happen to have so handy a word for it one may wonder. It seems doubtful if in Homeric times the Greeks did have a word for it. Very awkward it must then have been, finding utterance for certain ideas, or perhaps even having those ideas at all. Much simpler at any rate now that we do have a word.

Basic to the discussion throughout this essay will be the concept of 'the social cosmos'. To some readers the expression may perhaps be new. The novelty of the term need be no discouragement to those who would like to see it coming into current use. The more we use it the more conscious may we expect to become of that reality to which it refers us. And if it be indeed the case that man's inherited parochialism is now becoming a threat to his very survival, it may be all to the good if he can be furnished with a mental tool wherewith to think more readily in terms of the larger social milieu. The notion of the social cosmos might serve him as such a tool.

Your Own . . . in Fear and Trembling

Looking upward at the night sky, Pascal felt a sense of fear. Equally might Columbus have felt one, when with a chart based so largely upon conjecture, he set forth across the sea. In the exploration of the social cosmos it is open to any one of us to set forth in a coracle of his own. For this he may have been able to equip himself only with a rudimentary map. On this map he will make his corrections as he goes. Whether we call it his 'map', or his 'image', what in his private explorations he has to rely on is something distinctively and personally his own. One man, one social map, one socio-cosmological image.

It is true that in the domain even of physical cosmology, where there commonly are accepted public answers to the questions we would wish to raise, those answers, sponsored not merely by individuals but by the fraternity of science, are never in principle better than tentative. The orthodoxy of today may tomorrow be superseded. In the sphere of social cosmology it is less generally easy to speak of an orthodoxy at all. One might for instance hesitate to say of a given conception of the human psyche that it was orthodox. Still more, of any picture of the cosmos as a whole. Yet even here there are points whose importance lies precisely in their status as orthodox answers, and which it behoves us to notice as such.

The Whereabouts of the Thought-about

There is however this more important further point of difference between the two domains. Though Columbus might have been led to make changes in the position of his imaginary Japan upon his map, this will hardly have affected the position of the actual Japan upon the planet. If however all mankind were one morning to awaken every man with a changed conception of the social cosmos—or even were only one man to do so—the very nature of that cosmos would so have suffered change. Perhaps we ought to say that, along with man's notions of it, the very nature of the social cosmos is changing all the time. For that cosmos has its very being in the fact of being imaged, being conceived of, in the mind and imagination of men.

And now yet a further difference. Though two men's images of the total physical cosmos may differ, that of which they have their images is as objectively 'out there' as is say that particular item within it which we call the Nelson Column. Of the social cosmos, it is not in the same sense easy to speak of its existing, objectively, 'out there'. The social cosmos is indeed, as is its physical counterpart, a 'going concern'. But the going in this case proceeds only partly in the world of tangible reality. Partly also it proceeds in a different world, the world of diplomatic ideas. This latter, the world, shall we say, of 'diplomatics', exists indeed, but only in the same sort of sense as does, in my mind, a 'castle in the air'. That it does so exist in my mind is a matter of fact. But the world of diplomatics is not itself a matter of fact. Like fairyland, it is a mental construct. And what takes place within it does so not in fact but in idea. And it is here, in this world of diplomatics, that there occurs a great part of that going which makes of the social cosmos a going concern.

Outward Acts and Inner Meanings

It is of course useless to imagine that one can confine one's study of any branch of social behaviour solely to matters which can be visually observed. For in the processes of social coexistence there is so much that happens less in fact than in idea. In particular there is the idea of the role. As on the stage a man may be playing Hamlet, this fact being the key to an understanding of what he can be seen to do, so, off the stage, he may be playing probation officer, or referee, or inspector of taxes, or sergeant-at-arms. One man in his time plays many parts. But this he does not merely in successive ages of his earthly existence. He combines many parts at once. My neighbour, besides being merely that, may be also my guide, my philosopher and my friend.

But there is a further point to be made. There are roles, and roles. When President de Gaulle faces an illustrious company in Westminster Hall, he speaks not merely as the spokesman, but as the symbol, almost indeed the living embodiment, of France. Not merely does he speak as in the name of France. France herself, he at least would seem to believe, is speaking through him. For in the realm of diplomatics it is not merely men, even in their roles as rolesmen, that behave. There is a sense in which there occurs also the behaving of countries, that is, of states. Such behaving is not, like that even of the rolesman, real behaviour. Rather is it behaviour by imputation, notional behaviour, and notionally the behaviour of states.

If, never previously having seen a Chinese play, a Westerner, arriving to watch one, comes in halfway through, he is likely to be at several sorts of disadvantage: he may not know the language, he may not know the plot, and he may not even know the conventions of the Chinese theatre. So, though he may be afforded a good view of what is happening in fact, he may have hardly an inkling of what is happening in idea. Even if the spectacle is not completely meaningless to him, his appreciation of the performance can scarcely be that of the connoisseur. And the like might well be similarly true of someone placed in a front-row stall in the theatre of world affairs.

Among people who engage professionally in the analysis of human affairs there are those to whom is nowadays given the designation of behavioural scientists. Of these it may be assumed that many would resist the imputing of behaviour to agents other than physically existent human beings. There is even a behavioural approach to the study of international affairs. That however is not what will be reflected in this book. For it will here be assumed that of significant things that happen some have their deepest importance in their happening not in fact but in idea: and it happens that in idea as distinct from fact states also do behave. Where de Gaulle is perceptibly behaving in fact, France may be behaving in idea.

Not a Case of Either/Or

To think of the social universe as consisting only of men and women, and not of states, would be like thinking of a fleet at sea as simply a lot of sailors behaving—without reference to the performance of the ships. The naval historians will mention the ships by name, as if it were they that were behaving. One might tell them that they shouldn't, but they will!

Is the world then socially multiple or is it socially one? The catch in such a question resides in the disjunctive 'or'. It is the both-and rather than the either-or formulation that, in our answer, we require. For the social universe has its human dimension, wherein, in terms of political organisation, it is a plurality of systems, and it has its diplomatic dimension, wherein, in terms of diplomatic organisation, it is a single system, its units the sovereign states.

To specify all the sorts of relationships obtaining as between the people, the peoples, the interest groups and the other component elements in the social cosmos would be an interminable task. Even on a particular level the relationships may be of many kinds. But, for our present purpose, they would be found to vary in their importance. As, for International Law, it is the legal relationships between sovereign states that chiefly matter, so, from international relationships generally, it is reasonable to distinguish, as international relationships proper, those, of all kinds, obtaining between the sovereign states. Anyone within the cosmos can no doubt communicate, through the post office, with virtually anyone else at any level. But it is relationships between countries, manifested primarily in exchanges between governments, that, when speaking of international difficulties or misunderstandings, we chiefly have in mind. Could men effect a radical improvement in the relationships between states, many desirable things might be added unto them. But one does not affect the position of a shadow by doing things to the shadow. Neither does one affect the attitude of a state simply by addressing arguments to the state. As well might one address arguments to a statue! Only if one's arguments are overheard by human beings can they be expected to produce any effect. The bad relations may exist between the states, but it is between the governments

8   THE NATURE OF INTERNATIONAL SOCIETY

that the dealings occur and it is between the peoples, that is, the people who compose them, that the feelings may be running high. The feelings between the peoples may matter even where between the governments there are no dealings at all.

Peoples, but No Such Persons

Groups as groups do not normally engage in dealings with each other unless so organised as to have their official spokesmen. While the Nicaraguans and the Nepalese could be imagined as intercommunicating at a moment's notice on almost anything whatever, between the peoples of Wales and Scotland there is less manifestly any channel for a getting quickly into touch. Their footballers may meet. Their feelings toward one another may become important. Their beliefs about one another may come to matter. But international relations proper are relations conceived as between persons; and persons, internationally, Wales and Scotland are not. Whereas Nepal and Nicaragua are. And herein lies incidentally the value, for the eventual consolidation into an effective one-ness of the universal human family, of the notion of the state as 'person'.

Two Cheers for the Poet

Such then is the structure of world society. Omar Khayyam, when he sang of 'this sorry scheme of things', did not thereby imply that he would have been happier without one. What he wanted was to mould it nearer to his heart's desire. He did write as thinking in terms of *a* scheme. His emphasis was not it is true upon its diplomatic or international-political, aspects: but it is on these that we shall be putting ours. And we, too, like him, shall perceive that there already exists a scheme, a sorry one perhaps, but given, and a going concern. We might like to re-mould it, but its existence we can scarcely doubt. Yet, while perceiving it as given, we should not mistake its genesis. This scheme was not the work of Nature, or of any other such hypostatised and personified abstraction. It is artificial, man-developed—a 'socio-fact' in the jargon of some. What this generation can hope to affect is not so much the present inherited structure of the given scheme of things, man-created though it be: but, the manner in which the coming generation comes to read, re-interpret, and, in re-interpreting, to re-mould, the scheme. The 'scheme' at any given stage derives its character from that composite prevailing image of it which lives in the collective psyche of the given generation. Were every infant so conditioned as to grow up with a persecution mania, the scheme of things might well be even sorrier than already it is. And conversely, if men all saw their fellow-men only as fellow men, it might well be not so sorry. As the Jesuits would ask for control of the first few years of a person's life, as best enabling them to affect the rest of it, so may we of today think to avail ourselves propitiously today of the formative early years of what in its maturity will be the society of tomorrow.

The Second Best of Six Possible Worlds?

A scheme then there is. Datum number-one is that the social cosmos is organised already to a certain extent: that it is thus in effect a society, of sovereign states, whose dealings are conditioned by received assumptions, received, that is, in the relevant, official milieu; though the layman may never have paused to make them his own. Those received assumptions are datum number-two. The layman's personal interpretation of them will be his private affair. While even of the physical cosmos it is true to say that men construe it differently and that the prevalent interpretation becomes modified with the passing of time, still truer is this of the social cosmos. That then is datum number-three, namely, that the cosmos is composed, *de facto*, of human beings each with his or her private version of the assumptions upon which, as a going concern, the scheme of things is based.

In theory no doubt the global scheme might well have been different. And indeed we may conclude this chapter by suggesting the six most obvious possible formulae for universal co-existence on the planet. First, sheer rudimentary compresence, each man fending for himself in an abstract perfection of freedom (such being the freedom of the jungle). With the absolute freedom goes absolute mutual distrust and absolute fear. Second, ordered freedom, the order provided by a system of world-wide inter-personal relations (the phenomenon known as 'government' being as yet unknown). This is the purely hypothetical condition of a utopia which never was and presumably never will be. Third, freedom relative, or non-existent, but never freedom absolute, in a multi-governmental system of warring states. This is the hypothetical condition of an utterly Hobbesian international anarchy. Fourth, freedom relative or non-existent but never absolute in a world under one world-wide government only. A hypothetical possibility this, which may some day materialise, though of men's liking it when they have it there can of course be no guarantee. Fifth, relative freedom, at best, in a world enjoying a modicum of order through an inherited and ever-developing system of inter-governmental arrangements (this being what now we have). Sixth, and finally, the same, in a world enjoying a greater degree of order through more effectively-functioning inter-governmental arrangements. This last we shall perhaps do well to recognise as what we have to hope, and to work, for, here and now. And, if it is this that we are set on doing, it were well that we should begin by taking more intimate stock of that possibility number-five, the 'here and now' from which we must effect a successful 'take-off' if our attempted flight is not to end up in a swamp.

CHAPTER II

THE NATION AND THE IMAGINATION

In the Beginning the Words

In an essay which is to focus on what is international, early attention will surely be expected to the nature of the nation and of the state—even though, in books which are readily available, much discussion on such matters may already be found. Not all of this has proceeded from the standpoint to be reflected here. And the reader may presently care to consider just why this has been so. Was it because, while it was sometimes with words, and sometimes with ideas, elsewhere it was with realities that a writer will have been mainly concerned?

The reality, that is to say the social reality, 'out there'— which is the subject-matter to be studied—this reality includes numberless individuals nursing the images, experiencing the sentiments, thinking the thoughts, reacting to the symbols, and using the terminology, of nationhood—the words nation, national, nationality, nationalism are among those most constantly employed—and acting from feelings fostered by their thinking on this theme. The prevalence of the relevant ideas, the focus of emotions important for their bearing on behaviour —the mere prevalence, that is, of those ideas, irrespective of their inherent plausibility—will, by the student of the social cosmos, be perceived as a fundamental datum. The facts of modern social co-existence do indeed include, and are conditioned by, these ideas, and the ideas are fostered by the accumulating facts. (Which—the overt behaviour, or the body of ideas—is logically, or psychologically, prior need not be answered here.) As to the nature of the particular idea— of the 'nation'—we can no doubt agree that, rather than asking what in itself is this idea, the correct and up-to-date question, philosophically, is: What, in the relevant contexts, 'language games', 'forms of life', or, simply, fields of social experience, do those best at home in the pertinent conversational *genre* mean, and understand, by such a term as 'nation'? Not, What is the idea?, or even, What is the thing denoted?, but, What is *meant* by the term?

Words and Things—

In case the reader feels uncertainty on the point, some further explanation may be helpful. Let him dwell on the evident fact that, when given a word to define, the nature of our task is not always the same. For there are several sorts of definition, and different sorts of it are right for different words. What, for example, is a triangle? What is a bicycle? What a biped? What a sycophant? What an elephant? What an oracle? What a miracle? What a mirage? What a garage? Though similar in their form, by no means all of these questions are similar in kind.

Sometimes one is being asked to give the 'essence' of a species of thing. We may for instance know a mirage when we see one, and yet have no idea at all of what it is. Or again we may know just what an elephant is, yet not know wherein its 'elephant-ness' consists. We may not even know whether the question need have any answer, or whether, if it have one, this should reflect a truth as to the nature of things (in this case, elephants) or merely a convention on the use of a word.

and Something Further

For inland revenue purposes there might well be debate over what amounted to a garage, but scarcely about what conventionally was meant by the term. What constitutes aggression, or collusion, or subversion, may seem to be a question of conventional usage. Yet there may or may not in such cases be a settled convention to which to point. Indeed there is here a whole spectrum of possibilities, at one end of which we find what is termed the 'term of art'. We are asked, for instance, What is a 'negotiable instrument'? Here there is a correct conventional answer, whether we know it or not. Short of that, we may get a term of which the sense may be unambiguous but which different people differently apply. What is a lethal instrument? (What, in certain sorts of hands, is not?) At the other extreme, we get questions to which our only answer will

be an attempt to decide and express what precisely we ourselves
understand by a term—in the expectation perhaps that others
will concede that we are right. What, for instance, is justice,
what peace, what peaceful change? Not of every such term
will there clearly exist a common acceptation. What is
democracy? You think you know. I think I.

Notions and Elucidations

'Inside our heads' are ideas—such as those of human brotherhood, of the millennium, of social justice, of the Devil. To any
of these we may suppose there to correspond a reality, 'out
there'. We may suppose it, but can we be sure? If therefore
we are asked to discourse upon 'good' cooking, or good education, or good government, we may be wise not to pontificate,
but rather to invite our hearers to admit that we at any rate
have focused faithfully, and illuminated, the issues that seem
chiefly to arise. We may submit, but we had better not claim
to have shown, nor shall we simply assert, that things must be
as to us they have seemed. The elucidating of concepts should
in principle be a useful enterprise, if unemotionally attempted—
but a given attempt, with a given concept, may not after all
prove helpful to everyone, or even to anyone at all. The proof,
so to speak, of the clarifying is in the clarification. And if the
analysis carries no conviction, there may, in the circumstances,
be little more that one can do.

A Sort of Social Whole

Meanwhile, what we here were proposing first to elucidate
was the concept, or the notion, of the nation. How are we to
characterise this prevalent idea? It is, is it not, the notion of a
certain sort of social whole? It is the notion of something
participated in, and belonged to. The nation is a social whole.
And, as determining just what sort of a social whole: What is it,
we may be moved to ask, that, typically, the members of a
nation will be found to have in common?

Teams and Teams

These same eleven men who yesterday were a football side
may today be a team for playing cricket. Today, as yesterday,
their behaviour is intelligible in the light of the knowledge that

they see, conceive, understand themselves as a team, and, all acting accordingly, understand one another and function together, as together composing a team. Only, today theirs is a different behaviour.

Just as so many men may figure, and function, together as a team, so in principle may so many millions feel, and figure, and function, together as a nation. What, in those conditions, did we mean by a team? What, in these other conditions, do we mean by a nation? The team was no mere plurality of persons: it was a plurality cohering in terms of, and by virtue of, certain assumptions. In particular, its 'team-ness' presupposed a possible participation in a game. Now it is in like manner that the 'nation-ness' of the modern nation presupposes a participation in the life of the modern world. The social universe as we have it is such that, within it, a multiplicity of persons may be associated as members of a nation, seeing, conceiving, understanding themselves as such, and acting accordingly. The social universe ... such ... Something evidently depends on that. Save within a picture of the modern world, a picture of the modern nation can hardly be presented.

But, given our social universe as the going concern which it is, it is, conversely, as little intelligible without access to the notion of the nation as is cricket without access to the notion of a team. It is in teams that men indulge in cricket, and in nations that they participate in the politics of the world. And to define a nation otherwise than in terms of men's idea of it would be as difficult as in a corresponding manner to define a team. In these cases the idea, in the relevant heads, is crucial: whereas, by contrast, a constellation, for instance, may be defined without any reference whatever to what the component stars may be supposed to understand by a constellation: and even a swarm without reference to what the individual bees may understand by a swarm.

The Function of the Idea

We might go even further. We might observe that to say: There goes a team, is at most a kind of shorthand way of describing with what ideas and purposes in their heads certain men are proceeding as they do. What else, comparably, does the fact of nationhood boil down to than the compresence of (*a*) the idea of the nation-ness of a given postulated-as-existent nation, and (*b*) the consequences, in the world of overt behaviour, of the prevalence, in certain minds, of that idea?

That such questions should be conclusively answered is less important than that, with a sense of their pertinence, they should have been put. Life will go on, even though they receive no answer: but the individual, for having faced them, should be the better in a position to understand the life that so goes on. Let not the reader be upset by what may seem like a suggestion that the nation is perhaps not exactly the same sort of thing as he took it to be. Life, he may rest assured, will go on as before. And the way of its going will remain a reality: even as people go on thinking and talking in terms of the sun's rising in the morning. Like the sunrise, the nation is something the reality of which we tend, as if naturally, to assume. Indeed our impression, until we think about it, is that the nation is real.

This may be conveyed in a different way: by recourse, namely, to the expression 'in effect'. We say, for instance, of some exciting occasion, that it is 'all over bar the shouting'. It is not in fact all over, since in form it is still going on; but it is, to all intents and purposes, already over. Indeed, it is 'virtually' all over. It is really as if it were indeed all over. In short, it is all over 'in effect'. And so with the reality—that is, the quasi-reality—of the nation. In effect, whether or not in fact, the nation is real.

In effect, it is possible, for the social or diplomatic observer, to say, There goes—there goes to war—a nation.

For it is in the context of social and diplomatic thinking that the notion of the nation has its pivotal place. How far could a discussion proceed, in terms of either of these modes of thinking, without involving this idea? As well might geometrical discussion be attempted without reference to the line. There is a universe of thought and discourse which requires the idea of the line. The like is true of the nation. The political theorist's nation is every bit as real as the geometer's line: or the player's team.

The nation, then, is a sort of social whole. In this it resembles the tribe. And likewise the association. For the association, also, is a social whole. But of a different sort. For whereas, typically and in principle, it should be possible to say, of an association, what it is *for*, the nation, by contrast, and *pace* Aristotle, is less essentially, if indeed at all, the expression of a purpose. And again, an association is essentially a many, performing for pertinent purposes as a one. A nation is, by contrast, a one, reducible to a many: for what gives the nation its unity, socially, is its unity notionally. In the association's case the kernel of the matter is the prevalence of a sense of the need, for a specific purpose, to associate. With the nation, it is the prevalence of the image of the nation as such, linked with the notion of it, both of these being evoked by the name, and other symbols, of the nation. And curiously, it is the name and other symbols that sustain the continuity of that of which the image and the notion are prone to change. For, looked at from the viewpoint of the individual member, the nation appears differently from time to time: according, for instance, as his lenses are for the moment those of self-interest, of sentiment, of sociology, or of poetic awareness. And the given nation may equally be viewed through a variety of lenses from outside.

The 'in-fact' and the 'in-effect'

Qua social whole, the nation does no doubt exist in fact, just as, where play is in progress, the teams do exist. But whether either the team or the nation could exist in fact did it not also exist in idea: this one may doubt. For what gives it its possibility of existing in fact is, precisely, it would seem, its existence in idea. What gives it its actual existence is the attitudes and behaviour of enough of those belonging to it. And that behaviour is reflective of their feelings in relation to their image, and to their notion, of the nation. As is their image, such are their feelings, their responses and their behaviour. If it be asked: In what sense does the nation, *qua* unitary, really exist, an answer is that at least it really does in effect exist. In that sense at least it really does. And this after all is also really the case with much else that we have to reckon with in our social experience. What most commonly counts in the social universe is not simply whether something has existence in fact, but whether it has existence in effect. And in effect at least the team is real, the tribe is real and the nation is real. Did the image of the team not exist, the position would be otherwise. But exist it does—the image of the team—as does the image of the tribe, and of the nation.

The Status-sharers

What, then, in these circumstances, have the members of a nation in common? From the lines along which this tantalising question is often approached, one might suppose there must presumably be some factor—such as language, biological origin or religious adherence—which the members of a nation might in principle be expected to share. What however was it that the members of a team had in common? Simply the fact, was it not, of having been included, as its members, in the team. Need two Britons in fact have more in common than the fact of being Britons? Given the postulated existence of a British nation, with the attendant possibility, for individuals, of being members of it, the question is, Who is regarded as such? Regarded. That is just the word. For membership is a matter not of physical fact, but of regardedness—that is, of status, and status is imputed as existent not in terms of fact alone, but of fact as seen in terms of relevant theory. What constitutes membership? is a way of asking: What, in the theory of the matter, constitutes membership? What, that is, in the sight of the relevant theory, *is* membership? And, when given, by what criteria may membership be known? It is not merely punning to reply that the membership is something 'given'.

Suppose there to be created, by the act of its intending members, an Order of the Disciples of the Devil. What now will constitute such discipleship? The answer can only be looked for in the theory of the game—the game begun by someone's having said, Let's play Devil's disciples! Will it in such case matter whether the Devil do indeed exist, and whether therefore he can indeed have any actual disciples at all? Actual discipleship of the Devil is not being guaranteed: only a status is being established. Likewise, membership of a nation is in the last analysis submittedly a matter not so much of fact as of status. For the fact of such membership is the fact of having that status.

That Which Unites

The unity of the nation, whence then comes it? Whence, by the same or a similar token, comes the unity of a flock of sheep? Or of a constellation in the sky? Or of the class of blue-eyed babies? The unity is in each case in some sense a function of the way those things are thought of, the way they are seen. Beauty, someone said, is in the eye of the beholder. Be that as it may as touching beauty, when it is said of the unity of a social aggregate there is a sense in which it is importantly true. To see the flock now as many, now as one, is to appreciate the degree in which our world depends on us. It is to view the sheep through alternative lenses.

What was it, for instance, that the stars of our constellation had in common? Little, surely, beyond their amenability to being seen and conceived of as one? And it is this their amenability, along with our exploiting of it, that results in our imputing to the constellation, as a whole, of a reality and a unity which, when we reflect, we must see it to possess not objectively by nature, but merely by imputation.

The Great Bear remains a constellation whether the stars composing it are conscious of it or not. And a 'class' of blue-eyed babies could be, statistically, a class though its members were wholly lacking in any sense of class. But could a nation exist as a nation had its members no sense of its existence? Surely no more than could a *social* class. This element of consciousness seems, in matters social, to be of the very essence of this matter. Without the notion of nationhood, influential in the appropriate minds, the fact of nationhood could hardly occur. Neither, presumably, without the notion of class, could there occur social, as opposed to mere statistical, class.

Social Prevalence

If at this point it be asked in terms of what species of idea the nation, as thus existing in idea, so exists, we shall answer, the nation exists in social theory, socially prevalent. 'Social', as relating to society; and 'socially prevalent', as being sufficiently prevalent to constitute a fact of social life.

So, given the conditions described, the nation is indeed a reality—not by imputation only but submittedly also in fact.

For there does in truth exist the plurality of persons, having prevalent among them the ways of thinking, conceiving, feeling and imagining here germane. While therefore the nation and the constellation are in some respects alike, in this respect they differ. Both may be thought of as in a certain sense existent only in idea. But in the constellation's case the relevant idea had its residence in the mind of the onlooker only.

In common with the constellation it is basically by imputation that the nation has its being as a unit. But in the nation's case the imputing is performed not by onlookers only but prevalently also among those human units, themselves sufficiently real, that make it up.

Given its imputed reality, the social group is able to figure as such—in the imagination as well of others as of those, or enough of them, who compose it. And there are several sorts of group-ness. One sort is nation-ness, or nationhood. It comes of the imputing not of group-ness merely, but of that particular kind of group-ness which differentiates the nation. It comes of the prevalence, in the appropriate minds, of the appropriate image, the image not simply of a social aggregate, but of a 'body', a mystical body, and one of that particular kind which is known, and belonged to, as a nation. In like manner comes team-ness of the entertaining of the image of a team.

The notion of nationhood in general: the notion, that is, that there are indeed such 'things' as nations—along with the image of the given particular nation, and with the notion of its nationhood—these, suitably and sufficiently prevalent, and not any putative community of blood or language or religion, are all that the effective existence of a nation might seem to presuppose. Not, then, necessarily a community, actual or supposed, of blood or religion or language; for, given the social prevalence of the notion of nationhood, and the presence, in the world, of examples of the phenomenon to which it refers, the conditions for the acquiring of individual membership of any given nation can be just what legally or otherwise they may. In this respect there is thus indeed an analogy—if a loose one—between the admitting of new members into a nation and the including of new players in a team.

So much, then, at this point, for the nation. Let the reader, if he finds the discussion unconvincing, take time to consider just why. And let him incidentally perceive for himself how far it has, alas, proceeded in terms just of bald assertion and how far of exploratory surmise: and how far it has been a discussion respectively of words, of ideas, and of things.

The Question of Race

And what now, by comparison, of race? Is the race any more, or any less, of a reality, any less something given—objectively 'out there'—than is the nation? And, if equally real, is it such with equal reason, to equal purpose, in equal degree? Is it, for example, as real as is the nation in socially prevalent social theory? No: not, surely, in equal degree? And not for every purpose for which the nation is, theoretically, real. Meanwhile, however, like the nation, the race may be regarded, independently, from more angles than one. At any rate from two. As onlookers at life we may find it almost as easy to think —unthinkingly—of humanity as being divided into races as into nations. And, secondly, the individual may almost equally, though doubtless not as prevalently, feel a solidarity, even a kinship, with those that he thinks of as his fellow-members of a race. What makes the difference in the case of the nation is not that basically it rests on anything more objective than an idea: but that, in socially prevalent social theory as well as in social practice, there is so strong a tendency for the idea of the nation to be linked with the idea of the state. Racial self-determination is not after all a familiar principle. Whereas national self-determination is.

Race sentiment, race feeling, race prejudice, the idea of race —these are indeed among the facts of present-day life. Racial solidarity is no doubt, as a rule, rather more of a theoretical possibility than a fact. Though there is in principle no more reason why the negroes of the world should not—any more than should the workers of the world—respond, as one man, to a summons to unite—organising for the concerted exercise of their massed political strength—yet, even in an era of Afro-Asian assemblies and anti-colonialist fronts, such a consummation seems still rather far away.

Meanwhile the practice of organising, when appropriate, for the concerted exercise of their combined political strength is in the social thinking socially prevalent among the fellow-members of a nation seen as virtually a matter of routine. What in principle is the state, as we nowadays know it, but the machinery whereby the members of a nation—for the fostering and the safeguarding of interests which, as being the fellow-members of the given nation, they conceive themselves to have in common —play in with the expectations of the modern world?

We thus see that, whether race be biologically a reality or not, there does indeed obtain the *idea* of the race: and, whether understandably or not, there exists the idea of the nation—as well as behaviour informed by that idea.

The Postulated Presence

And what now finally shall we say of the state?

So familiar indeed is the associating of the nation with the state, so linked in common thinking are the two ideas, that it is not surprising that in unsophisticated minds they should sometimes be conceived as interchangeable. How often will one not indeed find a state referred to as a kind of group. An association, it is sometimes even said to be, of fellow-citizens.

And yet how questionable this conception is! For one thing, though in some sense the nation exists only in men's mental pictures, in another, very effective, sense, it exists 'out there', consisting as it does of real people, having the pertinent nationality in the eye of the law; whereas the state—the state of which the 'national' is a citizen—what else is it at bottom but an abstraction, not by, but in the name of, which, he is told what to do and where to go. The apparatus of government he so to speak can see. And the processes of government he can observe as they proceed. And all are more or less related together as if integral parts of a single concern. But is the machinery of government, considered as a single whole, what we do precisely mean by 'the state'? Or is it not, considered as a whole, merely the state machine? Surely it is at least possible, and perhaps rather common, to think of the state as standing above and behind its machinery, a reified abstraction, the repository of that authority in reliance on which the processes of government are carried on. In the sight of socially prevalent social thinking, the machinery of government is, submittedly, not itself the state, but rather the paraphernalia established for exercising governmental functions in the service of the state. Scrap the machinery and do you *eo ipso* scrap the state? Or might there not tomorrow, for the needs of the same, persisting, state, be established new machinery?

The same, persisting, state! What, on these assumptions, is it that persists? To say of a state that it persists is not to say that it persists as does a nation. In order to persist as does a nation it is not sufficient merely to persist in social theory. For as composed of flesh and blood the nation is physically, factually, there. And what is given in social theory is not *eo ipso* given in fact. Whereas, in the case of the state, the notion of the state, the state as given in social theory, is all that we have—even though its nature is conceived of, in social thinking, as if not notional but real. However real your reified abstraction may in theory become, notional at best, if it be but an abstraction, it must in fact remain. So, while the nation as composed of flesh and blood is in reality a reality, the state, as distinct from its machinery, from its citizenry, and from its territory, is a reality only in idea.

From its citizenry—yes. The state, it was contended above, is not itself a social whole. Its image, from the viewpoint of the citizen, is not the image of himself and his like, but of an institutional structure, an organisational set-up, or even, to borrow an unbeautiful term, an *apparat*. Whenever, in living together, men develop processes whose logic depends on the positing of that to which there may be imputed interests, attitudes and activities distinct from those of human persons, this same is true. Whereas the nation is indeed a social whole, the state is a social set-up.

Set-up of Set-ups

As it happens, there exist in the world a very galaxy of such social set-ups, having relations *inter se*. These relationships are made intelligible only by the imputing to the set-ups of what in fact they cannot have, but only can have in effect—the quality, namely, of being persons. Inter-state relationships are intelligible as being, conceivedly, the relations between persons. In effect, it is persons that they are—their personality being theirs not by nature but by imputation. And let us remember that what may especially matter, socially, is how things are in effect. In effect, the state is a person, having selfhood and so much that goes therewith—the possibility, for instance, of self-assertion, self-administration, self-frustration, self-worship, self-control. Self-control through self-organisation.

In matters, however, of social organisation, there are different degrees of intensity. For a group merely to have a leader, perhaps also a deputy leader, and roles assigned to the various classes of its members, is hardly yet to have a bureaucratic set-up. But organisation can involve the bureaucratic set-up too. In that event it may, as we saw, be helpful to distinguish between the group as so organised and the machinery which it so employs. While a trade union may have a mere minimum of machinery, a Church may have much. And a bank simply has to: indeed a bank *is* mainly its machinery. A university, again, is both of these at once—a community, that is, and also a machine. And the state? Seldom is it appropriate to equate the state with its citizenry: for these are better referred to as the 'people'. The state, as distinct from the people, is the mechanism, the organisational set-up, the instrumentality, by means of which the people's interests are sought to be served. It is a set-up conceived as a unit; its unity being that of the abstraction behind, as it were, and underlying, as it were, the system of its administrative machine. Basically, then, the state is simply an idea in men's minds, which they entertain as of a thing 'out there'.

Imputed Thing-ness

Reified abstractions, conceived of as 'out there'. An adjective with which conveniently to characterise such entities and to mark them off from those having an existence independent of our imaginations is 'notional'. The soil is real, the people also, their relationships too. But, like a Church, or a university, or a bank, the state is, from many important points of view, rather notional than real. And the notion that we have of it is the notion of a set-up. Not, that is, or at any rate not simply, that of a group. The practice of reifying abstractions is after all ancient and common enough. And in prevalent social thinking it is prevalent indeed.

Law, Logic and Psychology

Imagine there being formed an alliance between the Big Five banks. It is the bankers, not the banks—the men, not the institutions—that will have negotiated the deal. But what results from it will be a relationship not between the men, but between the banks as such. This, in the sight not of the law only, but of men and of society. In legal parlance, yes: but in common parlance also. In legal perhaps even *because* in common parlance.

Even before trade unions existed, as persons, in the contemplation of the law, they functioned, as persons, in the sight, and in the idiom, of common, popular, prevalent, usage. Collective beings are felt and experienced by men in society, and so by society (itself such a collective being), as persons.

And the law's way of thinking in this matter merely follows the generally accepted way of thinking. No need to speak of a *persona ficta*. No need to suppose that anyone, ever, actually came out with a 'Let's pretend . . .'. The pretending in such cases is, typically, as much of a 'myth' as is that original contract whereby men have been thought of as first having come together in society. This is, after all, only one instance of the pervasiveness, throughout men's social arrangements, of the influence of myth. Yes, it is the psychologists who may be invited to explain. The anthropologist has merely to note, and report, the pervasiveness.

A Subtlety of Adverbs

As in common, no less than in legal, parlance, the alliance obtains not between the bankers who brought it about but between the banks, so, in common and in legal parlance, an alliance made by statesmen obtains not between the statesmen, but between their countries. In common, and in legal, parlance, and also in the parlance of diplomacy. In the relevant variety, the 'diplomatic' variety, that is, of official thinking. In the orthodoxy, indeed, of the matter. And we need not suppose it actually to have all begun with someone's saying 'Let's pretend . . .'. Factually, the countries may seem to be geographical units and nothing more. But legally they are persons. Legally. In legal idea. And how comes it? Is it not because they are persons popularly, in ordinary, everyday, sentimental, poetical and human, idea? Ideally, shall we say? Conceptually? Or, again the useful word, notionally? Notionally the countries do exist as persons—as do the banks, the world, fate, the weather, and who knows what? For such, in the world of ideas, the fairy-land of our communal imagining, is what they are. Persons, not in fact, but as conceived of. Notional persons: let us leave it—but also let us retain it—at that.

What Explanation is Impertinent?

That the banks and the trade unions and the countries and the West and the World are popularly conceived of as if persons—this we can admit is a fact. But that persons they actually are—that we cannot admit. Conceptually, yes. Factually, no. Conceptually, the stars of the Great Bear are components in a constellation. They are seen and conceived of as such. But in fact they have no more in common than have any other selection of separate stars. It is in our imagination and in the world of fiction that we accompany Sherlock Holmes on his inquiries. It is by contrast *de facto* in the world of fact that we live our daily lives, even though, psychologically, it is in the world of our concepts that we live them, in the world that is, as we conceive it. But explanations in terms of fact for how things are in terms merely of conception—of prevalent, popular, social, communal, public, conception—explanations, that is, of how they *are*, as distinct from how historically and psychologically they came so to be conceived of—for such explanations we may expect to seek in vain. Accounting for a belief is not the same as proving the existence of the thing believed in.

Of how the sun contrives to be such an early riser there can after all be never a true explanation. For explanations are appropriate only of what happens in fact. What time does the sun arise—on a particular morning? To that question we can give no answer. All we can give is the time at which at any given point on the planet the sun seems to arise. And even this seeming is found to vary from point to point. The proper question to be asking in the presence of certain sorts of puzzle is: Are we asking a proper question?

There is doubtless a merely notional component in the

conception that any one of us may have about almost any event whatever. But there is a difference between the mere adulterating of fact by fantasy, and the treating of what is pure fantasy as if it were pure fact. It is the difference between a subjective account of an actual happening, and an account, however exact, of what has happened in a dream. To treat the subjective account as objective is not the same thing as treating the dream as fact.

The Gift of Personality

Let psychologists say, if they can, why it is that, whatever happens to them, men so commonly tend to ascribe it to some human, or quasi-human, agency. Happy he, wrote someone, who has been able to ascertain the causes of things. Happier still, don't you think, if he has found whom to praise or blame, and hold responsible, for them. Anyhow, happiness apart, man does tend to ascribe things to a 'will', or does so when he has such a word for it. And psychologists may at the same time explain why we so easily accept the metaphor of imputed 'personality'—personality attributed, for instance, to a place or institution, or, especially, to a collectivity. Let Europe arise, to do this or that. Dear London, welcoming me back. It is a graceful usage, neither novel nor unfamiliar. And if we do not personify, then we 'hypostatise', and we 'reify', at least.

What do we *not* hypostatise? The elimination of mosquitoes is in principle a concrete task. By contrast, the stamping out of malaria is not strictly a task at all. At most it is a result, the result perhaps of the elimination of mosquitoes. Though malaria is not a removable substance, usage does rather suggest that that is virtually what it is. The metaphor seems hardly to be a metaphor at all. Almost it is as though malaria were indeed a substance—if only in theory. And what is not possible, in theory? Legal theory, social theory, diplomatic theory—these all may hypostatise, and reify, and personify—to any congenial extent: and that they do. Social cosmology, by contrast, will be concerned to detect and expose, rather than itself to practise, such manoeuvres of the mind. This therefore is why it may applaud our reducing of the state from a thing that people encounter to an idea they entertain.

A World of Dreams?

But socially prevalent social thinking is familiar not only with the state, but with that still more abstract—since it is doubly abstract—abstraction, the society of states. Though we may refer to it as the 'family' of nations, it is of the 'society' of states, of sovereign states, that we are thinking when we turn to the problems of the state in its relationships with other states. And the question which suggests itself is this: Assuming, if we must, that for the purpose of internal domestic social thinking the state, though theoretically a reality, is in reality no more than an idea—what now is its status in the context of its inter-relatedness with other states? Can what when at home is no more than a notion become a reality when it goes abroad? The question may look tricky, but it is really not so tricky as it looks. And this is because of the fundamental difference between milieu number-one, the domestic, and milieu number-two, the international. It is as the difference between the wideawake world and the world of dreams. Or between the world of fact and the world of fiction. Or the world of life and the world of law. For it is the difference between the world of living men, observable with the eye, and the world of sovereign states, present only to the mind. It is, in short, the difference between the real, and a notional, world. And, in a notional world, what more natural than that the beings who compose it should be notional also? The sovereign states—and it is of sovereign states that the international society is composed—are, *par excellence*, notional beings. And, just as it is in the name of that notional being, the state, that government is domestically conducted, so in the name of those notional beings, the members of the international society, the society of states, do the processes of diplomacy keep proceeding on their artificial way.

It is not in fact a world of dreams. But it is indeed a world of notions. And it is because men take so readily to living in terms of notions that they can—as indeed they so evidently can—be so apparently at home in such a world.

CHAPTER III

PLOYS OF THE MIND

The Freedom of the Imagination

Human beings have an evident propensity, and certainly a remarkable capacity, for conceiving things otherwise than as factually they are. As an example of this there springs to the mind the little girl with a doll. We know it, and she surely also knows it, for the bundle of rags that in fact it is. Yet her treatment of it is not just an exercise in conscious make-believe. If playing is a matter of pretending things, then she is not merely playing with her doll. There is a factor more aptly referred to as fantasy than as play, a matter of feeling and 'imaging' things rather than of doing things. It would seem in short that the interpretation put by the child on the situation in which she finds herself is the resultant of an interplay between two analytically independent elements: the evidence of her eyes, and the promptings of her instincts. 'Throwing herself', as we might say, into her part as mother, she both knows and discounts the truth of the matter, namely, that she indeed is deliberately throwing herself into a part. One has only to reflect upon the ever-fluid, non-logical and composite character of one's internal vision of any emotionally potent facet of reality on which one permits one's mind unhurriedly to dwell, to acknowledge that if one's rambling thoughts remain at all attached to the relatively unchanging 'given', it is only by a very elastic string. Though it may well be that Freud's analysis of our thinking in terms of the dichotomy pleasure principle-reality principle should be accepted only for what it is worth as the oversimplification that it rather obviously is, this analysis does at least serve to remind us that it is not by the reality principle only that we naturally tend to be guided in our conceiving of the real. We do indeed have a remarkable capacity for conceiving things otherwise than as to our knowledge they undoubtedly are.

Why does the child hang up his Xmas stocking? Because he thinks Santa Claus is coming? Possibly—but not necessarily. Why then? Because in the official theory of the occasion Santa Claus is *supposed* to be coming. Factually he is perhaps not even expected. But notionally.

Or take the gracious practice of deeming honourable, in some unspecified sense, anybody who by whatever lawful means has found his way into Parliament: do we not esteem and trust him just a little bit more than we otherwise might do? In the theory of the parliamentary process, the players in the game are all of them as by definition honourable members. (It is tempting to believe that the knowledge of this may in some degree condition their comportment in the House.)

A possibly more apposite example of the dualism that can mark our appreciation of things is to be found in the daylight-saving fiction. By the stratagem of re-numbering the hours, we make it easier for ourselves to get up early. We both know and in effect forget that midday is not actually with us until an hour after our conventional noon. For we both remember and half-forget that it is by British summer time that we are proceeding and not by the 'true' time of the sun. Indeed we are probably all a bit dualistic in our understanding of much that we experience. At the theatre we are just as conscious of the presence before us of Sir Laurence Olivier as we are of the Hamlet whose role he is enacting. We similarly both assume and see through the imputed personality of the body corporate. And do we not all of us know how naturally it comes to the patriot to speak of his 'mother' country, or his 'father' land?

Eggs that Pass—in the Mind

Again there is conjuring. What a fascination it can have! Is it merely in its challenge to our astuteness in the detection of a trick? May it not be partly that there seems to be some plausibility in the performer's claim to have magical powers? In the theory of the conjurer's display, the moment when he makes a certain movement with his wand is the moment when the egg moves invisibly out of the hat on his right and into the hat on his left. This, the official theory of the matter, we very well know not to be true. Would we accept a bet at even a

30 THE NATURE OF INTERNATIONAL SOCIETY

thousand to one against its being proved to be true? Of course we would not. Yet, until we have fathomed the mystery we do, presumably, in a sense concede, or half-concede, the claim. There is an imagined, an imaginary, passing of the egg—a passing known to be non-factual, but conceived of as factual even so. A notional passing, let us say.

Something in the Head yet Nothing in the Cupboard

The case of Mother Hubbard's bone, though significantly different, in that it is here all just simply a mistake, is nevertheless instructively comparable in its way. Why did the old lady go to the cupboard? Not because of there *being* a bone in the cupboard. It was of course because she *thought* there was a bone. And there was indeed, in a certain sense, a bone, an imagined, pictured, expected, bone, in the cupboard as conceived by her. In the factual cupboard a strictly notional bone. A 'fictional' bone, does someone say? Fictional yes, but only in the sense in which the old lady herself is matter of fiction: the fictional notional bone of a fictional factual Mother Hubbard. The bone is no fiction of Mother Hubbard's. It is an element factually, not fictionally, present, but only in her fancied, her pictured, her notional, environment. In fact, admittedly, there was no such bone: not even fictionally.

What—no Sunrise?

'I doubt,' said a colleague, 'if there *is* an international society.' How then, he asked, could the study of the 'structure' of such a society become a subject in the university curriculum? Doubt it as he might, this could not affect the fact of that society's existence, in idea. In the idea, that is, in the light of which relationships between the governments of sovereign states had for so many a past generation been officially carried on. For the assumption of an international society, having a membership of sovereign states, 'persons' every one of them, with capacities appropriate to their role—it is on that, rather than on any matter of tangible fact, that official relationships rest. The assumption of such a society, the idea of it—or, why not?, the notion of it—with the notion of the personality of its members and of their subjection to international law; unseen as it may be, this is the premise, the 'dogmatic' premise, of the process in which the world treats itself, conventionally, as one.

France, in idea, and Britain, in idea, are not merely countries, but persons, and, with sufficient luck, good friends. The friendships, like the personalities, of sovereign states, are such not by nature but by imputation. As they are not naturally, but notionally, persons, so they may be notionally friends. For such in the official theory of their relationships they ordinarily are.

In the light of the facts (exclusive of the facts as to her state of mind) Mother Hubbard's movements made little sense. In the light of the theory of her moving, her moving made sense enough. Official behaviour, if sense is to be made of it, needs to be construed in the light of the theory, the official theory, of that behaviour. And in the official theory much may be notionally thus-and-so, while factually otherwise. Are France and Britain ever friends in fact? Do France and Britain, as capable of friendship or enmity, exist, in fact? What *is* France, in fact, but a stretch of territory? But what, by contrast, is France in idea?

Realism versus Realism

It is thus that we are led to recall our two different kinds of 'realism'. There is the realism that must deny that anything happens except in tangible reality; that must therefore deny that what has only happened virtually, or shall we say, only happened in effect, has happened at all. But there is also the second kind of realism, for which the happening-in-effect is also a way of happening. For the former kind, the earth may indeed turn upon its axis, but in no sense can the sun be considered as getting out of bed. For the latter, there is a sense in which the sun does indeed get out of bed; notionally, and as it were, albeit not factually, get up is precisely what the sun does do. And thus, to recognise that things happening in effect do indeed also happen—happen, that is, in a sense: this is itself a variety of realism. If to deny the sun's rising is realism, it is crude, rudimentary, naïve; whereas to assert the rising-in-effect is mature, sophisticated, refined. And the case for the sophisticated variety of realism is that it rings the more true—the more artistically, poetically, humanly true.

In the familiar story, it was the little child who insisted, when the emperor was displaying his wardrobe, that in fact he was not clad. His, we may say, was the naïve and irrelevant kind of realism—given, that is, the object of the exercise in which his elders were engaged. It is likewise a naïve and irrelevant realism that on Xmas morning denies the existence of Santa Claus. Or which doubts if the hostess is indeed quite so sorry as she seems at the going of her guests. It would require a particularly naïve kind of realism to offer comment on a game without any reference to the theory of the game. For only in terms of the theory of whatever game it is can any sense be made of what is happening at any point in the playing of it. It is therefore in terms of the theory, and not just of things to be seen, that a game as a going concern has need to be followed and understood.

The world official system, the universal social set-up, the global 'game'. Whichever we choose to call it, what we have here is a going concern, whose momentum is such that it is hard to imagine its being arrested. It looks like going on going on. Even if we be thinking to try to stop it, we had better try to understand it as it is. And for this purpose it is a special kind of thinking, to be undertaken in a special kind, so to say, of thinking-cap, and not just sharper eyes—a cap made for thinking in terms of entities which are notional, not real—that we shall require.

Conformism is Enough

When what we wish to explain to ourselves is the relatively frictionless co-existence of individuals in a smoothly flourishing society, we know how useful it is to make investigation into that body of shared assumptions, or belief-system, in terms of which they in common face their common problems. When, however, it is the co-existence of states that we would explain, we find a difference; it is idle to ask what beliefs are cherished by the states: for states, as such, have none. Men in general may have their beliefs, about states. But it is not in terms of these that the states have dealings with each other. Their dealings are referable not to anybody's actual beliefs, but rather to certain official dogmas, traditional in the relevant milieu, and retained as the premises for the persisting feasibility of forms of co-operation which nobody as yet would wish to discard.

What is one saying except that the world of international relations is a notional, not a factual, world: and that the existence of this or that possible element within it is a matter of 'doctrine'? A question, in short, to be answered in the light not of tangible factors but of the assumptions officially presupposed.

Fifty-seven of Them?

What then is doctrine and what are its kinds? Etymologically, doctrine is presumably teaching, learning, the substance of something taught. And if, while the earth is round, we teach that it is flat, the difference between matter of fact and matter of doctrine becomes plain enough.

Of what varieties of doctrine have we now become aware? Of what kind do we first receive a dose? 'The goblins will get you if you don't watch out.' Folk-lore? 'And the morning and the evening were the first day.' Myth? 'The music of the spheres', cosmological doctrine. 'The geocentric universe', astronomical doctrine. Horoscopes, astrological doctrine. 'All men born free and equal', social doctrine. 'Vox populi, vox Dei', political doctrine. 'Parallel lines never meet', geometrical doctrine. 'Original sin', theological doctrine. 'The id', psychoanalytical doctrine. 'Vicarious liability', legal doctrine. 'No parliament can bind its successor', constitutional doctrine. 'No taxation without representation,' politico-philosophical doctrine. 'God the meaning of human existence' theologico-anthropological doctrine. And finally—notebooks ready please—'Sovereign states subject to international law'— diplomatic doctrine.

Second-order Formulations

Now there is one thing that may be said of these many varieties: they are all, by the simple process of specifying in terms of what kind of doctrine it is that they have their ostensible validity, reducible to statements of fact. ' "All men are liars" is a lie.' That may well be a true statement of fact: for it may indeed be true that 'all men are liars' is a lie. It may equally, however, be true to say, of 'all men are liars', that it is a proposition of subjective anthropological doctrine. True statements of fact can thus be made about lies, and also about propositions of doctrine. Yet neither a lie nor a proposition merely of doctrine is itself a true statement of fact.

No doubt this sort of thing is all very obvious; yet it may just often enough be overlooked to make the stressing of it worth while, for safety's sake—when one has need to think.

Three-storied Universe?

The world society, the social cosmos—there could be other terms for it—is sometimes, in particular, referred to as the multi-state system (the system, that is, of the many sovereign states). But the subject to be studied is not just the system of states. It is human society, comprehensively, as a whole. Better then to call it the many-levelled society, with the multi-state system as the layer at the top, not altogether unlike the water-lily-covered surfaces of a series, or system, of ponds (the lilies drawing nourishment from mostly invisible sources down below). Two below-the-surface levels, at least, require separate recognition. Basic to the whole is the level of human life as physically, biologically, and psychologically lived—the life of men and of women and of men-and-women-to-be. And intermediate between the actual life of human units, and the notional life of states, there is the complicated habitat in which there live and have their hybrid part-actual-part-notional being the numberless and variegated assortment of groups, groupings and organisations, in and through which men associate together to strive the more effectively for ends they have in common.

Very important among the groups, no doubt, are the nations, very important among the organisations, the governmental systems. It is at this intermediate level between the solid earth of manhood down below and the stratosphere of statehood up above that, for the purpose of universal sociology, the multi-dimensional interplay of social forces goes perennially on. Soldiers fight, it is true, and soldiers die; but it is armies that win battles. It is as important to try to understand the facts of life at this intermediate level as it is to appreciate the distinctness, the difference in conceptual kind, of the life of the states 'up there'. If there is any single short formula wherewith to epitomise the conditions in which humanity seems now condemned if at all, if only for a season, to survive—it is 'Danger, states co-existing overhead!' Not—nations co-existing. Exalted as they are, and important as they are, the nations are not so inaccessibly intangible as that. The nations do have their home among the human groups; and as groups in general are not mere abstracts, neither are the nations in particular. They consist of human beings. But the states—the members of the international club? These, the states, are not groups; they are, on the contrary, countries—countries conceived of not as groups but as individuals. They exist at all, indeed, only as conceived of. For the country, in international society, is not a tract of territory (though it *has* one). It is a person, a notional person, that, and nothing more. The France of international society is not the France of geography. She is, rather, the France of diplomatics and of international law. Sometimes it seems that she might more appropriately have been designated Paris. But no. What gave, formerly, much of his importance to the King of France was—France, the tract of country. Without that, what was he? And what gives now her importance to France, the international person, is likewise mainly France, the tract. That, as well no doubt as its inhabitants, and much besides. We speak of 'international' relations. Small wonder if we are apt to forget that it is with inter-sovereign-*state* relations, on the level of the water-lilies, that we are primarily concerned. As men behaving in the world of fact produce changes in the world of law, to be appreciated in a special professional thinking-cap developed for this purpose, so men, including men playing roles in governments, produce, by their behaviour in the world of fact, changes in the notional world of diplomatics, some of them also incidentally in the world of international law—each of these worlds giving occasion for our wearing of a further kind of thinking cap.

The Limitations of the Single Eye

We may say indeed about social and political matters that there seem to be two broad types of thinking—thinking which takes as pivotal the dichotomy factual-notional, and thinking which slurs this dichotomy over. For 'sophisticated' realism it is necessary to retain and to practise the two types of thinking together. Relatively rarely does one encounter those who in their thinking about politics employ patterns appropriate to the processes and problems of both levels of experience at once. One should interest oneself therefore in the sociology of appreciation and study those forms of cultural conditioning which make men's thinking what it is. One should notice in particular the conditioning which makes men's judging what it is. For though judging is the function of the individual, it is by the individual-in-society that it is done. And society is not without its influence upon how it happens.

Is not Essentialism Essential?

No one ever physically encountered Nature 'herself', as distinct from natural objects and events. But what we do not and cannot encounter we can, as philosophers say, 'posit'. And having thus, by positing her, conferred on Nature a quasi-existence, we can thereafter 'postulate' her existence as, in effect, given. 'In effect.' 'Given.' Are there no such 'things' as Ignorance, Disease, Famine and Unemployment? Is there no such thing as War? Are there only ignoramuses, invalids, hungry workless people, and men sitting, or dying, in holes in the mud? A platonist may be pictured as one who sees war as not less real than is the sitting of men in the mud, unemployment more real perhaps than men without work. We can hold our breath for a time, and, for a time, with an effort, we can focus our imaginations on miserable humans rather than on human misery. But why try it, unless just to know what it feels like? Is it not more sensible to think about war and unemployment, while at the same time remembering why in terms of human lives we dislike them? To impute, as if without question, an independent existence to a 'universal', such as goodness—independent, that is, of the existence of things, and conduct, and people recognised, by us, as good—is to 'hypostatize', as we say, the quality of goodness. And we may go further, and conceive of it as thing-like, even as personal, nay, even as divine: in which case we reify it, personify it, deify it. Good things we see as having existence. Goodness by contrast is an 'essence'. If this imputing of reality to essences is not perhaps the only tendency to which the term 'essentialism' has been applied, it is what is meant by it here. And the question one is asking oneself is whether, were we not given to it, we should be able to achieve very much, with our thinking, at all. Is it merely a disability, this disposition we have to think of War as an evil to be combated and if possible eliminated rather than to think of the avoidance only of particular wars? Anyhow, be it a disability or not, the disposition is sufficiently common. The important difference is not that between thinking and not thinking of, say, War as such: the important difference is that between merely conceiving of War and conceiving of it as an entity independent of our so conceiving of it. To believe in essences, in the sense of conceiving them as entities independent of our conceiving, is the particular kind of essentialism which we may style 'ontological essentialism'. For ontology is concerned with whatsoever 'is', independently of its being known or thought about or conceived of. (Alternatively to being believers, in this as in other matters, we may be out-and-out disbelievers, or we may occupy the betwixt-and-between position of the agnostic.)

Now, if not all essentialists are of the ontological variety, what other variety is there? The other, very important, variety of essentialist is the one who, without necessarily believing in what he conceives of, nonetheless proceeds on the assumption of its independent be-ing. Has my country a manifest destiny? I may genuinely believe so, provided I am an ontological essentialist with respect to destiny as such. But, whether believing in destiny or not, I can nonetheless choose to proceed in practice *as if* I not merely conceived of, but believed in, the destiny of my country, and therefore of course the element, or factor, or principle, or what have you, to which traditionally, the designation of 'destiny' has been given. To have doubts about the ontological status of essences is not therefore necessarily to reject them. We may continue to conceive of them but not with the same 'logical' status as before. What we do not believe in we may nevertheless be content to 'postulate'. And this, if essentialists merely in the 'methodological' sense, is what we presumably do. Did the English, on the morrow of Dunkirk, believe in eventual victory? Who knows? The question was, wisely, not asked. What matters was that as good methodological essentialists they proceeded to proceed as if they did believe in Victory with a capital 'V'. Do we believe in fairies? We can act as if we did. Do we believe in the will of the people, in human rights, in the conscience of mankind? We can act as if we did.

Is not methodological essentialism socially essential?

The One-world Philosophy?

Near akin to essentialism—if not even perhaps a form of it—is a propensity no less important: the imputing, namely, of oneness to what may merely be the sum of many parts. To see the body corporate, the crowd, the flock of starlings, the statistical category of the workers of the world, not just as multiple but as unitary, to see the learned world not merely as so many allegedly learned persons but as that singular something to which they belong—to see it as indeed an 'it' and not merely a 'they', this too is an achievement of which few of us, if any, are apparently incapable. We may call it, if we like, a mere ploy of the mind. But it is the avoiding of it, the strict and consistent 'nominalism', the thorough-going 'methodological individualism', the denial that the committee, or the school, or the Church, or the team, or the nation, or the human family is anything more than the mere sum of its members, this it is that, like the holding of the breath, demands an effort which, for many of us, it is difficult to sustain. As we cannot hold our breath while asleep, so we cannot, in our unthinking moments, eschew the 'holism' which imputes their wholeness to social, and other such, wholes. For, like essentialism, holism, to many of us, comes 'natural': and, though we expel Nature with a fork, back and in she comes again (this last being a typically essentialistic formulation of what we are in reality saying about the way in which we think). Even if at the ontological level we feel constrained to doubt, since we cannot demonstrate, the reality of, say, the nation, we may nevertheless, and indeed we had better, on the level of daily political and social living, relapse at least into that methodological holism which allows to the committee credit for having done something on an afternoon when its members, having lunched over well, have not individually done very much.

Shifting Perspectives

Opposed, whether on the ontological or on the methodological level, to holism, are collectivism and individualism. Meet my family (holism). Meet the members of my family (collectivism). Meet my brothers, Tom, and Dick and Harry (individualism). Or again: Bring me my dinner; bring me all the things you have prepared for me to eat; bring me my soup, my meat, my pudding. Our union struck, we all came out, every man Jack of us downed tools. The Church disapproves, your country needs you, Cambridge won, let Europe arise, the new generation is in revolt (holism). All churchmen, all the young people (collectivism). Every good European, every young person (individualism). Is it useful to restrict oneself to one way of thinking and speaking, if all three have their valued uses? Is is not better to notice how intriguingly they live together, without necessarily causing confusion, in our mind? No doubt they might indeed cause confusion, in our thinking, but need they? Not if we appreciate and apply the relevant distinctions. Not, in particular, if, reserving the ever-debatable question of the 'ontological' status of essences and of wholenesses—the question, that is, of their independent givenness as presences 'out there'—we accept, though it were only for purposes of our thinking and our speaking and our concerted acting, such tools as our convenience may require.

Sceptical though we remain as to the objective existence of a Santa Claus, we may postulate it, none the less, as a matter of season-celebrating method. Knowing, for a fact, that the customer is wrong, we may, in point of selling method, behave as if he were right: that is to say, proceed upon the methodological premise that he is. Our ontology sees him as fallible, and in this case definitely wrong: our methodology treats him as if necessarily right. To underplay the logical distinction between the ontological and the methodological would itself be a blunder—of method. To deny it would be a failure of understanding.

Words, and Images

The personifying of the social whole: is it, as some have thought, no more than a clever dodge, hit upon at some point in the past, and adopted for its evident usefulness, its relevance to the survival of the race? Or do men, in speaking of groups as persons, so speak of them because it is so that they conceive them? Even if some don't, some, it seems, do, and probably always have done, at least since the Old Testament writers used Israel, in the singular, as their symbol. No need for the social cosmologist to assess the relative prevalence of these respective ways of using what all might agree in identifying as a metaphor. Suffice it to see, and to say, that the metaphor, as a verbal device, has the two sorts of use. Necessity we are told is the mother of invention: clearly metaphorical, the motherhood here ascribed. But what about love for the mother land? Is there no such distinctive emotion? Is the use of the mother terminology in this case metaphorical and nothing further? The question is whether the language which here does justice to the way we conceive things is strictly speaking metaphorical at all. If we do in fact conceive of death as stalking the land, and removing people with 'his' hand, then it is at least questionable whether in so speaking of him we are using language in even approximately the same way as when we describe necessity as a mother. Let it at least be accepted that a metaphor, if that we are to call it, may often be a significant index of how men conceive, and in that sense see, their world. We may indeed express ourselves in metaphors, but we can hardly think in them. Rather may we think in those 'images' of which the metaphors, if that we are still to call them, are the attempted reflection.

Fighting Ships and Warring States

The line between the mere metaphor, employed and enjoyed as such, and the reflection in apparently metaphorical language of the terms in which things are actually conceived, may be a shifting one. But analytically it can be important even so. 'When my ship comes home' seems to be strictly metaphorical. 'The ship of state' seems rather less essentially so, for one surely does tend to think of statesmanship in terms of helmsmanship. And the term 'fighting ships' is hardly metaphorical at all: it presupposes that ships do positively fight, that battles at sea are indeed fought between ships. Granted that not even in the theory of the matter is the state a kind of ship, or even a quasiship, it does rather seem as though in the theory of the matter actual ships do actually fight. Ought we to be protesting that strictly the ship is only a machine used, in the fighting, by the captain? Or that the captain-plus-crew-plus-ship are a machine used by the commanding admiral, or the super-commanding admiralty, or by the country as a whole, in its fighting? Once we progress beyond the point at which the fighting is done only by men against men, it seems simplest to see it as done by ship against ship, and to say that, if this sort of encounter is fighting only in a figurative sense, then in modern conditions there isn't any fighting done, at sea.

It seems simpler. Might we not go further and allow that it positively *is* simpler? The reductionism which, basing itself on analytically valid distinctions between realities like fighting men, abstractions like fighting states, and betwixt-and-betweens like fighting ships, resolves to think only in terms of the tangibly real, soon involves itself in artificialities of mental usage which are not really simple at all.

Take, for instance, the battle fleet. On one level, it can be conceived as so many thousands of sailors distributed between so many ships; on another, as so many ships manned by so many sailors; on another, as so many divisions, comprising so many ships manned by so many sailors. There is an obvious sense in which the ships do of course exist. They exist as ship-shaped physical things. But as feminine their existence is notional only, not real. The fleet as so many ships is not merely simpler than the fleet as so many sailors. The fleet as so many ships is also real. But the fleet as so many fighting ships, especially as so many female fighting ships, is partly notional only.

And what now of the states? Of these by contrast it must be said that their very existence is not less notional than is their femininity.

The Sovereignty of Theory

The world society as so many female states is notional wholly. It is, that is, a world not found, nor even perceived, but a world conceived of—and conceived of as peopled not by individuals, nor even indeed by peoples, but by 'countries': countries peopled indeed by individuals, and themselves conceived of as people. These countries—conceived of as people—as persons—each of them a distinct personality—are conceived as subject to international morality, and to international law, as well as to the restraints of good feeling among neighbours and friends. They are conceived of as alive, with minds of their own, aims, interests, objectives, policies, aspirations and scruples of their own, distinct in idea from those of their peoples and the individual people of whom their peoples consist. They are conceived of as capable of action and as acting—their action being conceived of as occurring as and when there occur the appropriate events, in the appropriate conditions, in the world of the tangibly real.

We do indeed speak of a gallant ship, and we do in fact seem to have the notion of the ship as gallant. We do report the battle in terms of the theory of ships versus ships. The only question is whether this theory is merely fashionable or whether it cannot, as a way of thinking, also claim to be 'correct'. For even if the language of 'fighting ships' may only be a fashion and not reflective of an orthodoxy, surely the contrary is the case with fighting countries—states at war. If France is the victor it is France indeed—not simply the people of France—that officially, that is in the official theory of the matter, wins the victory. The long and short of the matter thus seems to be that, though ships be but machines, countries, in the sight of the pertinent brand of theory, are not mere organisations or areas on the map. In the sight of 'diplomatic theory' countries, far from being mere machines, are persons—and international relations, in the sight of this particular brand of theory, are relations between persons, personified countries, countries, that is, in their character as states.

A Case in Point

Subtle as it may seem, the distinction we have here been drawing is fundamental: so much so indeed that the reader may be wondering why his familiarity with it has not simply been assumed. Does one need to labour the difference between night and day? The truth however is that our distinction is seemingly too fine for some.

On 19th April 1960 in an Easter editorial *The Times* provides us with a striking illustration. 'The international society,' it points out, is 'a metaphorical expression'. In the context this intrinsically acceptable proposition could have no point except to suggest as problematic the status of moral judgment in international affairs. It was as if the wording were a veil with whose removal a void would be exposed: as if, in short, the idiom of international obligation were being revealed as that of make-believe and nothing more. To postulate a moral order for undergirding the social co-existence of men and women might be to base oneself on solid ground: but not so for the co-existence of countries. Only in a manner of speaking could peoples, as such, transgress. Such, or somewhat such, appeared to be the implication of the passage.

Language can indeed be merely metaphorical. 'He was a mother to me' says hardly more than 'He to me was like a mother'. Though in either form extravagant, the remark has still the flavour of a bald reportage. But have we not also the languages of mysticism, of poetry, and of social convention, in all of which metaphor is ubiquitous? Would mere similes serve for conveying all that ordinarily finds a vehicle in these?

Granted that 'international society' is indeed metaphorical; so also is many another expression whose aptness is not to be discounted merely by describing it so. Where, with the 'de-metaphoricising' process, would the great newspaper wish us to stop? Is not 'the brotherhood of man' a metaphor too, to say nothing of locutions more sacred still? And are we in international dealings henceforth to rely on nothing better than the quasi-loyalty of quasi-friendly peoples and the principle of quasi-good-faith? What becomes of the Commonwealth of Nations, the Atlantic Community, the conscience of humanity, or, for that matter, the reputation of *The Times*?

If the toughminded reductionists are able to reduce the thinking and conceiving that these sorts of language connote to the level of the simile, it is goodbye to much that we might be loth to forgo, including our hope for the building of a peace. For the difference, superficially so nearly imperceptible, between the two kinds of metaphor is that, while the one is the compression of a simile, the other is the expression of a myth. And we ought not over-hastily to think to deprive ourselves of myth. If to postulate an international society is to reveal one's mentality as pre-scientific, how about one's respect for the sovereign people and the national will?

Granted that it is on man the mystic that the international order, in so far as we have one, must depend; so equally does the order on which so much is dependent nearer home. Almost it is as if the great newspaper were unaware that the foundations of society, even domestically, are credal rather than testably empirical, and under the delusion that the philosophy of obligation was more conclusively explainable with respect to the narrower sphere of social relatedness than the wider. One may be grateful for so timely an example of the kind of confusion that one is seeking to dispel. For while it is right to insist that the realm wherein states consort with one another is not just the realm of fact, this does not put it into the world merely of fiction.

CHAPTER IV

THE PROJECTED PSEUDO-WILL

Decisions and 'Decisions'

Typically, in games, somebody, for example one of two captains, has the opportunity to make a decision: for example, the decision as to which of two teams shall be the first to bat. And by which of the two captains it shall be so decided is 'decided' by—the spin of a coin. Strictly, rather, it is decided by the rule—or, still more strictly, by those who made the rule—the rule whereby the coin is for this purpose to be spun. The matter requires somehow to be decided, and a process for this purpose has accordingly been laid down. But *can* a mere process, as such, decide anything? It is said, no doubt, to be the rain, or the absence of it, which may decide whether the game shall in fact begin. The truth is that not everything which gets decided gets decided by anybody's deciding. For there is, for the relevant purposes, a process which beyond any likely question is the one for producing a 'decision'. What better example could there be of this than a General Election? The decision is made by the voter? By the voters? By which of the voters? By the majority of them? Not necessarily. The decision is made, rather, by a process, in which the voters, by voting, take part. It is the relevant rule that prescribes the relevant process for producing the relevant result. The electorate, not the voters individually, has decided—the electorate as synonymous for this purpose with the people—since with a system of popular sovereignty it is with the people that such decisions purportedly lie. The Election is the process for ascertaining the people's will.

Wills and Wishes

As a noun the word 'will' has various uses. By 'my will' may be meant the document in which my wishes are declared, or, those wishes as so recorded: or, that capacity in the exercise of which it was done. The document is single. Its contents, however many and varied, are brought within a single operation of willing. And, for doing this, mine is a single capacity—a single will. But what if the willing be done by more than one? A given content may be willed by one, or 'jointly' by two, or collectively by many, or it may 'in common' be willed by two or more.

'Communal' willing—if this we may call it—is a highly convenient device: one of the most convenient indeed with which social man has yet endowed himself. What after all is administration if it be not the art of getting, if necessary by cumbrous procedures, results for which the full formal responsibility can in some cases be brought home only with difficulty to anyone in particular!? Individuals may be party to what committees 'do'; but it is by the committees that the things are 'deemed' to be done. In the eyes of naïve realism, or of an adolescent scepticism, every decision is, and surely must be, the decision of some individual. It requires the sophisticated kind of realism to appreciate the sense in which decisions are made by notional entities, personified notional entities, notional persons having notional wills. Communal willing, though not a willing *stricto sensu*, not a willing really, is in effect a willing even so. And sophisticated realism, so far from ignoring it, sees it and accepts it for what it is: a willing in effect, a willing notionally speaking, a willing in all but fact.

Sophisticated Animism

To account for the apparent ease with which this communal willing is so universally accepted as though tantamount to a willing in fact, one may invoke the idea of a 'mystique'—the mystique, as we may call it, of communal willing. Primitive animism might see man's inanimate surroundings as a world of many spirits, each having some ability to will. Why this way of seeing should come so easy as seemingly it does we may not know: but it evidently does. There is more than a hint of primitive animism in our personifying of an administrative 'machine'.

Responsibility and Responsibility

In the theory of the matter—and here the theory is all that counts—it is not strictly a case of the members acting on the committee's behalf—or even of the members' actions being imputed to it. In the theory of the matter it seems rather that a process which includes the casting by members of their votes is *construed* as 'adding up to' action by the committee as such. The point is worth noting carefully, if only for the sake of precision in the placing of responsibility. New members do not individually inherit the responsibilities of the body which they join. All that they do individually incur is their own responsibility for what they may individually do: e.g., for what they may do individually toward determining the manner in which the committee's responsibilities shall be met—met, that is, not by them individually, but by the committee, as such. The orthodox interpretation is holistic. The committee is construed as responsible, and as acting, as a whole. And, just as the committee's responsibilities are those of the committee as such, so those, internationally, of a country lie upon the country and not upon its government or the members of it. The responsibilities of those individual members are heavy enough without their having to be mistaken for the country they serve. If the responsibilities of the country could be regarded as resting upon its individual statesmen, these last might have merely to disappear, and its creditors would be left 'to whistle for their cash'. As it is, while the politicians are mortal, the country, in principle, is not.

The Nature and Naturalness of the Artificial

No need here to describe the process by which a committee reaches a decision. So familiar is it that it excites as little curiosity as the beating of the heart. What may well, however, excite some curiosity is the question of how it comes to excite so little. For curious it certainly is, once one begins to be curious about it, at all. It is not as if anyone had ever said: Let's play committees, and proposed in what conditions the purported taking of a decision should be represented by what ritual. Which of us, the first time we heard of a committee's having decided something, had any difficulty in accepting the information

48   THE NATURE OF INTERNATIONAL SOCIETY

as though it were the most self-explanatory thing in the world? But that will, of course, have been because nothing prompted us to reflect. What everyone else took for granted it did not occur to us to question. But had we reflected, so far from continuing to see it as natural, we might well have found the process as artificial as is the bicycle, for getting about. Even so, bicycle movement is at least a method of movement, but is committee decision a method of deciding, at all?

Calculation and Calculation

What if it be suggested that a committee is merely a social device, for producing what it may become convenient to treat as a decision, and conventional so to do? The calculating machine may produce results, but they are not the results of a calculation. The point here is not that it is found so easy to have what is, after all, not a process of decision, but a substitute for a decision-making process. The point is that it is so easy to overlook the fact of its not being such a process at all. Realistically analysed it is a process whereby, settled rules of interpretation being applied to a procedure whereby certain votes are cast and counted, the whole is treated as if tantamount to the taking of a decision. It is clearly a case of the thing that is not being construed as the thing that is. The committee is as strictly a social device as is 'British summer time'.

How do we do it? Simply enough, it would seem. All it requires of us is that we postulate the committee's existence as a person distinct from its members, and impute to it what we conceive of as a will. Very artificial in its way. Yet all so simple. And the key to its simplicity is a propensity which we have for seeing the fully factual, and the merely notional, as if interchangeable elements. Notionally, not factually, a unity, notionally not factually a person, notionally not factually the exerciser of a will, the committee is as much an agent in our effective environment as are the mortal individuals of whom it is composed.

Given Grounds

'It doesn't matter what we say so long as we all say the same.' Cabinet decisions may have been hard to hammer out. The grounds to be given for those decisions may have occasioned less concern. For what matters in such things is not that the world shall know how the decisions came about, but only that the preamble—with the grounds it gives—shall have an apparent compatibility with what has been done. While the 'line' of a live individual may be largely affectation and so partake of the notional, the line of a notional person is notional only, being only notionally that of anyone at all. The mind imputed, holistically, to the meeting as such is, *eo ipso*, a notional mind, and its grounds merely notional too.

The Un-Willing Non-Houses

Thus the will of Parliament is the will not of the members as such nor even of either House as such, but of a notional, and notionally unitary, entity, the Queen in Parliament, both Houses of Parliament—of Parliament as a unitary whole. Parliament is thus credited with a single will: and to this will there is imputed a single content. To the question: 'What's wrong with Parliamentary sovereignty?'—one possible, if stupid, answer might be that it places authority where there is not in fact a will. How can responsibility reside in a personified abstraction? As well might it be vested in a personified thing, in one or other of the Houses, as a building (not that either of the Houses is in fact a separate building!).

Fact and Folklore

The question is, however, not commonly asked; and, if it were to be, few would be fobbed off with such an answer. For not only does constitutional theory vest authority in the notional abstraction—but precisely this is what the folklore of the British 'way of life', the British form of co-existence in community does too. It is not only in point of constitutional theory, but in point of folklore, that Parliamentary sovereignty is reckoned as being 'all right'—that it is deemed proper that people be required to defer, and conform, to Parliament's will.

John Austin's Point

The odd thing is not so much that we should feel in tune with the chairman when he assumes to voice the communal standpoint, or with the leader who proclaims that the nation is determined never to yield. What is, by comparison, much more odd is the tameness with which we accept the verdict of the electorate as decisive, even if a numerical majority of those voting might apparently have wished it the other way. It is almost as if, the voters being on one side and that mystic being, the electorate, on the other, the voters had got the worst of the affair. While we appreciate just what it is that has happened, and perceive in particular that the outcome of the process has been nearly as chancy as the spin of a coin, we yet accept the result almost as though it were indeed 'the verdict of us all'. It is by no means entirely as if we were doing this simply as, in game-playing, we accept the result of a gamble, the fall of the dice, the spin of a coin, or the disconcerting decision of an umpire. It is not mere good sportsmanship, or faith in the law of averages—to bring us better luck another day. No: it seems rather to be some kind of a genuine semi-belief in the last word's having indeed been spoken by what John Austin called 'the Sovereign Number', as represented by that most important part of 'it' which is the electorate conceived holistically as exercising a single will. No chairman, when his meeting is divided approximately fifty-fifty, would think to describe it as having arrived at a common view. But the fact remains that we do seem capable of believing in that mystic will to which, every so often, the re-election, or rejection, of a government is referred. And this it is that makes such sense as there may be in the notion of a world public opinion as finding its expression through a procedure as artificial, and as arbitrary, as is the procedure of the United Nations. The most we can confidently say, in rationalising justification of a very common attitude, is that, if there were indeed such a factor as world public opinion, and if this were not in accord with what was being asserted in its name, we should presumably have evidence of this being the case. It is a rough and ready method, but not simply a hit-or-miss one, of reflecting world public opinion—assuming that it is not just nonsense to be thinking in terms of any such factor at all. After all, the world is not less of a reality than is the committee, and if without arousing protests the competent spokesman purports to ascribe to the world, or to the committee, what he takes to be *its* momentary mood, it is perhaps as rational in the one case as it is in the other to let him have his way. We need not take such a verdict, so arrived at, over-

THE PROJECTED PSEUDO-WILL

tragically. The world (there we go—even we!) will understand.

Calling the Kettle Black

The make-believe of the purportedly democratic procedures under the Soviet system today is best identified as merely a special case of the kind of thing to which man has lent himself throughout his history. For allegedly communal willing is no modern invention. And a realistic analysis of it may need in any given case to probe behind the form of it and ask what it is that happens in fact.

Two Into One Makes Three

If the reader feels tempted to cavil at what to him may seem an over-pedantic, hair-splitting, academic and practically inconsequential distinction between the government, as a group of flesh-and-blood agents, and the state in whose service they act, let him consider an analogy which is perhaps not altogether too far-fetched. Let him think of that curious but endearing object, the pantomime horse. What is it but a bag, containing two performers, the one to operate, and be, the forelegs, the other, the legs behind. Does anyone in the audience suppose that a genuine, biologically authentic, horse is cavorting about the stage? Does anyone not well enough know what in reality is going on? But which is it that causes the amusement—the movements of the men inside, or the antics of the horse? Is not this a case where what matters is not what in fact is done concertedly by several, but what is deemed to be done by one? It is to the illusion that a horse is behaving in what for a horse would be so diverting a manner that the audience's amusement is due—even though all actually know it for an illusion. They understand well enough how what in fact are the movements of the men add up to what in effect, and in the theory of the occasion, are the movements of a horse.

The Theory of the Occasion

Is it really so altogether otherwise when the doings of a government add up to what in effect, and in the theory of the occasion, are the doings of a country? The foregoing is surely a more realistic statement of the position than is either the ignoring of the inauthentic horse in favour of a study of the movements of the men, or the imputing of the human movements, quite unequine in each case, to the horse. What is deemed to be happening is the prancing of a horse. That is what is happening in the theory of the occasion. No need to identify this with what is happening in fact. And similarly in the case of state behaviour what we are given, in the theory of the occasion, is the behaviour not of a government, or even of the members of a government (this latter being what we are given in fact), but the behaviour of a state. And if the horse has lameness, or obligations, or a thirst, these are not the embarrassments of those inside it. They may be thirsty on their own account. Or one of them, or neither. The obligations of a country are not those of its government or of the members severally or collectively thereof. They too may have obligations, of their own.

The Not-so-bad-ness of 'Bad Faith'

What has been said above about the communal mentality and about communal opinion is no doubt said at some risk of its not being universally understood. To refer to it, and to do so in such terms, is not necessarily to commit oneself to a belief in the existence of minds other than the minds of individuals. Even if one speaks in some contexts of a communal mind, or a national will, or, with Rousseau, of a General Will, or of the will of the electorate, one may be doing no more than avail oneself of a convenient formula—as when at a cricket match one may speak, only half in jest, of the weather, as taking sides against the team of one's preferring. It is the opinion which is communal, in that no one need hold it authentically as his own —all merely appreciating that it is for them the safe, the respectable, the seemly, opinion to profess and to cultivate. And similarly the communal mentality is the one which it proves socially convenient to assume. In all this there is an ingredient of what Sartre is blunt enough to characterise as *mauvaise foi*—which means play-acting a part without even being fully conscious that one is doing so; being false, that is, not just to others, but in a sense to oneself. But intermingled with this element of incomplete sincerity there is something more obscure. It is not a lack of frankness that prevents our calling in question the formal attribution, to a committee on which we are serving, of sentiments, whether of grief or joy, which no single member present shows much sign of feeling on his own. We do in some sense conceive of the committee as having an identity, a life, and a standpoint, and sympathies, proper to itself—independent of who at a given moment are present and voting. The sense in which we so conceive of it is not merely the sense in which we rationally resort to a well-tried social device. The explanation of our behaviour lies deeper than that. It may well be that we shall be safer in ascribing our capacity for ready participation in such goings-on, not so much to the rational as to the mystical component in our make-up. The language of communal willing is convenient precisely because it does indeed express what we mean. In a sense it seems true that the committee has willed thus and so, that the nation has resolved to make a stand, that the electorate has said no. It is the mystical rather than the rational component in our make-up that renders such statements so acceptable and so digestible. It *seems* as if they were true. We have almost forcibly to remind ourselves that they strictly are not. When the chairman articulates what he judges to be the sense of a meeting, he is indulging in himself, and appealing to in others, the disposition to believe in that additional personality which is that of the committee as such. The 'mystique'—neither more nor less. The mystique of communal willing: that might well have served as title for this chapter.

CHAPTER V

PHANTOM ALIBI

The Impact of the International 'Ought'

But what exactly, it may be asked, is the practical importance of the distinctions between the committee and its members, and between leaders individually, leaders collectively, government, people and state? The importance of these distinctions may be seen wherever a judgment is being passed upon the moral merits of some step in, say, a foreign policy. The country concerned is, let us assume, in the language of those whose criticism we are discussing, a 'Christian' country. For the individual Christian citizen the question might have been: What, as a Christian, can I countenance, and of what is it incumbent upon me publicly to wash my hands? The question raised, however, is neither: What am *I*, a Christian, nor: What are *we*, a Christian people, to do? It is: What is ours, a Christian country, to do? A Christian country—among countries not all of them Christian! Do countries, as such, have any distinctively Christian responsibilities to one another? Could we sensibly expect our non-Christian fellow-citizens to agree with us that they have? And, Christian criteria apart, have countries any kinds of responsibilities, other than legal ones, to one another? Have they in fact? Have they in theory? If so, in what kinds of theory?

Amongst others there are always the following questions to be kept distinct: (*a*) What ought I personally to do? (*b*) What ought my country's government to do? and (*c*) What ought my country to do? It is in the light of one's answer to (*c*) that one can proceed to consider (*b*) and of one's answer to (*b*) that one can go on to consider (*a*). When put in relation to a matter for our present decision, these questions are not immediately interchangeable. Nor are their counterparts interchangeable, when the historian, in his evaluating of policies pursued by others in times past, puts them to himself.

It cannot be said of all historians that they consistently bear these distinctions in mind, at any rate when reporting to us on what, by their researches, they have found. When Britain, for example, 'gave' independence to India, who in fact did what?

To the lawyer, as a technician, the answers to such questions are, or should be, tolerably obvious. If a treaty binds two countries, or, if one country is in default, it is in point of legal doctrine that this is so. But when a country has done its duty, to whom, by the historian, should be accorded the credit? Which thinking-cap should the historiographer wear? Should it be that of primitive impressionism, or of adolescent scepticism based on naïve realism, or, of sophisticated realism? For which kind of reader is he to cater? Not always does every history-book-writer seem exactly to know. But he does know, presumably. And anyhow, submittedly, he ought to.

The Historiographic Dilemma

Primitive impressionism continues, let us say, to hold 'Germany' answerable for the first world war. What the historian looks into is the contribution made, and in what conditions, by individuals such as von Moltke, Bethmann-Hollweg and the Kaiser. If on balance he finds himself concluding that primitive impressionism has had it broadly right, how shall he present this result? What he cannot do is to pose as personally any longer a primitive impressionist, for that, at least, he no longer is. If then he nevertheless puts it that 'Germany' was not blameless, this is not a simple statement of the facts that he has found. Nor, on the other hand, will he have been investigating a technically legal issue. The answer he is giving is a historian's answer to a historian's, not a lawyer's to a lawyer's, question. How comes he then to speak, if he does so, of 'Germany', as distinct, say, from certain Germans, at all? Are we to say that, as a lawyer in legal, and an economist in economic, categories, so a historian does his thinking in a distinctive kind, the historian's kind, of categories? As there is legal, and as there is economic, theory, is there, analogously, something to be differentiated as historian's, or historical, theory? If yes, then differentiated from what? The answer seems to be that the historian does indeed relate the past in terms not so much of fact as of theory; but—that there is nothing particularly remarkable about that. Nothing remarkable, because it happens to be what we all do, in so far as, though no longer primitive impressionists, we are not mere adolescent sceptics either. The only question is whether the historian, in using language appropriate to sophisticated realism, is always fully alive to what he is doing, so that he does not slip into thinking in terms of the primitive impressionism with which his language, in addressing his public, is consistent enough.

The Pitfalls of Linguistic Usage

For the sophisticated realist does, it is true, content himself with the language of the primitives. Only he does it with a difference. He does it, in short, with a sufficient awareness of the difference between the metaphorical and the specific, between the notional and the factual, between the conventional and the true. Those, for instance, who have fallen in a war: do we object to their being rated as heroes? Surely not. Yet do we by this our acquiescence beg unwittingly any questions of fact? Do we in our inner minds necessarily ascribe heroism to each and all of them, as if the alternative, cowardice, must necessarily have brought them through alive? Hardly. The truth probably is that, in speaking of the fallen as heroes, we no more impute actual heroism to particular individuals than we beg any questions in imputing honourableness to an M.P. Our conventional way of speaking of them may or may not reflect a conventional way of thinking, of M.Ps.

The idea that every fallen conscript was heroic, or that every little baby is a darling, or ever parent 'fond'—all these are conventional notions. So, presumably, is the idea that, say, Cambridge, as distinct from certain oarsmen, may win a boat race. Or that France and Germany may patch up a quarrel. Or that Germany may still be to blame. Or that Britain did the right thing in India. In our minds, along with these conventional notions, we as people of sophistication carry images, sociologically realistic, of the facts they imply.

Do Historians Pull Punches?

And if, as mere laymen, with our relatively lackadaisical thinking habits, we thus remain sensitive to the realities, how much more may this not be assumed of the professionals? The popular historian, we may perhaps be certain, remains perfectly clear that those non-existent characters, those notional entities, those mythological beings, Britain, India, Germany, really never themselves took any positive, fleshly, or even any metaphorical, hand in the events that he is reporting upon at all. They simply did not happen to be physically present on the relevant, or on any other, occasion. Like the lawyers, the historians may, as do the rest of us, have their wonted way of speaking and of thinking about the actual facts, but none has thereby any influence upon those actual facts, in so far as they are past, and done with. It is true that our popular historian uses his customary language rather as if he believed it to be literally true. But being, as we are bound to presume, not utterly naïve, he knows that Germany, for instance, was never involved and thus was not to blame. The only question is: Why then does he speak and write as if she had been? Is it that he is using conventional and simplified language for expressing something much more complex which indeed might be literally true? But, if so, what? After all, it is not unimportant for us to know whether, in grammatically blaming Germany, or France, or the Vatican, for something, the historian is actually declaring those 'persons' that he names to blame. In speaking of the sea as angry, we do not impute anger to the sea. But in speaking of France as helpful, or touchy, or vindictive, does not the historian sometimes come rather close to ascribing the qualities in question to France?

Of course he does, in common with us all. For, as the lawyer talks his theory, so do we, and along with us our historian instructor, talk ours. Ours, and his, is the language of a certain sort of theory, the theory, let us acknowledge it, of diplomatics, the theory in terms of which diplomacy proceeds.

The Expectations of England

It is true that the historian, in employing the idiom of diplomatics, may be yielding to a romantic streak in his personal image of the real. He may even have been reading poetry. Or remember Nelson, with his 'England expects . . .'. May that not have conveyed the very thought that was in Nelson's mind? Nelson's idiom had about it something of the poetic, something of the politically rhetorical, something of naval convention, something of personal primitive impressionism. But the historian knows.

So also should the social cosmologist know. What the cosmologist does, or should do, is, G. E. Moore-fashion, to ask for the 'analysis' of what people are saying. And the result may be as it were to substitute the physician's technical diagnosis for the patient's account of his trouble. The historian is peculiar in that, though his investigation be as strictly scientific as is the skilled physician's, the language in which he communicates his findings is more likely to be the language, misleading if not meaningless as it may be, of the patient. Diplomatic theory posits the personality, the presence, and the participation, of the state. So does popular, and poetic, convention. But cosmology must bear in mind that it is mere convention, and—shall we say?—nothing more.

When signalling 'England expects . . .', Nelson was not, presumably, invoking diplomatic theory. Nor was he composing poetry; or indulging in political rhetoric; or merely availing himself of a naval jargon. He was not just giving unstudied expression to the way he felt. Nor was he just using a metaphor for conveying a complicated matter of fact. What then was he doing? He was affirming in a straightforward and unadorned manner what was indeed, notionally, the then existing state of affairs. What he was giving was not merely his private interpretation: it was the orthodox social theory of the matter. It was a social theory whose prevalence and orthodoxy and natural acceptability were due precisely to the ease with which people like Nelson, and the rest of us, could feel and think that way. And historians too.

Two-track Minds

One might imagine somebody, not simply because he was naïve but because he was timid, thinking to resist in himself a disposition to feel sentimental or romantic, lest he lose altogether his capacity, at need, to call a spade a spade. But others of us, and thus do we hope to get the best of both moods, believe we know very well when to be sentimental and when severely matter of fact. At one moment man is pining for his dream cottage; at another he is resenting its perforated roof, its rudimentary plumbing and its distance for the bus. To the mother whose infant is at one moment the little darling, it will, presently, be again the little wretch. The world of my illusions and the world of my experience play Box and Cox. Life is a thrill and a burden, both.

Our moods, let us recognise it, vary between widely separated extremes. The mother is well aware of being ambivalent in her feelings for her child. When poetry has momentarily possessed me I may feel sincerely what I say of the angry sea. Soon, a prey to seasickness and hence temporarily allergic to the very thought of poetry, I resent, without reason, the sea's behaviour, yet do not impute it to anger. The historian, blaming Germany, is not always entirely innocent of the primitive impressionism that saw Germany herself as also in part to blame. But now, in the disciplined spirit of a scientific social cosmology, he consciously re-construes his language as merely the conventional shorthand formulation of the fact that individual Germans seem deserving between them of so vital a part of the blame that a feeling that Germany is the culprit comes natural, objectively dubious though this, as a way of putting it, may be.

Dishonour where that is Due

Notionally, action occurs on a number of levels. Factually, it is all individual, and all blame for it individual blame. Official indignation may be expressed at the behaviour of collectivities holistically conceived, or of organisations seen as persons. But genuine indignation, if realistically directed, will fall only upon individuals, whether severally, or in common with others. Yet this is not of course the way in which the behaviour of countries is commonly appraised. Instead, the state is conceived of as if itself a living person, and its relationships as if those between individuals in a context of private life. And, with a major premise, What is wrong for the individual cannot be right for the state, one quickly arrives at a verdict of Guilty-my-Lord—and with no recommendation to mercy—against whatever state it may happen to be. One's gaze tends so often to centre upon what is notionally, not actually, the case. Officially, of course, whatever has happened is what has happened in the official theory. And in the official theory it is indeed the states and governments that do what is done, and should accordingly have the credit and the blame.

It is, in the eyes of the academic observer, bent on tracing responsibility to centres of real, not just of postulated, volition—to the wills, that is, of real people—it is in his eyes that the official picture becomes a veil that he must thrust aside. For if this be not done, the possibility is that a phantom will serve as a scapegoat, and guilty flesh and blood get off scot free.

In the United Kingdom, for instance, the power of ultimate decision lies, in formal theory, in a specific quarter, namely, with the notionally-single electorate—conceived holistically as the unitary seat of a single will. And persons of flesh and blood are each of them responsible only for such part, whether actively or by omission, as they may individually have had in causing or permitting 'it', the electorate, to behave in such a way. The procedure of such ultimate 'decision-making' is strictly speaking such that it seems almost frivolous to ask for solid evidence of anyone's being existentially responsible for it at all. It is a system whereby results can be got without anyone having to be identifiably responsible, unless notionally only. How much more congenial—and how much more customary—to remain on the level of things primitively notional, and, ignoring the multiplicity altogether, either blame the state itself, or else assign to some single individual a responsibility out of all proportion to any personal opportunity he may ever have had for controlling the flow of events.

The Knight that Failed

In imputing personality to the state, as the member of international society, modern social theory does nothing very new. It merely takes advantage of a rooted disposition of man's emotional and mystical self. The folklore or mythology which sees international relations as those between personified states is as dominant today in personal, prevalent, collective, and communal, calculations as it can ever have been. In recounting therefore the evolution of those quasi-interpersonal relations, the historian is merely attuning his idiom to the ear and the understanding of the common reader. That he should find this so easy a thing to do is most convenient. What is indeed remarkable is the ease with which he does it, even when presenting the upshot of inquiries all of which have been concerned with the doings of flesh and blood. Contrast the judge. The judge of course is well aware that what his language reflects is not the facts as they nakedly are, but those facts as they figure in contemplation of law. But the historian seems scarcely to remember that in his kind of summing up it is the position not in fact but in terms of a sort of mythology that he is giving. That there has been a migration in his thought from one to the other of two logical planes, that of the factual and that of the notional, he scarcely seems to know. Certainly his reader is not warned of the transition. Rarely is he advised against attributing blame to Germany when it is Germans only who have been shown to him as deserving of censure.

There is as little intrinsic validity in imputing blame to a country as a country as in reporting a sea as angry or in calling silly the knight on a chess board for succumbing to a pawn. But, rather as we may be tempted to impute folly to the chessman, or wrath to the sea, so in the same uncareful manner may we find ourselves blaming Germany.

Do we never then regard it as proper for a historian to end an inquiry by blaming Germany? We do, do we not? Do we not, in effect, assume that there is a species of doctrine (we might call it 'historical doctrine') which, like legal doctrine, deems things to be such as they strictly are not? If so, we shall presumably claim, for the words of the historian, that they are not just metaphorical, nor even merely the simplification of a complex truth, but aptly reflective of what we are here calling historical 'doctrine', a species which imputes personality to the country as such. Or that at least is what, in logic, we might be expected to do.

International law does, of course, notoriously see the country as a person. So too does diplomatic theory. And so, it would now appear, does 'historical' doctrine. So too, come-to-think-of-it, does the doctrine, the social doctrine, of the man-in-the-street. But, by contrast, so definitely *not* does the analysis performed by an austerely realistic social science. So rooted in our colloquial speech and thinking is the convention whereby countries count as persons, that the social cosmologist has almost to apologise for the pedantry that requires him to insist that they are not.

Why Blame Anybody?

The truth is that blaming an individual and blaming a bank or a sovereign state are different sorts of blaming. The more one reflects on what an individual has done the less may be one's disposition to excuse him. But the more one reflects on the behaviour of a sovereign state or a bank the more does one's mental picture of whom it is that one is blaming dissolve before one's mental eye, giving place to a fuzzy vision of various individuals contributing each in his degree to a process whose outcome one deplores. One should recognise that the vivid understanding of what really happens when a state commits a wrong is not readily to be squared with the attributing of blame to the state, as such, for what 'it' has 'done'. If he himself is to be distributing praise and censure, let the student clear his thinking on what exactly he is doing, on what grounds, and with what philosophical warrant.

Sometimes it may be easier, yet still emotionally satisfactory, to say of some process that such a thing ought never to have happened, without then bothering to specify who, for the fact of its so having happened, should bear the blame. In life generally, and especially in international relations, it is useful to remember that the attributing of blame may well be idle, and better done without. But is this the idea with which historians most commonly write? And their readers most commonly read? The transition from the sifting of evidence on what happened in fact to a judgment in terms of what may be held to have happened in theory is seldom explicit. It is almost as though the transition were not made consciously at all. As though, that is to say, when statesmen performed certain motions, England, a person distinct from those statesmen, was understood as behaving—not figuratively merely but in fact. Allied intervention in the Russian civil war of 1918–19 forms, for instance, a complicated story. Why should it be necessary to establish that any single country had any precise conception of what it was about? If Soviet doctrine sees the U.S.A. as having deliberately assailed the infant U.S.S.R., one ought not indeed to complain. For are not western historians often themselves a party to the use of just such language? The mythology of the matter is treated as if it were history. And the 'persons' who acted are then thought of as still today alive, and still of course to blame.

CHAPTER VI

EICONICS AND EIRENICS

What is the Point of It?

Fine distinctions, some of these, that we have been drawing. Some people, perhaps many, are rather allergic to fine distinctions. About such people, that philosopher-statesman Lord Balfour is credited with a characteristic remark. 'I am told people complain that I am given to drawing fine distinctions. I am. High policy depends upon fine distinctions: and, if people find they cannot understand them, they should entrust their affairs to those who do.' Those sentiments, if not the whole truth, are certainly a part of it, in regard to the problem of peace.

Yet the question may still be asked: Why all this emphasis on the non-factual character of the units which in official theory make up that international society whose affairs, when all is said and done, are factually of such concern to us all? To put in doubt the common-sense supposition that the nation is every bit as real as its members is not, for instance, to require of the reader of these pages that he take now a vow of lifelong abstinence from the attributing of motives to the state. Is it likely that such a vow would not be broken?

What then is the point of it all? Partly the point of it is to sound just a gentle but solemn note of warning, by underlining the perils of an idiom which blurs, for example, the true responsibility for what men do as parties to the so-called behaviour of the state.

Let's Not be Hard on the Sea

What is merely a notional responsibility comes readily to be thought of as if it were the genuine thing. And, conversely, the man who was willing to die for his country—as it was imaged by him—comes to be spoken and thought of, as having been willing to die for his friends (quite regardless of whether in fact he ever had any friends). Or again, it being seen as good to uphold the authority of the United Nations, the United Nations comes to be thought of as if by its nature capable of having and exercising an authority and a judgment of its own. Almost it is as if the angry sea were to be conceived of, anthropomorphically, as literally angry. When France is officially disappointed, the disappointment is, in idea, not that of Frenchmen only: it is imputed not just to Frenchmen, but to France. France's mission is hers, not theirs, even though it is only by the exertions of Frenchmen that, her, France's, mission can be fulfilled.

Thus among the various forms of 'reductionism' against which we do well to be warned is the one which sees international politics as involving the behaviour only, and hence the relationships only, of fleshly human beings.

The Ignorance of Learning

A student who finds no trouble in differentiating between the cricket championship in which it is the counties, or cricket clubs, that compete, and particular matches, in which it is teams—and who knows that, though teams play each other, it is really the players that play—such a one may nevertheless be beguiled by the perspicacity of a nominalist when in effect he discloses to us that a government is nothing more than a plurality of human individuals. Yet what else, in a sense, is a cricket club? And yet it is the county, and not the players playing for it, that reaches, or may do, the head of the table.

The truth of course is that those with understanding of the matter see what happens in terms at the same time of counties, of clubs, of players and of teams. It is as if things were occurring simultaneously on four distinct planes of co-existence. One movement by a single player may affect at once his place in the public esteem, his side's hope of victory and the prospects of his club and county in the championship. For in the pertinent theory all these alike can be affected by that single movement—occurring not just in theory, but in time and space. Who would think of seeking to reduce it all to terms of what individuals do? And similarly, amount though they may seemingly do to so nearly the same thing, it is saying not just one thing, but four things, to remark that a statesman is well disposed towards a certain country, towards its existing regime, towards its government and towards the members thereof. Like anyone else, the statesman will have a conception of the government as distinct from its members, of the regime as distinct from the government, and of the country as distinct from the regime. And distinct they in each case are. Thus it is probably between the regimes in the U.S. and the U.S.S.R. that the present-day tension goes most deep: and it is as members of a government, serving their country under a given regime, that the individuals concerned, whatever their personal sympathies, think and act.

Men's Bodies and Bodies of Men

To 'institutionalise' a process is to give to it a kind of life, and a life force, distinct from those of the people whose behaviour it evokes. An organisation is a type of institution, and its momentum is that assured to it by the institutionalising of the activities that keep it on the go. To interpret the process of history in terms only of the behaviour of individuals is even less convincingly representational than it would be to do so in terms only of the functioning of organisations as going concerns. It would be as though a rugby football match were construed as the playing together of thirty men rather than as the playing against one another of two teams, of fifteen players each. The match in fact is meaningless unless appreciated as involving both the men as observed through one lens and the teams as seen through the other, of a pair of mental binoculars designed for the synthesised appreciation of both. What is thus true of teams and players is likewise true of states, and other organisations, and of statesmen, officials and citizens, as such. An intelligence capable of appreciating rugby football need feel only slightly the strain of watching international politics simultaneously on so many planes.

What are little Families Made of?

The point is not that there never will occur contexts in which the use is socially convenient of language which blurs the boundary between two universes of thought and discourse. The point rather is that these universes are indeed analytically distinct, and that to overlook their distinctness may result in what it may perhaps be appropriate to call a 'category mistake'. An example of a failure to clarify the said distinction is provided by much current talk on the topic of the Atlantic Community. Except as between human souls, community *de facto* can hardly exist. Where, however, it is absent in fact, community may yet be supplied with some sort of existence in idea. And, as between countries, community can of course only exist in idea. Of which, then, is the Atlantic community composed—of countries, of peoples, or of people? That Canada and the United States are members of it, this it would be unconventional, not to say scandalous, to deny. But are not Americans and Canadians, also? Whatever answers one gives to them, it is as well to have noticed the queerness of such questions as this.

The Two Civitates

In a passage, which is, as it happens, being written on Christmas Day, it would be easy, and seasonable, to enlarge upon the brotherhood of man. A single world society. Why not a single brotherhood? To talk of human brotherhood would not involve the coining of a novel concept. What is wrong with this expression—that one need hesitate to bring it in? Nothing wrong with it, within the 'language games' where it applies. Only, these do not happen to include that particular game of which social analysis is the name. Brotherhood is an ideal. It is scarcely a 'realisation'. It is not a reality. Were the ideal, even though only as such, a sufficiently influential factor, today, in the doings of men, it would fall to be noted and reported upon as such. But as a proposed analytical tool, for the mental taking into grasp of things as they happen, it is not at present required. Were it the only formula for abstracting from the organisational fragmentation of the human world and focusing on the essential singleness of human society as a whole, 'human brotherhood', with appropriate explanations, might become for sociology a term of art. But such in current linguistic practice it is not. Nor, submittedly, would it in current or readily foreseeable conditions be a useful one. For, though brothers may squabble, the term brotherhood carries a suggestion that by rights they shouldn't, and even perhaps a clouding of the sombre truth that they so commonly do. And sociology needs in the main to have its focus on the fact that they so commonly do.

Doctors' Mandates

When Eisenhower, as if not merely in jest, conceived of the governments as withdrawing so that the peoples might have the peace they all desired, it was as though he had suggested the abolition of workers' and employers' organisations so that men and masters might live together in harmony. It is the old fallacy; the doctor's presence, if it fail to preserve life, is *eo ipso* to be considered the cause of death. *Ergo* to preserve life, abolish the cause of death, the doctor. To preserve peace, abolish the cause of war, the diplomat.

The truth is that it is largely owing to the doctors that the preserving of life can be thought of as something to be hoped for and attempted at all, and it is only thanks to inter-governmental arrangements that the conception of peace as the normal condition has ever been able to beguile the dreams of men.

What the governments are of course engaged in is not introducing frictions into the sphere of individualistic human strivings, but so regulating the inevitable tensions as to save men from the logical consequences of their inveterate disposition to seek their own good even if to the frustration of other men's seeking of theirs.

The Role of the Role

If Ruritania were in reality a person it might be possible for the spokesmen for Utopia to appeal to her in human terms and evoke a human response. But it is to President X and the Government, not to Ruritania, that their appeal must be addressed, and for President X it is a question of what he is to do, not with his own, but with other people's interests and resources. It is not from mere close-fistedness that he may balk at the idea of being apparently generous. As an editor must be taken as expressing the views not of himself but of his paper, so does a government express views as on behalf of its country.

Physically, superficially and visibly, conversation between countries is conducted by men with men. But it is by men in the appropriate roles, not just by men as men, that this is done. What men do in their capacities as 'rolesmen' is not to be confused with what they do as merely men. 'Prime Ministers,' remarked a newspaper, 'are human'; and that was why Mr. Macmillan wanted to choose an election date 'to suit himself'. But it was as leader of the Conservative Party, not just as the individual careerist, that Mr. Macmillan had the choosing of a date. To choose except with regard to the party's, and to the country's, interest as he saw it would have been to betray a trust. There are choices which, as a lackadaisical individual, he might casually have made but which, as a rolesman, he scarcely could.

Levels of Relationship

In point of form the states of affairs existing internationally are states of relationships between states. Of these states of relationships many varieties have been seen. Even as between a given pair of states the relationship is never simply static. And its determinants are bafflingly complex. In an important sense it is a function of the relationships between their leading men. Also, though less importantly, a function of the relationships between their peoples. And conversely the relationships between the leaders reflect changes in the relationships between the states. Never, for instance, should one assume that because one has heard how things stood, this morning, as between a Nehru and a Chou, one ought to know how they are likely to be standing at the same time tomorrow. Even when they quarrel, their quarrels may but be 'the renewal of love'. But in that case what enjoins the renewal is the overall situation, not a mere impulse of the heart. 'We never jobbed backwards,' recalled Macmillan at a famous moment, meaning presumably that he and Eisenhower had attempted no joint autopsy upon the Suez affair. Why? Because the movement of events just had not happened to require it.

The states of relationships between peoples may in themselves be important also, as either a support or an impediment to those between their leading men. Can an Eisenhower safely afford to invite a Khrushchev to the U.S.A.? The moods of the peoples can, however, to an impressive and disturbing extent, be 'engineered'. Almost we can account for them as merely reflective of the relations between the states. Communal feeling may run high on issues towards which individuals as individuals could, in other conditions, with almost equal ease have been led to feel another way. 'Who are "our gallant allies" this morning?' Given leaders who are sufficiently secure in their domestic saddles, it is remarkable what changes in the relationships of peoples may by their endeavours for a time be brought about. The Briands and the Stresemanns of the 1920's prefigured the de Gaulles and the Adenauers of today. Yet in this very comparison there is of course a warning. Like a certain type of psychiatric sufferer, a state may have more 'faces' than one. And indeed it normally does. A charm which is switchable-on this morning may be switchable-off this afternoon. And, like an improvement, so also a deterioration, in the relations between the states, may not be slow to have its effect upon the relations between the peoples.

Where do We, She, They, Come In?

Analysis appreciates the words we use as clues to the thoughts we entertain. In matters of external affairs, men talk of 'we', 'they' and 'she'. We the British; they, H.M.G.; and she, our country. 'We' may be very suspicious of 'them', and solicitous for 'her'. It is 'she' who commands 'our' allegiance. When through 'their' activity, 'she' becomes bound, 'we' feel bound as well, even though technically 'we' are not bound, save by 'our' allegiance to 'her'.

Because Egypt had quarrelled with Britain, Egyptian athletes had to miss the Olympic Games; just as, in brighter diplomatic weather, the prowess of Egyptian runners might have brought prestige to Egypt. We all understand well enough that this is so, but do we trouble to follow out its implications? That would be to wear for the while the thinking-cap of Social Cosmology—or, in the terminology of the London curriculum, the Structure of International Society.

Whose War?

When, facetiously, Noel Coward produced in wartime his song, 'Don't Let's Be Beastly To The Germans', he was showing up the idiocy of those who had not accepted the implications of a war. Though we might blame ourselves, no one else in those conditions could reasonably have blamed 'us', for being 'beastly' to the Germans. Not by our own choice, but by the vicissitudes of history, 'we' had been given a predicament to which no response short of being beastly to the Germans would have been an adequate response. Our beastliness in behaviour was in no sense revelatory of any intrinsic beastliness of disposition, but only of an adequacy of appreciation, a capacity for taking the situation in.

Conversely, when in ordinary times we casually entertain, express and act upon, slapdash, uncomprehending, and intolerant, assessments of the attitudes and actions, including the more 'beastly'-seeming ones, of others, we are failing in fairness not merely to them, but to ourselves and to those whose fortunes we affect. For we are making a less than adequate response. If we would understand our own situation, it is indispensable that we understand theirs too. And, that we understand in particular why their behaviour is not always particularly well calculated to give us the pleasure that we feel to be our due.

In nothing is an innocence with respect to the 'structure' of the social cosmos so commonly betrayed as in the standpoints from which laymen will refer to the problem of the avoiding of war. If it is not actually assumed that war only happens because someone has wished it to happen, it is all too frequently implied that enough people have merely to want it not to, for it to become effectively avoidable. That the structure of international society is virtually unalterable, and that the possibility of war is a built-in feature of that structure, seems not to be universally perceived.

Whose Emotions?

In his *Journey with a Pistol*, an ex-subaltern of the 8th Army tells the tale of a campaign from the viewpoint of one who did not personally get much emotional satisfaction out of it. In particular he recalls with what feelings he would read in British papers of churchmen exhorting their congregations to hate the enemy. No one whose job it was to kill the enemy, lest by the enemy he himself be killed, had needed, he explains, in order to perform the killing which the occasion required, to hate the man he sought to kill. Moreover it would over such long periods have been practically impossible to keep up the necessary hating, had hating been necessary at all. But in fact it was fear, and the sense of self-preservation, which had sufficed to ensure the killing.

The suggestion seemed rather to be that, if the soldiers could dispense with the hating, the civilians need not have hated. But this is as inconsequent as it would be to say that, if the trombone player in a municipal orchestra need not worry about who is paying for the hall, no one should need to consider whether, and with what arguments, the rate-payers should be invited to do so. Without a public willing to foot the bill, the concert would not be happening. Without public support for the war the enemy might be having it all his way. The home-front communal will to resist is a prerequisite if the soldier is to go to the desert at all. All that need be asked of him when in the desert is that he grasp the predicament in which he had better be the first one to kill. It is not the bellicosity of the soldiers that accounts for the war. Nor is it as if in 1914 any at all of the British people had hated greatly the Germans. By 1918, however, it had become rather necessary that they should. And both communally and severally they had by that time come to do so. Yet the war remained a war between the countries, not between the now mutually antipathetic peoples.

Sorts of 'Good Understanding'

Similarly when peace is said to rest on a good understanding between peoples, this carries no assurance that if through interchanges of students and sightseeing parties a person-to-person familiarity at the popular level is achieved, the relations between the states as such will necessarily have been brought any closer to the desired condition. That condition is a state of affairs at the *diplomatic* level: and it is a function of much else besides the state of feeling as between the generality of the citizenry on either side.

The situation in which the individual statesmen find themselves is to be understood only in the light of the one in which their government finds itself, and this again only in the light of that in which their country finds itself. The individuals in question may fail to figure out for themselves the differences between the three situations.

Once again we may note that the only actual behaviour, the only actual doing, of anything, be it the right thing or not, is the doing of the individuals concerned. But, while in one sense the behaviour is theirs alone, it is also at the same time proper to be interpreted as behaviour of the government, which in turn is proper to be interpreted as behaviour of the country as such. To say that the country behaves is to use a metaphor, but not more so than it is to say of a committee, or even of the electorate, that it behaves. All of which is sufficiently obvious, yet possibly just worth underlining. For it helps us to recognise how it is that, while the behaviour is without doubt the behaviour of the individuals only, the relationships affected, and the obligations fulfilled, are those not of the individuals but the states. The individual may of course have a duty to his supporters, and a duty to his constituents in general, as well as a duty to his government, and a duty to his country. To the foreign country he need personally have none. It is his country that will at this level have the obligations. Meeting in a top-level tête-à-tête, the interlocutors may owe nothing individually to one another. But their countries may be owing each other a lot. And if, in the outcome, a country and its individual spokesman both emerge with enhanced prestige, this constitutes two developments, on two separate levels, and not just a single enhancement of prestige. And, like actual behaviour, so also actual emotion, occurs only at the level of flesh and blood. If the pantomime horse behaves sympathetically, the only actual behaviour involved and the only actual sentiments, are those of the legs. And while the forelegs may be feeling one way, the hindlegs may feel another.

Who in Fact Does What?

The members, then, of international society, while deemed to do much, do not themselves actually do anything. Instead, things are done as in their name. So familiar is all this that we tend as a rule to content ourselves with talking of the policy, and comportment, of the governments which 'do' the things. This is all right, so long as we appreciate that, being adopted in the name at once of the government, and of the country also, these courses are not adopted by the government as in its own interests alone.

Whose behaviour then do we, in the international context, have occasion to appraise? The behaviour, someone may say, of sovereign states. So to sovereign states we duly ascribe their responsibilities, and so we develop our classifications of them into good states, states not quite so good, bad states and states not quite so bad. For that is the way things do tend to strike us. It exemplifies that primitive impressionism on which in the rough and ready assessments of everyday we so commonly are content to rely. It is nevertheless not strictly realistic.

The more fundamentally valid approach to the apportioning of credit will suggest the question: Whose doing was this?—and *not* simply: Through which committee was this put? Otherwise it is rather as if we were to blame the pantomime horse when Mr. Hindlegs was dragging his feet. For while, officially, behaviour is what it is in theory, responsibility for it, existentially, can lie only where it belongs in fact.

The House that Who Built?

Whatever the poets might have felt and written, or the politicians have said, it was not, technically, by the peoples, but by the governments, that negotiators were sent in 1945 to San Francisco. It was the governments—though presumably with at least the acquiescence of their peoples—that co-operated in the framing of the Charter. And the terms of the Charter were presently to become binding, not upon the peoples, but upon the states. Incidentally, one cannot say of the document that it was written by those who did not sufficiently understand their social cosmos, for this one cannot know. What one can indeed, however, say is that, if they did indeed well understand it, they may yet have had a reason for electing not to seem to. They may, for example, in the body of the Charter, have fallen back upon an almost certainly unworkable plan in recognition of the stark impossibility of arriving at agreement on anything that could seriously be expected to work. In any case, if there was indeed a defect of understanding, this failure will have been a personal failure on the part of human individuals, and not of states. And yet the agreement concluded was an agreement neither between the peoples, nor between the statesmen, but between the states. Not between the peoples, but between the states. Here indeed is one of those disconcertingly nice distinctions for which we were warned to be watching. Had we not now been supplied by Kenneth Waltz with his analysis of war as incidental to the normal functioning of the international set-up, and had he not used in this connection the image-terminology of Kenneth Boulding, we might have found it less easy to separate in idea the peoples in whose name the Charter was devised and the states in whose name it was signed. As it is, we should have little excuse if in our thoughts on the possible avoidance of war, the problem, that is, of peaceful co-existence in the international society, we did not put the spotlight on the water-lilies, albeit not to the total obscuration of the levels down below. And, if it is to Kenneth Boulding's seminal essay *The Image* that we owe our fresh awareness of 'eiconics' as the up-to-date approach for the social sciences in general, so it is to Kenneth Waltz that we may make grateful acknowledgment for the specifically 'eiconic' treatment he has given us (why not call it 'eirenics'?) of the problem of the avoidance of war. His book *Man, The State and War* shows tellingly the weakness of every explanation which derives from any single-level understanding of a world where things happen interdependently on three levels at once—the levels, namely, of what we have seen as the pond-bottom, the lilies, and the water of the pond.

The Buffer States

Even were league-of-nations number-two to follow its predecessor into the diplomatic discard, there need be nothing to prevent the instituting in its place of league-of-nations number-three. The world might yet have time enough for that. Were the world's only hope dependent upon men's being brought to behave more reasonably toward one another, it might be a poor hope indeed: but since it depends not upon the behaviour simply of men but rather upon the behaviour of states, and since this depends upon the nature of whatever game they may be playing, need we assume that the world's hope is after all so poor?

Peace then, fortunately, does not appear to depend directly upon better relations coming to be established in the human family, for it is not between members of the human family that wars occur. When war occurs, this is between the non-human members of that non-human family, the family of states. Do away with those members and you do away with that family, and with war proper—and with peace proper—as well. How much more physical bloodshed might thereupon ensue between members of the *human* family is quite another question. The world's great hope lies in what for us is so happy a circumstance, namely, that we inherit a global social order in which the cause of international peace is in a certain sense insulated from the causes of human quarrel. It is between man and man that the quarrels occur, it is between states that peace must be maintained. So, be it repeated, the problem of peaceful co-existence among countries is a different problem from the problem of peace among men. It is true that this problem—of peaceful co-existence at the diplomatic (waterlilies) level—has still to be solved. That it admits of solution has still to be shown. But that it admits of *no* solution, this equally has still to be shown: pending which, the search continues. It is in the realm of a more advanced social technology than we have today that the solving, if ever we come to it, will be accomplished. But if it is to be a technology in any way relevant to the condition to be treated it must be grounded in such a deeper understanding of that condition as can be looked for only from those who address themselves to the problem in authentically socio-cosmological terms. As fundamental science is the necessary avenue toward an improved technology proper, so does the problem of peace and war invite attention to that subject which probes into the underlying structure of that society in which wars arise. Who among us would wish to call a halt to such inquiries?

CHAPTER VII

POND-BOTTOM PURVIEW

The Proper Study

Communal willing, communal judging, communal feeling—the social cosmologist must at all times have as a staple preoccupation the 'sociology of knowledge' in its relevance to these. And in this matter let him not be baulked by names. Since names are a question merely of convention, it does not essentially matter which names we employ. But our subjects of study themselves are essentially, and not just conventionally, whatever it is that they are. If conventionally given a different nature, a subject becomes a different subject: whereas, though conventionally given a different name, the subject may stay the same. And the subject which is the subject of this essay stays the same one, however we may choose to name it. Essentially, with whatever name, it remains a study of men behaving, in society which conditions their behaviour, on assumptions which are revisable, and to ends which tend endemically to conflict. It is thus the study of man: and on the face of it, one might suppose, it must therefore be a kind of 'anthropology'. But if so, it is anthropology with a difference: as being studied in a particular period, for a distinctive purpose, and with its focus on selected elements, aspects, strands, levels in that reality which is the life, in co-existence, globally considered, of social man. We might, even so, be content to call it a kind of anthropology, had we not, for specifying its purpose and its focus, a choice of more distinctive names. 'Social cosmology' is one such name.

Globally considered, human society is at once a compresence of people, of peoples, and of communities of other kinds: as also of organisations of all kinds, and of associations, of movements and of groups. Recognition of this, and of what it comes to, means awareness of the insufficiency of any analysis in terms of countries only, or peoples only, or organisations only, or only of beings of flesh and blood.

Multi-dimensional Matrix

Consider the archipelago. We may see it as so many islands, their coasts washed by the waters of a single sea. Or, as a single sea, its surface interrupted by so many islands. In terms of land, it is plural; in terms of water, one. So is it, in a sense, with the social universe. In terms of sovereignties it is plural. Of social substance, one. Socially it is a single non-compartmented jelly. It takes the whole of today's world situation fully to characterise any part of it; and it takes the whole of yesterday's world situation partly to account for the whole of today's.

There is however this decisive point of difference. The water of the archipelago we might imagine drained away, leaving an uninterrupted land-surface. Or we might alternatively imagine all the islands becoming submerged beneath the sea. But we cannot conceive the diplomatic set-up as surviving the disappearance of its social infra-structure. Sovereign statehood might in theory be transcended. Social co-existence hardly. The conditions of such co-existence: these may improve, or they may worsen. But, while men co-exist, a social co-existence theirs will be. It is the conditions of this co-existence, these conditions as obtaining now, that have to be studied and understood if we are to understand a situation obtaining now. And foremost among the conditions is the very texture of the social cosmos as such. Not just its legal structure, nor its political, or economic, but its social, cultural, and psychological structure too. Which of us can claim to have been born with a comprehensive, or even a barely adequate, understanding of these—or to have acquired such an understanding simply in the process of his growing up?

Group Appreciations

'Birds of a feather . . .' But there are feathers and feathers. The flocking together may be that of persons with a common object of worship, or taste in fun, or objection to being pushed around. But especially there occurs the flocking together of those with a common interest to sustain and defend. For instance those who care in common for the countryside, or the traditional Sunday, or the fate of captive peoples. The important distinction here is the one between the non-organised, and the organised, groups. Voegelin writes of a people becoming 'articulated for action', and being consequently in a condition to be spoken for by a representative. In the life political—a life which belongs to the stratum of public experience lying as it were next above that of individual existence, and below the formalized procedures of the state—there are many significant factors, but none more significant than the pressure-group, with its authorised, possibly salaried, spokesmen, and its common, or even communal, standpoint, which its spokesmen have it as their office to assert. A pressure-group is an organisation, with the qualities of a going concern. Its going is on largely predetermined lines, lines determined by its purpose. And, in a world of competing purposes, it is for the service of their own particular purposes that such organisations exist at all. A pram factory may be convertible to the making of weapons: but a trade union to the fight against restrictive practices, surely not. The expression 'non-partisan pressure-group', were anyone to think of using it, would therefore be a contradiction in terms.

But the organised pressure-group is merely a familiar example of something met with in a wider field. For a given judgment there are at least four sorts of status. It may be purely personal; or it may be prevalent; or communal; or official. Official statement: 'He's a jolly good fellow.' Communal echo: 'And so say all of us.' Prevalent opinion: 'He is, isn't he?' Personal thought: 'I can't say that I've ever been able to see it.'

Boys and Blood and Fishes

When Aristotle so sweepingly announced that man was a *politikon zoon* (a polis-maintained and polis-maintaining creature, shall we say?) he was, in a sense, setting a bad pattern for us all: for he was enunciating, as of man as man, what he had noted respecting the free citizen of the Athens of his day. The *polis* as he in his day had known it was a set of arrangements far from typical of what, whether thereabouts or anywhere else, had occurred in the world up to then. What was valid of man as citizen in the *polis* was not necessarily assertable of man as man. Nevertheless Aristotle has at least the virtue of having excluded the idea that man was by nature a hermit. However autonomous in principle, man does indeed relate his living to that of other men. Men think, judge, behave in relation with their like. They consort, they condone, they condemn with 'the boys', or, as Hitler expressed it, 'with the blood'. And as there are feathers and feathers, so is there blood and blood. If A's associates think one way and B's another, A and B will be predisposed, almost as by iron necessity, to differ. For their perspectives will not be interchangeable.

Let there be no mistake about it: social cosmology is a monstrous, non-natural sort of subject. The gymnastics which it calls for—emotionally, intellectually, perhaps even morally—are such as can be congenial to none but a few, to many would be distressing and to some would be beyond their power. Ordinarily, we humans originate and mature as dwellers in some particular pond. From ours into other ponds there may be ways of passing, but, whereas in ours we should know ourselves at home, in others we less probably can. Nor would we feel at ease were we not in any water at all, but for ever looking down upon our pond, and those of others, from the sky. Ours normally is the viewpoint of those among whom we were born, the perspective, that is, of our particular pond-of-origin. Everything else is 'out there'. Where we belong is 'in here'.

Eels' Eyes and Eagle's Eye

Now social cosmology is in principle committed to observing all the ponds alike as though from the sky. Though getting occasional glimpses of what is within them, all that it sees distinctly, and characteristically considers as from the outside, are the ponds. The layman's way, by contrast, of regarding international matters is to see them as belonging 'out there', and their study as involving a sort of excursion deliberately undertaken from 'in here'. The supposition might naturally be that it was the peoples, living separately their collective lives each in its particular pond, that will have developed a system of relations *inter se*. Historically, however, we know that that was not how it went. Our international 'society' began, rather, as an 'international', not of peoples but of princes. And, spiritually at least, these, the princes, may have been even more at their ease in the company of their fellows 'out there' than when together with their peoples at home. When speaking as prince unto prince, the typical prince might have had the sense of being above, rather than in, his patrimonial pond. Though the princes might differ much, and the populations more, from one another, the ponds, as seen from the air, might have differed very little at all. And the fact that in their communal mentalities the peoples may vary so profoundly is not insisted upon, if indeed it is noticed, in the theory either of diplomatics or of international law. This is because, in the place of the princes, it is rather the ponds than the people within them that now compose the society in question. No doubt, it is now, in principle, the populations that mainly determine the behaviour of the ponds, but it is as between the ponds, not the populations, that officially the relationships obtain.

Looking out, therefore, from 'in here', at international affairs, there is little to inform, or remind, us of the way things may look from inside the other ponds. We may know a bit about it. But imagination is a sluggish affair. We are few of us aware of it enough.

Every pond has its view of the sky, and its distinctive prevailing picture of how things are 'out there'. But what of the inside of another pond? It is as difficult explicitly to reckon with what in a neighbouring pond may be taken for granted as it is to appreciate how relative to our own local history are things that go unquestioned in our own.

Home-embroidered Mental Habits

By most of the world's people for most of the time the affairs that we class as international are seen as in the perspective of persons who have never except in imagination gone far beyond their pond. This applies even to how issues are envisaged by some who may have travelled much and far. For it is with their cast of mind and forms of thinking, not with the condition of their passports, that we here are concerned. The thinking here in point is collectively, not individually, pursued. It may be merely prevalent, it is probably to all intents collective, and it may even have the status and the traits of what we have called a 'communal' mode of thought. As Marx was chiefly interested in the consciousness of classes as such, and as Hitler addressed his message to the masses, not the few, so those whose study is the social cosmos will be wise to reckon with the typically Ruritanian view of Utopian policy, rather than with the insights of some exceptional Ruritanian who happens personally to have made a study of Utopian affairs.

When Ruritanians consider collectively their external relations, theirs is no academic undertaking. Typically their purpose is to develop a consensus, on a line. At a council of war, the one question is: What tactics? Not: Have the enemy a case? Talk in a party caucus is certain to be partisan. What Butterfield has so magisterially referred to as the 'embattled systems of self-righteousness' are maintained in vital being on the premise that the question of their righteousness is not going to be reopened while the struggle is on. The smugness, the moral self-pluming: these are merely the self-administered shot-in-the-arm which, to the pond-population, gives the unity which gives the strength which gives the survival-value for a tomorrow full of perils yet unknown.

Existential Sovereignty?

The collective cause is the cause of collective non-extinction. The collective memory may on some points be a long one, and on future possibilities the collective prevision may be persevering to a degree. To follow understandingly the thought-process in a neighbouring pond one would want not only to enter into the lessons and resentments there inherited from the past but also into the fears of possible evils that threaten in the time to come. In form, the relevant relationships are those between states. States themselves, however, have neither bogies nor nightmares nor stereotypes nor myths. It is at the level of the peoples that these elements occur. For the states there speak the leaders. Of husband and wife in England it formerly was said that, in the eyes of the law, they two were one person, and he that person. Sometimes of a given household it may, with point, be asked, Who, here, wears the trousers? Who, now, wears the trousers in the countries of the cosmos? The position may vary a lot. Here it is the dictator. Here the Party—which means those who within the Party wear the trousers. But who in the democracies, that is, the *free* ones? If we take the garment as symbolic not of the intelligence but of the will, then in the free democracies, though others wear the thinking caps, it is the people that wear the pants. In terms of willing, as opposed to thinking, had the leader and the people to be seen as one person, the people would be it. Anyhow, not a Führer. Not, in the free democracies.

Actually there are within the ponds two sorts of cap, the one for facing problems as they exist, the other for rationalising the collective feeling and for matching so to say the pants. Duly to understand a country demands an appreciation not merely of the logic of the studies pursued in cap number-one, but the illogic, or, as some would say, the 'psycho-logic', of the passions developed in cap number-two. And the feeling and the thinking both occur, we remember, deep down at the bottom of the pond. A treatment of international issues which was a distillation, however reasonable in style and phrasing, from that local line of thinking could hardly be acceptable as sociocosmological lore.

The Stuff of Society

To the anthropologists, 'acculturation' is a long familiar concept. For the social cosmologist, too, its importance is great. Like the recruit in the army, the new boy in a school may even be put into uniform, so that it becomes harder to tell him apart from the other boys. Uniform is merely an outward sign, but what it shows is that the wearer is now no longer just a distinct individual, but one of a category whose members are for important purposes interchangeable, or, as a lawyer might put it, 'fungible things'.

The newcomer, however, who has merely put on his regulation clothing cannot as yet be considered effectively to have settled in. It is necessary that he acquire also as it were a standard-pattern mind.

The difference presumably between the 'free' world and the world of the 'people's democracies' is that in the non-free world, except within a strictly delimited area of public debate, there is officially no right of private judgment. The communal viewpoint is not something generated from below. It is fostered, by hothouse methods, from above. The communal orthodoxy is not something that was previously merely prevalent. It is what is to be *made* prevalent now.

Sometimes, of an army, it may be questioned whether it is controlled by, or controls, the state which it ostensibly is there to serve. So likewise one may wonder, of a political party, whether it shapes or is shaped by the doctrine that it exists to apply. As Mirabeau saw Prussia not as a state having an army, but as an army with a state, so has the U.S.S.R. been seen as a doctrine having a party, the party having a state, and the state a bomb. It is because those going concerns, the states, are as organisations so powerful, and so powerfully entrenched, that they have of necessity to occupy the forefront of our stage. But the fact that they are so far from being the only organisations so entrenched—this is what makes our subject so complex, and so demanding upon the mind. For while, in form, the relations are those between the states, and while in reality the behaviour is that of individuals, in effect it is in the organisations and collectivities that the thoughts and feelings which determine the behaviour and the relationships chiefly have their seat. For the behaviour of the individuals is a function of their feelings, and these the feelings of individuals are conditioned by how the collectivities feel.

The fact, of course, is that at the social level it may here be class, there religion, there race, there tribal affinity, which gives its flavour to the rivalry and competition that are the stuff of social life. It might suit Marx's purpose to focus on the element of class, and indeed that might have been all that he himself was sufficiently aware of. But his interpretation of history never was sacrosanct, even among his ideological brood. Other observers will note the multiplicity of different 'publics' which together compose what too commonly is comprehensively referred to as public opinion. Rare must be the situation in which the single state is sustained by a single public, with a single communal stance. The problem of the symbiosis of mutually allergic cultures occurs as well within states as across the boundaries between them. Misunderstanding between the cultural groups within a single country may in fact be hardly less serious and less demanding of attention than as between countries as such. Peaceful co-existence as between the cultures may be as much of a problem for the future as is that between the states.

It would not indeed be inappropriate to see the social cosmos as a multi-state society existing, paradoxically, in what is primarily a multi-cultural world. It is largely in terms of cultural influences playing upon them that individuals react to situations as they do. If of religious experience there is a distinct epistemology, so is there also of political experience: and for the peculiarities of that experience in a given civilisational setting it is cultural factors that are accountable in the main. What gives their quality to the inter-state relationships is by no means only the interests whether of individuals or of groups, but the ideas collectively cherished and the emotions collectively felt. The socio-psychological map of the world may be thought of as largely reducible to a cultural map.

Pluralistic Clubmanship

Acculturation is largely a matter of the 'internalising'—or assimilating—of a folklore. 'When I was a child I thought as a child.' 'Now that I am a man . . .' And there are men, and men, Prooshians and Rooshians and Turks and I-tal-ians! Always no doubt there are the deviants. But no functioning society is founded upon them.

For the individual, in a free world, there may be safety in numbers. Joining more clubs than one, he may move from social circle to social circle, his idiom, his bearing, his very way of feeling changing with every move. The point is that it is he that has to change. His milieux remain tradition-bound. And the tradition is that the individual do conform to the local type, quaint though it be.

Sub-cultural Thoughtways

And quaint indeed may it be when it comes to modes of thinking and of judging. Types of thinking have a way of being stereotypes. The proverbial Frenchman's idea of the Englishman, the Englishman's of the heathen Chinee: exaggerations these were, yet of something sufficiently real, the tendency, namely, as an element in the folklore valid within a given community, for images to become implanted which have little necessary relation to that for which they stand. And acculturation includes the acceptance into a person's private portrait-album of those versions, often travesties, of the truth which in a given social circle are the stock-in-trade of those who set the talking tone on matters of common concern.

So, at a school, might the 'new boy' consider coolly how to brief himself for the 'doing' of his 'stuff'. For this involves saying his stuff, and presupposes knowing his stuff: and, if people in general did not know, and do, and say, their stuff, how could society continue as a going concern? Conformism, even in ways of thought, may moreover be not only convenient. Commonly it is also congenial to the human mood. The explanation for this may well be Darwinian: the survival value of not becoming a deviant, a straggler from the herd. When the leader cries: Let's! the expedient reply is: Yes, let's!!

Dressing safe

Who is the educated man, the man of culture, the cultivated man? Not seldom he is the man who has acquired a particular culture. Too often, that is, for the interests of general enlightenment, of insight and of truth. Ours is a multicultural world. If now no longer literally, then mentally and temperamentally, our fellows, and conceivably we, are given, on public occasions, to appearing in national attire. This multiplicity of mental costumes may make a pretty sight. But what hope of world community if men's minds are all laced up and buttoned up—the unprotesting prisoners of communal ways of thought? Nor is it for public appearances only that we so strangely get ourselves up. Some of us seem as if we slept in our office attire. Uneasy indeed would lie the head that wore a crown, upon the pillow. Why is it that so many do their better thinking in their bath? Why have men withdrawn into the desert?

Sometimes, if only for our self-esteem, we might do some reality-thinking. First, we might lower the lights, lest we be seen as if in thought. Whether we shall publicise tomorrow the results of our adventure, we need not now decide. The good rule appears to be: Don't. Not if you value your standing in your cultural tribe.

The Cave-man in Us

Of the de-parochialising of collective thought there can be little prospect. What social cosmology perhaps will ensure is the momentary readjustment of the thinking of the adult-minded seeker after insight into all that is. Others may in general be content with what is current in the pondy deep. They will hardly see very much of the cosmos from there below. Like Plato's sage, the social cosmologist may need to commute between the daylight and, dare we say, the darkness—accepting the pain of seeing nothing very plainly until his eyes have re-accommodated themselves now to the one perspective, now to the other. If the pond be deep enough, those for whom it is their habitat may have lost the very possibility of distant sight. Sometimes some national ponds seem deep enough for that.

CHAPTER VIII

CONVENTIONAL 'CONVICTIONS'

Why think?

Among the curiosities of language is the way in which a verb may occur in senses both transitive and intransitive, and distinct. 'To reflect' is a case in point. It would seem that man's addiction to reflecting in the one sense is what saves him from overmuch reflecting in the other. Why if you can read editorials should you yourself do any thinking? Such might be the motto of the talker.

For in many matters man seems content for his mind to function like a faulty mirror, giving back what impinges upon it blurred and distorted, if in principle unimpaired—but incidentally unimproved. That it has been given to him in order that he may find his own intellectual salvation, is a truth which comes home to him only if he pauses to reflect: and, since this he so little does, he does not see the need to do it.

Those who would wish to change the world by leading others to think differently have first to find a way of leading them to think. The opinions that men hold are commonly not a result of any thinking, on their personal part, at all. Rather they are the reflection in their minds of other men's reflections.

There are in short two main ways in which our situation, economic, social, political, conditions what we do and say: by affecting such thinking as in fact we do, and by virtually determining whose opinions we accept. Sociology has a branch, the sociology of knowledge, which shows us how strongly our own opinions are affected by where and how we are placed. The worker, for instance, tends spontaneously to see things from the angle of 'the' worker. That he merely tends to do so is partly because he at the same time tends to see them from other angles too. Today's pedestrian, being tomorrow's motorist, does not take the purely pedestrian view of the traffic problem, even while going on foot. He who, while the importer of some things, is at the same time the exporter of others, may be ambivalent in his thinking on tariffs, and the like. And the same sort of sociology also helps us to see in what way, and whence, men's derivative opinions are typically derived.

The question of the way in which men independently think is noticed here partly to stress its complexity, but chiefly to underline its relative unimportance, given that in practice so little of man's thinking is independently done. This chapter is concerned less with how men think, or think they think, than with how they manage to manage without thinking very much. It may be that if men's opinions are to be altered it will not be merely a matter of leading them to think.

Autonomy and Other-directedness

'If you want my advice, there it is: but of course it's for you to decide.' Thus many a candid friend to many a troubled soul in many a moment of indecision. There comes indeed a stage in life when even the person reared as the member of a Church has need to use his individual judgment and make his own decision as to how far he will continue to defer to the hierarchy: whether to subordinate his judgment to that of the institution is thus itself a question for his judgment. Or, in a now familiar jargon: whether he is to remain 'other-directed' becomes a matter for 'inner-directed' choice. For ultimately it is on our own judgment, ours personally alone, that our behaviour is based—for how else, as being indeed *our* behaviour, could it indeed be ours? Though you threaten me with death if I disclose not my secret, it still is for *me* to decide. What is done under duress is in this sense freely done in as much as it is done at all. (*Coactus volui.* Though under constraint, I did indeed consent.)

And if our decisions are ours alone, what then of our opinions? Are these all of them in the same degree ours? In a sense of course they are ours as though by definition. But in a more important sense they may well be so only in form. For simply to say that an opinion is ours may be to obscure a gamut of distinctions.

What is it that makes my opinion distinctively mine?

Surely, the fact of my having arrived at it independently. And this may be only quite exceptionally the position. There are so many matters on which I may prefer to think as those around me seem to think rather than make my own approach. This is the case of simple 'other-directedness'. Or again, I may live in a milieu where some particular opinion is not prevalent merely, but orthodox: in which case I may feel bound to be satisfied with that. Or, it may be a question not merely of a milieu, but of an institution to which I belong and whose official 'line' is mandatory upon me as the well-conducted member. Fifthly, there is the curious case in which an opinion wins acceptance by others and by me, because, although no one in particular may be known to have held it, it has come to be ascribed to what only notionally and as by imputation has a mind. 'This is the voice of America.' 'London rejoices to hear . . .' 'England expects . . .'

Picking up the Moral Tune

If therefore we take some such specific example as my view, say, that democracy is good, this may be either (*a*) privately mine, or (*b*) found current by me among those I consort with, or (*c*) communal in a sub-culture that I belong to, or (*d*) official in the organised set-up to which I belong, or (*e*) attributed, by the paper I read, to 'the Public'. Of particular interest, under (*c*), is the case of the young trade unionist, or the novice in a religious order, or the new recruit. In each such case the tyro may typically be alert to learn the attitudes appropriate to the middle-of-the-road exponent of the sub-culture into which he has moved. What, he may almost be heard to inquire, is it the 'done' thing to feel, think and say, about this or that? What, in short, in this corner of the canteen, this common room, or whatever it be, is the 'line'? He may of course be mistaken in supposing that there really is such a line, in the sense of either (*c*) or (*d*). But, thinking to detect a (*b*) and being in fact influenced only by an (*e*), he may suppose himself to have evidence of a (*c*).

The Heteronomy of 'Private Judgment'

The prestige of a possibly unprepossessing point of view gets presumably a certain reinforcement if plausibly attributed to some such holy abstraction as The Public, or The Establishment, or The City. The politician who dismisses a suggestion on the premise that 'the Country would not stand for it', may have in mind nothing more than a handful of marginal voters, but what in terms he in effect is doing is endorsing the myth on which democracy in theory rests. Is 'the Country' more strictly self-existent than was that *Volk* in conformity with whose requirements Adolf Hitler went upon his way? Explicitly, Hitler professed to rely on a partnership of minds, the People's and his own, or rather, his own and the People's, so intimately interwedded as invariably to think as one. A mystical body, that *Volk*, as he would walk and talk with it: certainly no dull plurality of bovine individuals. For the members of the Party, what resulted was a duty, not merely to act, but to think, feel, and speak, accordingly. No mere matter, this, of voting as directed in a three-line whip. Though the Nazi might claim credit for the correctness of his views, others knew, and so did he, how little he would himself have dreamed of doing any independent thinking. That would indeed have been almost unthinkable. Not merely for him as one of the Party rank-and-file: but simply, one almost might say, as modern man.

Meeting the modern man, the student of politics should ever be ready to ask himself: Is this that I am hearing the frank avowal of a personal conviction? Or is it some 'party line'? And he will recollect that such 'lines' are not those of the bigger parties only. There may even be individuals who talk like one-man parties in themselves. It is as if they had a pre-formulated programme attachment to which, despite dawning doubts as to its wisdom, was felt as a matter of loyalty, to self. As in public life, moreover, so also in everyday social affairs, there are those who live in terms as it were of a private 'official' doctrine. Not: What is the truth on this point? but: What on this point is my line? That is what they seemingly ask themselves before 'taking', even independently, a position on anything at all. But mostly it is by their achieved and cherished solidarity with others that people are precluded from reappraising situations towards which their 'official' attitude is becoming difficult to sustain. Opinion among, say, the miners, on what touches their interests as the miners, is likely to be the opinion not just of individual miners: but rather that 'communal' among a miner 'public', an opinion which the miners individually may well be heard affirming with all the personal fervour of zealots reciting a creed. And what matters in the life political is not simply the arguments of the intellect. It is the faith which puts vitality and venom into the activity of the individual as a sharer in the life and attitudes of the group.

The Unfree Mind of the Unfree Man

As a case in point, we may recall Mr. K., on capitalism as depicted by Marx, and, as displayed to him by Mr. Lodge during his visit to the U.S.A. What differences there might be, between the two sorts of capitalism, Mr. K. professed not to see. Was this his mere obtuseness? Not necessarily. Was it not simply his reiterating of the party line? Given the nature of his party, Mr. K. could scarcely have confessed himself a convert to that capitalism with which communism was still in principle at war. For, whereas one might often be warranted in supposing that a nobody was speaking the truth precisely as he saw it, one should never too confidently expect this of a public man. Certainly not of a Kremlinite when, with everyone's eyes upon him, he is on a mission to the West. Whereas one might normally expect to be told: 'You can't say that. It isn't true', one is, in public life, more likely to be told: 'You can't really say that sort of thing however true you may think it.'

This is why some see so little magic in the idea of a meeting at the summit. The very expression 'at the summit' has an ironic aptness; since it is of the sitter on a summit that it may be most tempting to ask that he 'come off it'. It is difficult to conceive of individuals meeting on a summit, and appealing to one another to do that: but oddly enough this is just what they presumably are expected to do!

The Substance of Society

In so far as society functions with success this is partly because it is formed of individuals so emotionally and psychologically constituted as to lend themselves to social co-existence. Not all of them may do this with equal freedom from spiritual unease. But society functions as it does because enough of its members have sufficiently little difficulty in behaving as is conducive to its functioning. In behaving, that is, congenially: doing their social 'stuff'. And this without distress: because feeling congenially, thinking congenially, understanding, interpreting, pronouncing congenially. Doing, that is, and thinking, and feeling, and talking, their social stuff.

The thing about congenial thinking is, of course, that it may or may not be sound. Its content may or may not have a likeness to what is true. Freud in his analysis of our thought drew a distinction between the 'pleasure', and the 'reality', principles. Congenial thinking is related not to reality but to the convenience—that is, in the Freudian sense, to the pleasure —of the group. And, commonly enough, it is in terms not of testable truth but of mythological doctrine that such thinking is typically pursued.

Whereas the seeking and finding of truth requires use of the intellect, what socially congenial thinking demands is deference to the group. In Hitlerian language, it is thinking 'with the blood'. In ours, 'with the boys'.

Myths Good and not so Good

As doctrinal sustenance for the rising Nazi movement, Hitler and his aides developed, deliberately, a communal mythology. It was not necessary that the votaries of anti-semitism should personally have encountered, or had cause to dislike, a Jew. The disciples were fortified in their folkish solidarity by an image of themselves as threatened in their communal existence by a supposedly identified foe. What anti-semitism meant to the Nazis, anti-this or anti-that or anti-something-else may mean to many an ardent young political bulldozer of today. The matter is however much too delicate to bear closer consideration, except by the individual reader in the privacy of his self-examining heart.

Before dismissing as irrational, self-deceiving, and therefore contemptible, the intellectual practice of what Hitler recommended as thinking 'with the blood', it behoves us to consider whether this is other than just a special case of something to which many besides the Nazis have at all times and in all societies been only too commonly prone. It was as trees walking that in the Gospel narrative the man born blind first glimpsed his fellow men. It was as bees buzzing that we probably all of us first got accustomed to hearing them. Change the bees into B's, and a range of illustrations is provided for our theme. 'B' stands for so many apposite categories of our contemporaries. If the curate feels no compulsion to think with the bishops, the employee may be tempted to think with the boss, many a rank-and-filer with Big Brother, many a climber with the best people, or with the bright-young-people (*alias* possibly in these days the beatniks), or simply, as we saw, with 'the boys'. Yes, especially with the boys. Whether, for the world and for its hopes of happiness, regrettably, or not, the disposition to conformism in thinking-practice is hardly less prevalent in what Frenchmen call the *évolué* (the no longer primitive tribesman) than in the typical member of the tribe. The one kind of B-thinking for which we can, it would seem, look with least confidence among our fellows is thinking with the brain. There was something disconcertingly human about those Nazi enthusiasts.

The Law of the Community as the Lore of the Few

Less irksome it is, and so more congenial, to preserve one's group-orthodoxy unimpaired no less in thought than in expression: to blink, that is, the distinction between what is matter of fact and what matter of doctrine; and to treat the socially reiterated as if objectively true. Yet the difference between the orthodox and the proven or self-evident is obvious enough, however unorthodox the attitude of those who harp on it 'out of their turn'.

As perhaps our best instance of an orthodoxy, we may take the sufficiently familiar example of the law. 'The' law is that obtaining in a particular society. The study of it means the acquiring of a corpus of concepts, standards of appreciation and points of view which for the relevant purposes are in the relevant milieu the stylised and institutionalised substitute for a fresh examination of the given. Not all legal systems are equally sensible, or equally not. But in the case of every legal system there can be little room for deviants on the Bench, or among those aspiring to sit there. Not: How does this strike me? but: How do things stand in contemplation of the law? is what the judge is concerned to consider.

The legal profession is a fair example of what by some would presumably be called a 'sub-culture'. And the sort of thing the members of that profession share, namely an esoteric orthodoxy, is what those of other sub-cultures may similarly be found, amongst themselves, to share. This is just the point of our calling them a sub-culture. A farmer may have bred a special strain of cattle, or a gardener of peas. So, in any given sub-culture, there is maintained in vigorous vitality a peculiar breed of preconceptions, prejudices, partisan points of view. Occasionally into the herd there may be born a queer exception. A monster we may call him. If a 'sport', then hardly a 'good' one. An outsider, really. Out then with him! *Raus!* The swastika-dauber is alas only an extreme exponent of a mood which in less recognised forms has its parallels elsewhere. Which of us is not conscious of antipathies that we harbour as being what it is the 'done', rather than the strictly fair and reasonable, thing to entertain?

Politically Sealed Lips

Given that a particular evaluation has become so to say canonised in the local tribe, while few can afford to show uncertainty about it, there is one, namely, the politician, for whom it is as law. Nearly everything of any importance that is said politically is said by someone speaking in a 'role'—as the spokesman, for instance, of some section of opinion. That things said in that capacity may be other than objective is sufficiently plain. They are virtually certain to be other than objective. One might indeed speak of there applying in politics an 'iron law' of partisanship. Especially instructive to look out for will be those truths which by their nature are such that, while there are those who cannot officially afford to perceive them, there equally are others who can ill afford not to, at every opportunity. The Oder-Neisse frontier, for instance, is still technically provisional. This fact the Polish Premier cannot afford to mention, whereas the West German Chancellor can scarcely afford not to.

The difference between the roles of the politician and the analyst is as that between the two uses of 'reflect'. The social cosmologist, being *par excellence* an analyst, and not a politician, has a special responsibility for reflecting upon such truths as, in a given milieu, no politician can afford publicly to perceive. Also, for not exercising this his special responsibility irresponsibly. Indeed, his judging of judgings has need to be practised with special anxiety on judgings of his own. If, with the psalmist, he may pray to be given understanding that he 'may live', he should supplement this with a further prayer, for judgment, that he may have a better understanding, that he may live to better purpose.

One Man, One Justice?

Group thinking has typically its roots in the specific historical experience and the given social milieu. There it develops concepts which tend to be taken as having reference to the ontologically real. As, from his inspection of certain shapes, the geometer abstracts his idea of 'the' triangle, and goes on then to posit 'the' triangle as a form laid up, so to say, in the heaven of things intelligible, so may the moralist picture 'justice' as an essence, for the 'true' definition of which he may proceed to seek. The practice of conceptual analysis is generally indispensable to those who in common would wish to think things through. 'You try to verbalise your conception, and I will mine, so that, comparing them, we may together approach the true definition of justice as she is.' She, justice, is the projected image, the reified embodiment, of man's *idea* of justice, an idea born of his experience. Positively it may be difficult to show man's idea of justice as everywhere identical. But negatively justice should at least be the opposite of injustice, an idea derived from an emotional experience which presumably is everywhere sufficiently the same.

What is the Norm of Normality?

A comparison between ideas of justice can be instructive to anyone, both in showing him the diversity of men's understandings of life, in exposing the relativity even of his own idea, and in clarifying for him its implications. What must vitiate any such search for philosophical insight is a disposition on anyone's part to suppose that there is necessarily a true definition, and that it happens to be his. That would be like assuming that English, not being foreign in England, cannot anywhere, or for anybody, have the aspect of a foreign language. It would be like supposing that man is typically man, so that woman is an inferior form of man. Or, that British democracy is democracy proper, so that anything differing from it is called democracy only by courtesy at best. When polygamy is rejected as not just relatively but absolutely wrong, or eggs and bacon seen as 'the' authentic breakfast, a pattern of social thinking developed in given conditions is used for the discrediting of social arrangements obtaining, however successfully, in the conditions of some other social milieu.

One had better give thought to what this means. The French word *mentalité* is useful here. What gives to any communal opinion its endurance value is its attunement to a mentality that is communal, and not just prevalent only. It is owing to the inadequacy of our insight into others' mentalities that we find it hard to fathom the attitudes that we meet with in them and with which we may have to deal. Too readily do we ascribe to others what we would consider a normal mentality, meaning something not unlike our own.[1] If Mr. Neville Chamberlain may be taxed with having revealed, in 1938, a lack of anything, it was not a lack of courage; but rather perhaps of the ability, or even the urge, to get on proper talking terms with those with whom at a critical juncture it fell to him to parley. Advisers whom he might have expected to understand better than he himself did the mentality of a Hitler he seems to have brushed aside. The two men seem scarcely to have found a common wavelength: and for this the blame may not have been Hitler's only.

Patriotism is not Prosy Enough

Hitler was *par excellence* the bulldozer. He was born to change things, to smash and build anew, to do battle for a cause, the cause, as he construed it, of his *Volk*. It is not just the emotions of men individually that make the world go round. It is group emotions chiefly, those, that is, of men in their

---

[1] Utopian as it perhaps must remain to be wishing for a world in which at long last the peoples will have come to understand one another, it may yet be not beyond the limits of the realistic to be striving, and contriving, for a state of things in which they do at least appreciate that they don't. And what a progress that would be towards the target of an eventual all-round limitation and reduction of misunderstandings!

multitudes reacting collectively to group situations. To reason the world out of its susceptibility to nationalism would be almost as impracticable as to argue the eternal mother out of her feeling for her child. The nationalistic passion is not something whipped up to serve a purpose defined by reason. Reason is on the contrary called in to serve the cause that passion has espoused. Between the oratory, and the poetry, of patriotism there are obvious affinities, and the status of what either has to say is scarcely that of scientific 'truth'. The critic who assesses poetry in terms of its testable-truth-content is off the point: and so is the sociologist who shows surprise at the interlarding by politicians of their analyses of the outlook with an admixture of myth. Political edification and academic enlightenment are different things, serving different objects. To measure the one by the standards of the other is a category mistake.

Nationalism may well have been a cause of war, as has vitality of dog fights: but we have not abolished the dog. Whether we find good in it or not, nationalism is a fact of our environment, like the warmth of the sun. We have air-conditioned offices—but not yet a reason-regulated cosmos. Even at its worst nationalism is a social malady with which at the best we may long have to live. Not that it is altogether beyond treatment. It may, moreover, become, on the other hand, an element of social health.

But even so the forms it takes can be repellent to the unsympathetic. He may be tempted to call it a form of madness. Yet that it is not. Nationalism is an emotion developed by individuals collectively. For while the feelings of a man are some of them distinctively his, others he derives rather from his rootedness in a group. To explain a given display of national feeling we need to know the occasion of it. This has only to be such that members of the group have come to competing with one another as exponents of the *Geist*, and mere emulation will do the rest. Who among them really has what emotions in his heart is almost an independent question. The play, as such, is the thing. What a terror Adolf Hitler might have been on the stage! The student of affairs should note the great variety of worlds and should see the world of diplomatics, and within it the several sub-worlds of international organisation, as so many environments, the breeding grounds of cultures and sub-cultures of their own.[1]

Whose are the Normal Norms?

Of Frenchmen such as are accustomed to assuming that every anglophobe manifestation in the Paris Press must have been 'orchestrated' by the Quai d'Orsay, how can it be hoped that they will not make similar assumptions when criticism of French policy appears in the London papers? As a better-informed Frenchman once said on the air: 'I explain all that to my countrymen, but the truth is, they just don't believe me.' The reader may be too young to remember the alleged remark of the Yugoslav when in 1945 Churchill had lost the election: 'I suppose they'll shoot him now?'

The sobering aspect of the use by African leaders of the one-man-one-vote slogan is not that they should be clever enough to use it, but the readiness of so many reasonable people in England to find it reasonable that they should. For these tend to define 'the reasonable' as 'what we are used to here'. Man may presently get to the moon. Then, who knows, his very notion of the reasonable may well be rejected. He'll be asked, perhaps, not to talk that earthshine here.

Travel, as ordinarily understood, takes place within the earth's gravitational field. Space travel becomes realistically thinkable only when thought of in conditions not ordinarily applying to travel. This means, not that the intending space-traveller must correct his assumptions about ordinary travel: what it means is that he must relativise his idea of the 'ordinary', and hold together in his mind the ideas of two different kinds of travel, each as ordinary, in its own conditions, as the other.

The Foreignness of English

And what thus applies to thinking about travel applies comparably to thinking about politics in areas beyond a given country's jurisdiction. If, say in Ruritania, the jury system is not found to work well, this is not necessarily a reflection on Ruritania. If in revolutionary France a democracy was

---

[1] Each such milieu may be marked, in Wittgensteinian jargon, by one independent 'language game' or 'form of life'. 'When in Rome . . .'. Remember Bernard Shaw's '. . . their tastes may be different'.

understood to mean a homogeneous society based not on tradition but on abstract ideas, this was no condemnation of a form of government rooted in centuries of British experience. The man, it has been said, whose only speech is English is obliged, when he goes abroad, to shout: for how else is he to become intelligible to those who fail to follow what he says in normal tones? Anyone whose patterns of social thought are strictly parochial must needs discuss matters international in terms of these, irrelevant though they be, for how otherwise can he hope to contribute to a debate? The physics teaching, however, which shows the earth's as but one instance of a gravitational field, or the language teaching which shows English as no less foreign a language than any other, does for the child's education rather what social cosmology should do on the validity and status of those concepts which he uses in his 'ordinary' political thinking.

The Relativity of the Commonsensical

The concepts of classical physics and of common sense have not, it seems, to be abandoned even by the pioneer in quantum-theoretical inquiry: but he does have to do without them, and use others, rather odd ones, we are told, when at work in that special field. So too, the social scientist, when exploring the relationships between the notional and the true, must accept the experience of wearing an unfamiliar thinking-cap without discarding his ordinary one. He must not so extrapolate from the findings he has come to with the old one on as to prejudge what shall result from his wearing of the new. And similarly with the dualism of the domestic and the diplomatic systems of social arrangements. If, for instance, he is, in discussion of international procedures, to use the term 'democracy' at all, he should explain in what, necessarily very special, sense he deems it helpful to use, in that context, such a term as democracy at all. So, also, if he is to use in an International Relations context the term 'the rule of law'.

CHAPTER IX

THE MYSTIQUE OF THE LAW

A still Unsettled Question

It is necessary, if we would understand the social universe, that we appreciate the status within it of international law. In learned writings on this question the core of the matter has not always been approached. It is this core of the matter that there will now be an attempt to expose. And let it be insisted, lest there be any misconception on the point, that the question for inquiry is the nature of human society and the status of an element within it, and not just the uses of a word. Semantic analysis has its importance but linguistic conventions are not the only significant facts of social life.

A World that Never Truly Was

Let the reader conceive a world consisting of self-contained kingdoms, each ruled despotically by a king, and each as separate, constitutionally, from the others as, geographically, are islands in a sea. Let him imagine those kings the members of a club for kings, their membership being, of course, subject to their recognition, as binding upon them, of the rules. Within his own domain each king exercises sway through ministers who, acting together, run also a system of official representation abroad. A king falls ill: but his ministers carry on doing things in his name. He becomes a chronic invalid. Still they carry on. He dies without an heir. His subjects ask his ministers to remain in office, becoming responsible now to them collectively instead of to the no longer existing king. The representatives abroad now represent not the king but the kingdom. The idea catches on. And presently, the other kings also disappearing, the club carries on as a club, not for kings, but for kingdoms. For purposes of club membership the kingdoms are conventionally conceived of as persons, persons of like passions in the main with the kings they supersede, and, like the kings, having things done for them by ministers, and representatives appointed by these ministers, in their name.

In place of the kings we see two sorts of personified abstractions. Two sorts, not one. This is the important point. Represented abroad are the personified kingdoms, standing in the stead of those persons, the kings. Served by the ministers at home are the personified peoples, standing likewise in the stead of those same persons, the kings. The kingship in its external application has passed to the kingdoms. In its internal application it has passed to the peoples. In its external application, kingship meant and means simply eligibility for membership in the club. In its internal manifestation it meant and means ascendancy, supremacy, top-dog-ness. Kingship in these two independent meanings, being now vested in different abstract entities, becomes two different factors, in the one case a characteristic of a country, in the other of a people. Two different factors, both called kingship. 'Kingship' thus has now two different meanings, which no one need confuse. And the point of the story? The point of it is that that is also what has happened to the term 'sovereignty'. It has now two different meanings, which no one need confuse.

A Law for Sovereigns

To say that no one need confuse these two meanings of sovereignty is not to say that no one ever does. In particular, people ask: Given that sovereignty means topness, how can all the members of a club be sovereign? How can they all be top? We must be careful at least not to fall into that one! Fitness for membership in a club for top-dogs is easily described. Being dogs, being top (in their own kennels), being all equally dogs, all equally accepting the conditions of membership of the club. Or alternatively, not being physically dogs, but only notionally—being deemed to be dogs, conceived of as if dogs, having dog-ness ascribed, imputed, to them.

Countries, whether kingdoms or not, being deemed to be persons, conceived of as if persons, having personality imputed to them—these are duly qualified for membership of the club, under all the conditions attaching thereto—and especially the condition of subjection to the rules, to the system, that is, of international law—the law described by Vattel as a law *for* sovereigns.

Membership of a club is not a physical condition, it is a social status: and its implications can be known only by knowing the nature of the club. What it means to be a sovereign state is understandable only incidentally to an understanding of the nature of international society. As membership of a club depends on acceptance as a member by the other members, so does membership in international society, the club, the 'international', that is, of sovereign states; and in this society membership is understood not as sovereign statehood merely, but as sovereign statehood subject to international law. The possibility of a recognised sovereign statehood, divorced from subjection to international law, no more arises than does that of membership of the Stock Exchange divorced from subjection to the rules of the Stock Exchange. It is technically unthinkable. That is why you never find it thought of, by sovereign states. What they do think of is how, consistently with their continued technical subjection to international law, they can most successfully pursue the aims they have in view. In this sense they resemble business men with a reputation to safeguard or to lose.

Necessity the Mother?

A sizeable library might be filled with the writings of those —most, if not all, of them men of great learning and high repute—who on one side or the other have contributed to the great debate about the basis, and nature, of the binding force of international law, as law. On the one hand there are those who see it as somehow binding by the dispensation of Nature. As physical necessity expressed itself, or was supposed to express itself, in the laws of physical nature, so social necessity, or moral necessity, or jural necessity, or biological necessity, or necessity-just-like-that expressed itself in the law of nature and of nations. *Pacta erant servanda.* Pacts were binding, because—well, because they *were*—in the nature of things.

But were they? Are they? In the nature of things? Is it not rather that they derive their binding character from their status in the sight of the law? Is it not the law, rather than Nature, that makes them binding, legally (not just naturally, and perhaps not naturally at all—but non-naturally, legally, in the sight, not of nature but of law)? The cart being drawn by the horse, it is implausible to say that the horse moves forward because pushed by the cart. What moves the horse? What gives its binding force to that law which gives their binding force to those pacts which, under its mysterious aegis, are concluded? In opposition to those who so inconclusively have argued that law as such is binding by nature, there are those who have seen it, by contrast, as binding by virtue of consent. The positivists, to give them their accepted name, see the states as having in effect, constructively, if not historically and in fact, agreed that there should exist a legal system binding upon themselves as sovereign states. This is not the same as saying that the system is made up of provisions all severally so consented to: for it is the system, surely, which lends its legal force to that consent. It is the system itself, as such, that is being held to have derived its binding character from some sufficient sort of consent. What remains of course a mystery is how any sort of consent could in fact be sufficient to give binding force to a system, as a system, of law.

Holmes the Homeless?

The fact however is, is it not, that in asking how in fact a legal system comes in fact to be a binding system, both schools, backers on the one hand of Nature and of consent on the other, have made what it is now the fashion to describe as a category mistake. One does not ask where, as a matter of history, Sherlock Holmes had his home—still less where his maternal grandmother had hers. The way of life of any character in fiction is, as such, a matter not of fact but of fiction. Where in fiction, where in the story, the fictional character had his home, if any, or his grandmother, if any, hers, if any, is a question to which the sufficient answer, and so the correct, though scarcely the true, answer, is a matter of fiction. And as things can correctly be said in terms of fiction concerning what exists in fiction, so in terms of doctrine may things be correctly said concerning what exists in terms of doctrine. The answer, if any, to a question concerning something which is so in point of doctrine will be correct, or incorrect, in point of doctrine.

And if, like the question concerning Sherlock Holmes's grandmother the question is difficult to answer even in what would be the appropriate terms, in terms of *fact* it is no more susceptible of an answer, either accurate or otherwise, than is a question of fact concerning what has existed only in point of fiction. That the law exists is a sound enough assertion if by sound we are understood to mean sound in point of doctrine. That the law is thus, in terms of the relevant doctrine, *deemed* to exist—that too is a sound, probably even a true, assertion in point of fact. But what is not sound, because it cannot be true, in point of fact, is that the law exists in point of fact. For in point of fact law as such exists only in point of doctrine. And to ask or offer an answer in terms of fact to a question arising, if it arise at all, only in terms of doctrine is to fall into a category mistake. Anyone who makes this mistake in respect of the binding force of international—or of any other kind of law—has the consolation of knowing that in doing so he is in a numerous and illustrious company: but that does not render him right.

Worlds Distinct but not Apart

Any question presupposing that the legal relations between banks, or the legal relations between brothers, for that matter, are elements in the world of fact as distinct from that of law, involves similarly a category mistake. And while social relations between brothers, as distinct from legal relations, may be said to subsist in fact, between banks as distinct from the bankers, even the social, no less than the legal, relations subsist essentially only in idea. In the theory, the doctrine, the idiom, the way of thinking, that prevails in the relevant society, the banks are persons, having relations *inter se*, just as brothers in fact are persons having relations *inter se*. And over and above these, their social relationships, subsisting, in principle, as matter of fact, the brothers may also have legal relationships, subsisting in principle, as matter of legal idea. We may speak of course of happy relations existing *de facto* between banks, meaning *de facto* between the bankers. We may speak of friendly relations between countries, meaning absence of animosity between their peoples. But the formal relations between banks, as such, independently of the bankers, and of the states, as such, independently of the statesmen, are relationships subsisting not, in principle, in the world of fact, but in the realm of official idea. The relations officially conceived of as obtaining between what are officially conceived of as persons distinct in principle from their populations, whether individually or as human aggregates, are relations officially conceived of rather than relations obtaining in fact. Loose language however suggestive of, is not necessarily conclusive of, a category mistake having been made: for those who get their language picturesquely oversimplified may nevertheless be keeping their mental pictures realistic and precise. Not always is there a mistake being made. The point is that there often is one, and that when this is so, it is likely to be in the nature of a category mistake: for it is likely to be a question worded as arising with respect to the world of fact when in strictness it has arisen only with respect to the position in a world of doctrine—of legal doctrine, of social doctrine or, above all, of diplomatic doctrine. To show, or to question, something's existence in diplomatic doctrine it may be suggestive, but is scarcely sufficient, to point to something as existing in the world of fact.

A Set of Ideas

Law is a factor in the social scheme of things, consisting of a set of ideas in principle belonging together as elements in a logically coherent system—a system deriving its character as law not from the quality of its component ideas but from its status as a factor in the social scheme. For law is not simply a set of ideas, it is a social institution, not even conceivable— as law—in separation from the social milieu in which it has the status which is the very essence of its 'law-ness'. And, as law —that is as being, by status, law—it is, by status, *binding* law— for as little can one conceive of a law that is not binding law as one can conceive of a circle that is not circular. It is of the very nature of a circle to be circular, and of law to be binding. The imputation to it by the society it serves of its status as law is by the same token an imputation to it of binding character. Not naturally, but in point of status, it is binding. So far from the members of the society having rendered it binding upon them by any virtual equivalent of a formal consent, the membership to which they lay claim in the society in question is a membership in subjection to the law of that society, for such is the nature of that society. It is a society which has, historically, taken shape as a society of members subject to that law. Their subjection to it is no more detachable from their membership than is its binding force from its character as law. And to ask for evidence of their subjection, or of its binding character, or indeed of the existence of such a society—if this means asking for evidence of a *fact*—is, as it happens, a category mistake.

A Faded Myth

The student should know now to listen very critically to anyone who thinks to persuade him that international law is essentially a form of 'natural' law. Unless either the one term or the other is so defined as to make the statement tautological, the statement is incorrect. But it is worse than that: for while intrinsically false it has something of the appearance of being true. If international law were natural it would not be law—not in the sense in which the law obtaining in any modern civilized country is law. For law, let us say in England, is a human achievement, as much indeed as is the invention of games—with which it has not a little in common. The playing of games is possible because man's mentality lends itself readily to association on a basis of make-believe. The players in a game are living as it were in a little world or sub-civilisation of their own. And what makes their behaviour rationally intelligible is their acceptance, conventionally, of assumptions not true of the world of common day. And if this is true of the game as a sub-civilisation so also is it true of civilisation in general. Man by virtue of his game-playing capability lends himself readily to life in an environment other than the merely natural.

The Basis of Social Co-existence

Conceiving themselves as living in a society, the sovereign princes conceived themselves as living under law. This was analogous to a company of friends hitting upon the idea of indulging in a new kind of game. Some newly invented games do not take on. Others one will see being played. The game of let's-play-international-law took on, got going and is going on still. And the same may, with non-essential differences, be said of any other operative legal system. Once we remember that social co-existence, like the playing of a game, proceeds in the light not of things as they are, but of assumptions of a conventional character—in the light of how they shall be *deemed* to be—we see in what sense it is that law of any kind exists, and on what terms its existence is feasible.

What matters for the possibility of such a 'game' is not that the players should be all of a single heart and mind on what makes the game worth playing. On the point and purpose of their playing they need by no means be at one. Enough that their outward behaviour be in close enough accord with the requirements of the theory. But with respect to the status and content of the theory, given that they are men, not ants or bees, a certain semblance of agreement among the players, some approach as Boulding might put it, to the sharing of a public image, would seem to be a *sine qua non*. For it is on their sharing of such an image, of what they are involved in, that their co-existence and co-operation in community are basically dependent.

Why no Orthodox Answer?

On the function of law in the national community Karl Marx propounded a quarter-true idea, the error of which is made particularly apparent if the attempt is made to apply it by transference to the explaining of the function, internationally, of international law. Marx represented law as essentially, and not merely in special instances, an instrument of exploitation and oppression. What is true of Marx's idea is true likewise of any other theory which likewise makes law to be necessarily something imposed. Is there—and if not why is there not—an orthodox answer, to this question on which Marx's answer has above been described as only quarter-true? On what level of inquiry does this question arise? Is it on the level of legal theory? On the level of the physically real? No, it is on neither of these levels.

Where Have Law, and Music, Their Being?

Our question does indeed arise on the level of reality—but it is on the level of social, not of physical, reality—and our inquiry is sociological in type. Here sees the student of social phenomena a going concern. In this going concern an evidently important component element is law. What function, he may ask himself, can law be observed as fulfilling within the structure of this going concern? An analogous question suggests itself. What function does the musical composition fulfil within that going concern which we know as an orchestra performing a symphony? Physically there is a good deal going on, and what is physically happening is far from pointless. What gives it its point is however its relationship to something not physically existent in the world of tangible fact. For, in what sort of a world does the composition have its existence? In what sort of a world exists any piece of music while not in process of being performed? Or any poem not presently being recited or recalled to mind? Or any story not presently being told? Or any slander not presently being repeated? Or any recipe not at the moment being used? The legal formula is preserved on paper: yet its preservation on paper is not the same thing as its existence. Need a story, in order to exist, be available on paper? Need it even be remembered? How many stories have existed and then been lost? Do they in being lost so cease to exist? What if the same story should tomorrow suggest itself to someone anew? Will it now be the same story—or only another exactly like it? Such questions are not all as trivial, or as playful, or as impertinent, as they may seem.

As the orchestra operates in terms of a creation say of Beethoven's, so does English society operate in terms of the English Common Law, and so does the supra-national diplomatic society of sovereign states operate in terms of International Law. International, like domestic, law is not a policeman, or a prison, or a gallows, or a judge, but a set of ideas. Like domestic law it is binding. Like domestic law it is, as it were, being played. Just as a game, a composition, a play, is at a given moment being 'played', so also at this moment in history are a multiplicity of systems of law, each of them a distinct set of ideas, being played—among them the international system.

Whence the Circularity of the Circle?

What gives to International Law its binding force is what gives it its very existence—namely the thinking, that is, the conceiving, which makes it so. Men, in order to play law, need to conceive law and to conceive it *as* law, to conceive it as binding. For law, *as* law, *is* binding. By definition therefore International Law, *qua* law, 'is' 'binding'. The system is, *qua* law, a binding system.

And now, given this binding system, what of its detailed requirements? How came they to be law? How came they to be binding? How otherwise than simply by coming to be severally included as its component elements in the given, functioning, legal system? Coming so to be included means becoming law. As the promise which I give in a contract becomes binding in terms of the theory of the contract, so the contract as such is binding upon me in terms of the theory of the law. And the law? The law as such is binding on me in terms of the theory of the Constitution. And the constitution as such is binding in terms of . . . what?

Whence the Orthodoxness of the Orthodox?

As the idea of the binding force of contract as such is logically 'pre-' any particular contract, so, that of the law as such is logically pre-legal, and that of the constitution logically pre-constitutional. The idea of the possibility of a binding constitution is a logically pre-constitutional idea: and it is at the logically pre-constitutional level that the question, How *comes* the constitution to be binding? may arise. It is on that level that, if it is to be answered at all, this question must be furnished with an answer. The difference between this question and the question: How comes the contract to be binding? is not that the one question can be answered and the other not, but that the one can be given an orthodox answer, while the other cannot. There is no orthodox answer to the question: How comes it that the constitution as such is binding? There may of course be plausible answers, palatable answers, popular answers. But the binding force of the constitution, while orthodoxy assumes it, is not something that orthodoxy explains. It is matter of basic social dogma. It is the dogmatic premise of the functioning of the constitution, its existence, that is, as a going concern. And as the orthodoxy of the idea of the constitution's orthodoxy is basic to the constitutional process, so to the diplomatic process is basic the idea of the orthodoxy of the diplomatic theory in terms of which international law is binding on the sovereign state. The idea of the existence of states as persons, of their sovereignty, of their constituting a society, of the existence of international law and of international morality, and of these being binding upon the sovereign states —such are the dogmatic premises of that on-going game of diplomatics whose playing at the supra-national level is fundamental to the maintenance of such rudiments of order as men presently enjoy in their global affairs.

Does Enforcement Create, or Does it Presuppose . . . ?

What is it that accounts for—and what exactly is it that constitutes—the actual playing of a game of law? What, for instance, in the case of the Law of England? English law is not merely enacted, interpreted, applied: it also is in some degree enforced. Is English law being played merely in that it is being enforced? Or is it being enforced by virtue of its being played? A society playing a system of law seeks to enforce it upon any marginally co-operative members, just as an orchestra might scowl at a performer who was getting out of time. What accounts, however, for the music's being played is not the scowling, but the disposition of the members in general to play, and if need be to scowl. Had a functioning society to be thought of like that of a lion-tamer whipping his lions around in a cage—then international law just would not fit into the picture. So much the worse, must we not then say, for such a version of the picture? But if it be likened to a *game in progress*, it does. Imagine international society like a game in progress, the players being the sovereign states. Imagine the game as blending the characteristics of chess, of poker and of American football. Realise that, as the notion of law implies the notion of binding force, so the notion of disposition to play the game implies disposition to submit to the referee, that incarnation of the rules of the game, of the theory, that is, determining what is proper and what improper and what obligatory in the playing of the game. The game goes on because, the players being agreeable to its going on, enough of them are continuing in submission to the rulings of the referee. The international game goes similarly on because the players, the states, continue in principle, in profession and purportedly, to subject themselves to the requirements of international law. Even after entering the Rhineland in March 1936, Hitler was at pains to contend that in doing so he had not got 'off side'. The absence of a referee might be fatal to the playing of rugby football: but it is not quite fatal to the playing of the game of diplomatics. What happens is that the game goes on and the argumentation about alleged past infringements of the rules goes on as well.

Is a Light, when not Alight, a Light?

When is 'law' not properly speaking law? One answer might be, when it is not functioning as such. The same hat formerly fashionable may be now no longer in the fashion. What was a fashionable hat is no longer a fashionable hat. The same idea, formerly erroneous, may now have become correct (e.g. that Queen Anne is dead). The same fact once unknown may now be known. The same idea once heretical may now be orthodox. The same rules once not in force may now be in force. In virtue of their being now in force, legal ideas have now a certain sort of orthodoxy. They are the orthodox answer to the question, What, on such and such a point, is the law? The question arises: Are they the orthodox answer because they are the law, or are they the law because they are the orthodox answer? It is confidently submitted that their being orthodox flows from their being the law, rather than the other way about.

Why, when Playing Ball, do People Play at all?

Having thus considered in what sense international law is binding, it still remains to discuss why it is not only recognised, but treated, as binding. Why, though not necessarily enforced, is it at all complied with? The answer is: Because the on-going global diplomatic process is indeed like a game, and like any other game, it has to have rules, and compliance with those rules. The question: Why in practice is the law respected? may be met with another question: Why on a football field is the referee obeyed as he is?[1]

It is after all not in the nature of the law, but in the nature of the international society, that one must look for the answer to the question: Why in practice do states obey the law?

---

[1] Every large-scale society, be it free-democratic or totalitarian, or be it the society of states, has its own particular 'game'—played, or misplayed, in accordance with its own conventions—save in terms of which its functioning will not be understood.

CHAPTER X

SOME MORAL NICETIES

Angles on Moral Norms

Why, we have asked, do states obey the law? Why, we might have asked, does anyone obey it? To this some might answer: Because he knows, or because he considers, or because he feels, that he ought to. But what precisely do we mean by this 'ought' with respect to which men may report themselves as having knowledge, or beliefs, or feelings—if not all three, or at any rate two, of these at once? If we are to think about 'ought-ness', we had better reflect a little on how far we ourselves would claim to have knowledge, or beliefs, or feelings in reference thereto. It might be difficult except in the presence of some specific moral issue—some concrete question of 'oughtness'—to examine ourselves realistically as to how exactly we can describe our position in this matter.

Let us first of all note that for the focusing of moral issues there are three distinct perspectives: those (*a*) of the social analyst, with his interest in the ways that men behave and are expected to behave; (*b*) of the moralist, with his evaluative standpoints; and (*c*) of the social practitioner, the live individual with his participation in the struggle of life and his involvement in the particular situations where the moral issues present themselves for appraisement. To the social scientist the given elements include the given norms. With respect to these his interest is in at least three questions: (*a*) What are the norms in a given milieu? (*b*) How far is respect for them expected (in the sense of foreseen as likely in practice to be shown)? and (*c*) How far is it expected (in the sense of demanded)? The social analyst as such is not interested in the intrinsic value or validity of the norms, but in their status as obtaining in a given 'world'.

To the moralist the norms are standards, criteria, canons,

yardsticks, touchstones, ideals, wherewith as from the sideline to test the propriety of behaviour not his own. To the participant they are a framework with reference to which he renders his responses in the hourly routine of living. What to the moralist are predilections are scruples to the practitioner.

Behaviour as Affected by Norms

Behaviour in social situations is, we may say, affected by (*a*) what people in such situations are supposed to do; by (*b*) what in fact they generally do do; by (*c*) what it would be congenial to do; and by (*d*) the scruples whereby, in the circumstances obtaining, the congenial is rendered inadvisable—these scruples being in part inspired by (*a*) and (*b*) and in part, with some people, by (*e*), namely considerations of an ethical nature having weight with them individually or as members of special sub-groups, rather than having the status of common social norms.

It is a natural assumption that the norms whereby one values the conduct of others are those by which in like conditions one's own conduct would, one believes, be guided. Few of us admit that our judgments upon others are harsher than those we would be content to have passed on ourselves. If in similar circumstances we were to behave like that, we should, rightly, we tell ourselves, feel ashamed, and would feel no surprise at being frowned upon for it by our neighbours. Such seems to be the implication.

The Claims of the Sociological Approach

There is nothing inherently objectionable in the role of the moralist practising his appreciating of behaviour in the light of moral norms. What is regrettable is the way the attraction of that role may draw people away from the independent role of social analyst, or social physician. What the sociological approach should produce is not a de-moralising of the student's view of politics, but an improvement of his spectacles.

Aspects of Ethical Judgments

We all have our feelings on moral issues. How we will have come by them is a question on which Freudian psychology, and metaphysical speculation, may alike purport to assist us. Enough, for present purposes, to note that we often are not at a loss to know and to specify just how something strikes us, as considered from the moral point of view. We may note too that on a moral issue we may often have little difficulty in sensing the existence of a prevalent, or communal, or at least a fashionable, standpoint, as one which, as seeking social respectability in our milieu, it is propitious for us to espouse. We also may note that, whatever our feeling and whatever the fashion, the judgment in such cases involved usually admits of being so expressed as seemingly to claim a universal, and not merely relative, validity, and that what makes this all so easy is the fact that the very framing of the question to be answered will commonly not have been undertaken until it was known in advance what the answer was to be. If we wanted one answer then the question arising was: Are we in favour of peace? If the other, then: Are we in favour of appeasement? Either way, our formulation reads as if dictated—inescapably—by the very nature of the case.

Belief in Others' Badness

It is among the facts of life—whether international or not—that man's brother does not hold him guiltless. People do in fact find fault. Herein they expose their basic position on two metaphysical points. They show themselves to be assuming that man is indeed possessed of that freedom, failing which no imputation to him of responsibility for his doings would make much sense at all. And they show themselves as further assuming that in matters of conduct there is, not just conventionally, but ontologically, an opposition between the right and the wrong. Bad behaviour may be iniquitous, as bad weather never is. For the badness of bad behaviour is a moral badness. Men do therefore seem to assume the reality of a moral order, not just as a mental construct invented by a particular community but universal in its embrace. They do not prove this and might be hard put to it even to pretend to do so. But they assume it, as a rule without any question. It appears in short to be a key ingredient in their understanding of life.

Why So Certain?

If he happens to be a theist, the student should ask himself whether he thinks anyone is in a position to say with certainty what, in a given situation, the will of God prescribes. If, on the other hand, he is an atheist, or an agnostic, he should ask whether he does not, even so, believe in the ontological validity of the right–wrong antithesis. If not, has he any ground whatever for maintaining that anything ever is right, as distinct from supposedly right? Believing, if he on the other hand does, in the validity of the distinction, he should ask himself whether either he or anyone else has good reason to feel confident of knowing what in a given situation the distinction requires.

Acknowledgments to Parmenides

A man may believe absolutely that God's will should be done, and yet not claim to know with certainty what in a particular matter it requires. A sceptic too in things religious may as a moralist equally accept as absolute the distinction between right and wrong; and yet, here again, not claim in a given situation to know with certainty which is which. And this even with respect to the behaviour of others, though on this it seems in general to be so much easier to pass confident judgment than on one's own. A world in which no one believed in the objective validity of the right–wrong distinction might have its drawbacks. But hardly less would a world in which everyone felt certain he knew what in practice was right and what was wrong. The Greeks had a distinction—between *doxa* (opinion as available in say art) and *episteme* (knowledge as available in say mathematics). (Plato probably believed that *episteme* was in principle not ultimately unattainable in matters of right and wrong. But as yet, as he saw, what men had had in such matters was nothing better than *doxa*.) Even when my opinion is elevated into an orthodoxy, mere *doxa* it remains. It is one thing to fight and die, to murder and destroy, in defence of one's opinion because one believes it is the right thing to do. It is another to claim that one knows it is the right thing to do: or to claim that one's opinion, one's orthodoxy, is *episteme*. The crusader is one who is not merely confident that his orthodoxy is the truth, but also that it is his duty to impose this belief upon others who take the like view of theirs. In the seventeenth century relative domestic peace was achieved in England because men with opposing orthodoxies agreed in effect to live and let live. Were the world as a whole to follow England in the adoption of this principle, the future for mankind might be brighter than it now appears to be. But even in England men are not all of them equally convinced that it would be right to apply in the world as a whole this principle now traditional domestically within the U.K.

Puritanism in Odd Places?

There thus would seem to be six questions on which it is well, if one can, to clear one's mind.

(*a*) Does one believe that there is a will of God for mankind?

(*b*) If yes, does he believe that he, or anyone else, can be certain of what it is?

(*c*) Does he believe that the antithesis right–wrong is objective and absolute?

(*d*) Does he believe that he, or anyone, can be certain as to what, in any given situation, is, for anyone involved in it, the right thing to do?

(*e*) Does he believe it can be right to co-exist peacefully with those who do not share his conviction as to what is right and what is wrong?

(*f*) Does he, where he happens to have the means of doing so, believe it right to impose upon others conformity with convictions which they do not hold on what is right and what is wrong?

The chiefly important thing perhaps is to recognise that it is possible, while believing in the absoluteness of the right–wrong antithesis, to doubt if anyone can say with certainty what in given circumstances it implies; and, in any case, to believe that it is not necessarily wrong, and may even be right, to respect in such matters the freedom and the duty of others to live in terms of their own convictions rather than of ours. Even to believe that one knows what would be right for others does not entail believing that one should make war upon them to compel their conformity with what one 'knows'.

Whom and What Does One Blame?

It is wise, particularly in relation to international politics, to be awake, even though one have no remedy for it, to the war between one's intelligence and one's emotions; and to be on guard for the moments when it is by one's emotions and not one's intelligence that one's judgment, and actions, are chiefly determined. No one, presumably, in his more coldly self-critical moments would be heard to reproach himself for being a man and not a woman, or a mortal and not an angel. One accepts no responsibility for how one was born. And does anyone in his fairer-minded moments blame a bluebottle fly for having been born a bluebottle? Yet which of us, when pursuing, to destroy it, the not-intendingly-offending fly, does not blame it for being what it is? Do we when thinking judicially blame the child for his parentage, or for the sins of his forebears? Do we not acknowledge to ourselves that the threatening part of the Second Commandment bespeaks a philosophy of punishment the strict fairness of which, in human terms, can only remain a mystery? Yet does this suffice to enable us, as rational people, wholly to jettison the pre-civilised mentality that issues in attitudes of that kind? Which of us is not basically ambivalent on whether one is really entitled to accept credit for the achievements of one's ancestors, or the greatness of one's country? Which of us wholly rejects the idea that the Germany of tomorrow (meaning in practice the Germans of tomorrow) will at least be more to blame than we are for the misdoings of the Germany of a generation back? As the individual quite reasonably feels to blame, still, for his failings in the past, so, in idea, has she the person Germany to accept responsibility, and Germans of today to share the odium, for her misdoings under former dispensations.

Should Batsmen Take Wickets?

In the kind of comments we commonly hear on what governments do, there is often a seeming indifference to the facts of their concrete situation; and especially to the choices effectively open to them at the moment of their choosing as they do. Criticism seems mostly preoccupied with showing that politicians are not so high-principled as they may look. Almost every popular judgment upon a government's action tends to run in moral terms. Often of more interest might be a view on the virtuosity, rather than on the virtue, of the action. Governing is the filling of a role, which itself is never the invention of those who come to fill it. The role is an incidental feature of the multi-governmental and inter-governmental global set-up which is the source of its meaning. A man may be better at bowling than at batting, but even so one does not fault him for not bowling when it is now his turn to bat.

If then one is to evaluate behaviour, one had better have some claim to understand it—and what behaviour is it possible to understand save in the context in which it occurs? If one is to evaluate behaviour—even that of a statesman—it is necessary that one understand its context—and this means knowing the world situation—and therefore the world. Watch a surgeon at his work: does one think to appreciate his performance by criteria other than those germane to the judging of surgery? Is ingenuity in ethical speculation an alternative, for his purposes, to skill in the use of the knife? Why then, for the purposes, hardly less specialised, of the practitioner of political therapy?

The patient who engages a surgeon to perform on him a certain operation would reasonably complain were he to find that the operation done on him was a different one, at which the surgeon just happened to be better.

Those in governmental seats are there to do a given, and not some other, job. A sound performance will be accounted such in terms of the tests for the doing of that particular job. The conduct of foreign policy is a particular kind of job, and the Scriptures, for example, tell us little that is specific on how it should be done. Diplomacy of course is one thing, and war another: but, for all the grace and elegance of its manners, in its preoccupations and practice diplomacy is apt to be more like war than like tea, or even croquet, on the lawn!

The Propriety of Partisanship

While one cannot in strict fairness blame a fly for being a fly, one might if so-minded, blame a dipsomaniac for having taken to the flask, or even a miner for having taken to the mine. Why one should think to do this, rather than to praise him for it, is hard to see: but still, one presumably could. Less easy would it be to blame him in theory, as now a miner, for feeling, and making a virtue of, his solidarity with others similarly employed—not perhaps on issues of every kind, but in situations affecting particular interests which the miners have in common. And if the miners happen to have organised themselves for the collective protection of those interests and to have entrusted their defence to paid officials, it would be odd to feel irritation should those their spokesmen, in their approach to issues of professional importance, fail to avoid the attitudes of the partisan.

One does not expect a leader-writer to take a line other than that of his paper, or counsel for the defence to make a gift of arguments to the prosecution, or bankers not to be grimly alive to the financial aspects of programmes that they are invited to support. The editor, the barrister and the bank-manager are professionals, filling well-defined roles, in relation to which society has routine expectations. For the purpose of its fulfilment, the role may be more significant than the one who fills it. Like the miner and the trade union representative, these others, the banker, the barrister and the editor, are parts in the social mechanism, functioning in the manner required by their place in the machine. The mining, the representing of the miners, the leader-writing, the defending of the accused and the handling of the moneys entrusted to a bank, are jobs proper to be done—by persons of whom the relevant expectations will socially be entertained. For behaving consistently with these, will anyone think to hold such 'rolesmen' worthy of reproach? For altruistic courses not compatible with them, will anyone wish to excuse them? Can it ever be wrong for a statesman to do as best he can such things as must be expected of a statesman?

Where Scruple Comes In

Between subordinating politics wholly to ethics on the one hand and dissociating them altogether on the other, there lies the intermediate possibility of considering in the appreciation of any political issue whether there are ethical elements involved, and attaching to these such weight—but such weight only—as one reasonably can. Is not this after all what we do in our personal affairs of every day? Our practice, typically, when weighing, say, a business opportunity, is to form an impression of what, ethics apart, would look like a profitable course, and then to consider whether, from the angle of business ethics as we understand them, we need have any scruple in taking it, perhaps in some modified form. We do not, in business, feel simply indifferent to ethical ideas, but it is to an ethics applying to business as such that we so pay heed.

Who at a poker table would forbear to mislead an opponent, within the limits defined by ethical considerations pertinent to the playing of poker? If no deception were considered admissible how, at poker, could one hope to hold one's own?

'Strategics' is not poker; and 'diplomatics' not pure 'strategics'. Nor is domestic of a piece with international politics. Scruples, when we feel them, are always about behaviour in some kind of context: and always the nature of the scruples is conditioned by the nature of the context. A private-affairs context is not the same as a context of business or diplomatic affairs, or even of domestic-political affairs.

Fewer, or More, than Two

If asked, then, whether we therefore recognised a dual standard in matters of right and wrong, our answer would have to be: No, not exactly. For, according to how we look at the matter, ours is either a single standard, or else a combination of many more standards than two. Viewed as single, it is the standard of doing always the best that the circumstances allow. Viewed as a plurality, our standards are one for each distinctive set of circumstances. As aesthetic considerations may enter into surgical deliberations, and functional into architectural, so may ethical considerations arise in every department of human enterprise. Why is there any doubt, or confusion or puzzlement about that? How else, in practice, has the problem ever been viewed? In practice? The trouble it would seem arises when, not in their personal activities but in their assessing, as from an armchair, of those of other people, men of doctrinaire disposition assume to pass judgment on issues of policy or diplomacy by bringing the case before them under some sort of abstract canon of behaviour, an item in some sort of pre-formulated code. What such judgments presuppose is that the difference is known between rightness and wrongness, even as is the difference between darkness and light.

The Rightness of the Right

Actually it is right choosings that we want, between concrete alternatives, not rightness, as opposed to wrongness, in the abstract. The concrete alternatives require to be understood in their concrete immediacy before the nature of the possible choices can be seen. For example, regarding the telling of the truth: By what general principle can one resolve to be guided? To tell the truth so far as circumstances allow? But that only refers us back to the study of concrete conditions. And it is on our appreciation of these that we base our decision on how much of the truth we ought to tell. If we judge it right to tell part only of the truth, we judge it absolutely—repeat absolutely—and not only partly or relatively, right. What we have to watch for in others and to correct in ourselves is not a lack of moral principles, but a lack of moral scruple. Whether in business, or in games, or in teaching, or industry, in marketing, or politics or diplomacy, a desire to do only what is right will best express itself in a genuine endeavour to see in the various situations what in each case the right thing will be. And we shall not claim that the right, the absolutely right, thing to do will necessarily be a good, even a fairly good, thing to do. Sometimes the right choice is one between two evils.

Eyes on the Road

For an understanding of life as it is lived, it may be more important to consider the floor upon which Nature might seem to have meant men to crawl than the clouds among which, defiant of Nature's apparent intentions, they insist on aspiring to fly. Survival first, says Aristotle, in effect—and the good life only afterwards. In practice a state, however exceptional, is less likely than is the exceptional individual to lose contact with the solid ground of self-regard, far into the stratosphere though its dreams may mount. Any proposed arrangements for having states live with their heads in the upper atmosphere had better therefore be compatible with their feet remaining on the ground. And the serious student will discover that it is harder getting acquainted with the conditions on the ground than with the standards up there in the sky.

Demonstrables, Provables and Merely-arguables

And now, what amounts to a further difference between the political and the sociological, the ideological and the scientific, ways of talking. It illustrates the distinction between issues inviting proof of what is believed to be the correct answer and those inviting argument for what is believed to be a tenable answer. This has been put as the distinction between 'inquisitive' and 'deliberative' questions. To the question: Did Napoleon win at Waterloo? the answer would be categorically no, the justification here being the consensus among historians. To the question: Who did win at Waterloo? the answer would not be categorically Wellington, the objection to this being the absence of such a consensus. If nonetheless someone were to insist on answering categorically Wellington, his argument would presumably be the existence of at any rate a near-enough consensus among enough historians.

The stickler for precision, one must assume, will note these several possibilities, and will qualify his answer, Wellington, with the words 'to my way of thinking', or their equivalent. He might for instance cushion his answer with the mention that it has been conceded, if indeed it has been, by a respectable minority even of German historians. But the politician, if of the 'Wellington won' school of thought, may be likely to declare his conviction as if reporting a fact of history just as far beyond debate as is the death of Queen Anne. At least that is what he will be likely to do if he expects to get away with it. He may even avail himself of the tactic of the U.N. delegate in the margin of whose speech there were detected the words: 'Weak point. Shout.' As a politician, however, he may equally know when to pose as the strict thinker, with his cult of scholarly detachment, and his avoidance of over-confidence in the statement of a belief that it was indeed Wellington and no other.

Sociological Plausibilities as Arguables

When, in his hostility to what he termed utopian socialism, Marx essayed to marry socialistic ideals with sociological understanding, an understanding at which he apparently thought he had arrived by scientific research, we ought hardly to blame him for presenting his conclusions as if beyond debate. It was in those days widely seen as the essence of a scientific conclusion to be beyond debate. Nowadays by contrast we appreciate that it is no more than a high degree of probability that even in the physical sciences the empirical method can provide. Inquiry in say the social sciences domain is not therefore to be belittled as less than scientific merely because its findings must be tentative at the best. What one does nowadays, or should do, is notice the different sorts of results to be sought for in different sorts of inquiry. In mathematics, demonstration, as before; in statistics, probability; in the natural sciences, verifiability; and, in sociology, sometimes verifiability perhaps, but sometimes plausibility only. International Relations, as a line in sociological reflection and inquiry, need make no apology when able to offer plausibility and nothing more. But plausibilities themselves are not, of course, created equal. Some are more so than others; more plausible, that is. A due combining is called for of caution with courage. Caution in the testing of impressions, courage in speculation and in acting upon the best impressions one has been able to form. Even in the gathering of impressions the investigator can proceed at least in the spirit, whether with the techniques or not, of science.

Values as Arguables

So far our illustrations have been on issues of historical judgment, judgment on what might be regarded as issues of historical fact. The line between matters of fact and matters of value is however a blurred one. Whether 1066 was a good thing might perhaps be discussed as if a simple question of fact. But whether Cromwell was a good man would probably be recognised as a matter for argument. Here again the politician may be disposed to use the adjective as if the judgment were beyond debate. The sociologist by contrast will specify whether there is a consensus, or a near consensus, or no consensus at all. How many young students have acquired the scruples and mental habits of the social scientist in this regard?

Sometimes, moreover, even a consensus may be matter

merely of verbal form. No harm, for instance, in speaking non-tentatively of 'good' Queen Bess, since here the epithet has become so conventional as to be meaningless. No harm for the like reason in speaking similarly of the naughty 'nineties. But it might be better not similarly to speak of 'good' Lloyd George, for might there not be reservations to that?

Now in matters of taste, it may in the last resort be not worthwhile having an argument. And in matters of value the cautious commentator should be happy to offer his view, as persuasively as he may, and as relying, if he can, on such near-consensus as he may believe there to be.

Definitions as Arguables

More complex is the matter of definitions. One does not need in a mathematical statement to begin with one's personal definition of a triangle. Neither in a discussion of seamanship need one say what one means by a yardarm or a sloop. Nor, perhaps, in an economics seminar, need one mention what one understands by diminishing returns or full employment. One can use economic terms in the confidence that there is a consensus among 'those who know about these things' on the proper definition of such terms.

How many a statement made by others, and how many indeed that one might oneself be moved to make, would not be better justified if prefaced by 'to my way of thinking', this giving to it a second-order, in place of its first-order, formulation and ensuring to it a possible factual validity which it will have been a category mistake to put it as possessing before! How many an affirmation about what 'ought' to be—'by rights' —would not be better justified if so prefaced! But, so far from expressing themselves simply in terms of their personal judgments as such, men purportedly supply information on how things objectively are. So far from saying that X seems to us to have in justice a claim to this or that, what we baldly assert is that X is being denied his 'right' to it. The difference is one of metaphysical vision, and not of idiom only.

The Ontological Status of the Moral Order

Let the reader therefore consider what precisely he himself understands by rights. Does he ascribe to them an existence independent of the milieu in which they are claimed, acknowledged, presupposed? Does he believe man's rights to be his by nature—whether by his nature as a man or by that of human society as such? Or does he see rights merely as part of the social apparatus of a given society? Let him consider which position in this matter is his own.

If rights, and the moral norms which safeguard them, are grounded in nothing more cosmic than a local folklore, if they are part merely of a given society's cultural patrimony, a monument to the social artistry of past generations, how can they be thought of as having, intrinsically, any real, as distinct from merely notional, theoretical, claim, upon the obedience of an autonomous being? Is the 'ought' which supports the moral norm a merely prudential 'ought'? Does one not feel a difference in quality between the moral, and the prudential, ought? And if one's sense of this difference had to be dismissed as mere illusion, what does one suppose would become of a society if a high proportion of those who in that society set the standards were to become persuaded of what one had thus come to see? Do such leading elements in any dynamic, robust, and forward-looking society regard the norms of their society as merely prudential? Is it not of the very essence of their 'ought-ness' that men should believe it to be rather more than that? The student will do well to give some thought to this cardinal conundrum. And, having done so, he will also of course do well to preface his conclusions with those five little words: 'To my way . . .'

CHAPTER XI

THEORIES AND THEIR USES

A Matter of Status

There are indeed so many ways of thinking. Each of us may have several of his own. In our study of the social cosmos, if it is to be realistic, we must be careful to discriminate between what with us is a matter of conviction and what a mere matter of convention; and between those convictions born of observation and reason and those that we hold as articles of faith. And we may try likewise to distinguish between these several possibilities in the status of what others have to say. Indeed it may be opportune to reflect here a little further on the variety of the purposes to which, in whatever sort of society, men's propensity for theorising may be seen being put. It is a variety surprisingly wide.

Consider a familiar ceremonial. They stand there, a man and a maid, before a priest, in the presence of a congregation. What can be seen now to happen is indeed *seen* to happen. What results is less easily 'seen'. The link is established. The pair are joined in matrimony, in the sight of God. They are made man and wife, in the sight of the law. They become a married couple, in the eyes of good society. In crude fact, they stand there very much as before. To one who had no notion of what legal theory was, it could mean nothing to say that something had happened in the sight of the law. We all however know what legal theory is, and what socio-cultural theory is, even if we do not call these sorts of theory by their names. In crude fact, the pair are what they were before; but in socio-cultural theory they are a married couple. Some day there may be a divorce, but then the link will not be severed as with an axe, for the link is anyhow not a physical link. It is a theoretical link, or several such together in one: there are the spiritual link, the legal link, the social link.

The very word 'link' is, of course, a metaphor, taken from the world of fact for use in the world of theory. The legal link is not merely a link; it is distinctively a legal link, or as the Romans put it, a *vinculum juris*.

Or take a different occasion. Men are standing about in white, with others looking on. In the eyes of a barbarian, who knows nothing of games (those manifestations of civilisation), they are just men standing about in white. But in the sight of cricket theory, they are more than that. They may be merely men playing cricket. They may be two clubs enjoying a 'friendly'; they may be counties deciding the result of the championship, or, who knows, a Test Match may be in progress with commentaries being heard throughout the world.

Or again, in a certain building, with certain preliminaries, a certain person utters the words 'la Reine le veult', and so at last a Bill becomes law, and what until now was permissible or not permissible as the case might be, becomes not permissible or permissible as the case may be. What happens in fact receives its meaning from the theory of the occasion, and the occasions of the marriage, the cricket and the legislation are different sorts of occasion. Yet you and I take it all in our stride: for no, we are not barbarians; we are the cultivators of theories.

Sorts of Theories

There are at least three ways in which two answers may differ. They may be different answers to the same question, or answers to different questions of the same kind, or they may be answers to questions of different kinds. All theories may be seen as answers to possible questions, and it is important to notice into what different kinds the theories may fall.

Suppose that at some wedding the ring had been mislaid, and that they made do without it. Says one: 'I have a theory that the ring does not matter.' Says another: 'I have a theory that the ring is indispensable.' These two have each his personal theory as to what is the orthodox theory and whether it be legally orthodox, or orthodox also in the theory of the Church.

'I have a theory,' says one, 'that the apple leaving the tree is pulled down to the ground.' 'I,' says another, 'have a theory that it is pushed.' Each has his personal theory, not in this case as to what is the orthodox legal, social or religious theory, but as to what is that physical reality which the physicists are perennially out to explore. In this case the theorist answers a different kind of question, not a question as to the requirements of the law, but a question as to the nature of the universe.

An important activity these days is meteorological forecasting. A body of theory has been progressively built up in the light of which anticipations are hazarded with respect to the morrow's weather. The forecasting is not distorted by the wishes of those who do it, and their theory is solely concerned with how changes in the weather come about. A hardly less important activity is business forecasting, which comparably depends upon theories as to how things in the world of business come about.

At the card table one would sometimes like to know in which of two invisible hands there lies a certain card. If one is to make the best of one's opportunities, one may 'place' the card where, within the range of comparable possibilities indicated as relevant by the 'bidding', one would most like to find it, and one then proceeds on the theory that it in fact is there. Here we see yet another kind of theory. Investments in stocks and shares are made on the theory that particular securities are more likely to rise than to fall, and the particular investor may at the same time make hedging investments on the theory that prices may move another way. Life is largely like that. We proceed not upon certainties, but upon theories as to what *may* happen, more likely than not—though sometimes indeed not even that, for there is such a thing as backing a forlorn hope.

What makes for success in a battle is the sufficiently clear understanding, by enough of those engaged under a single command, of the theory on which on their side the battle is being fought. The Commander-in-Chief, having 'placed' certain opposing forces where he would expect to find them, proceeds on the theory that they indeed are there, and on a theory as to how to make the best of the situation. During World War II, co-operation with the U.S.A. made us familiar with the expression 'the overall strategic concept'. What was this but the theory on which the victory was to be fought for? Two kinds of theories are here involved; those of meteorology and the like, which aid the understanding of the conditions in which the war is being fought; and those which one may call practitioners' theories, which provide a doctrinal basis for a common programme for those whose combined activities must bring the victory.

A layman in such concerns may confess to being uncertain as to how far what is known as 'economic theory' comprises elements of the quasi-meteorological and, on the other hand, elements of the battle-winning type of theory. When we differentiate Marxist economics, liberal economics and socialist economics, it is because, different sorts of victory being fought for, different sorts of theory are entertained.

Observe little children in the road. If theirs is a game you yourself remember playing, you are in no difficulty; but otherwise what you have to divine is the theory of whatever game theirs is. And if you are a social anthropologist observing the rituals of some hitherto unvisited tribe, your question will be the same one—what is the big idea? What is the underlying theory? What do they think they are at? And among anthropologists each may have his personal theory as to what is in fact the theory underlying what is happening.

Sorts of Orthodoxy

It will be seen that theories on which battles are fought, theories about the weather, and theories underlying tribal ceremonial, are theories of different kinds. To which of these three kinds, if to any of them, belongs the orthodoxy of religion, the orthodoxy of superstition, or the orthodoxy of the law? Assuming that a tribal ceremonial will not have been in the nature of a legal transaction, it is evident that what the anthropologists are discussing, and what, at the wedding, members of the congregation may be discussing, are points arising in different sorts of theory, and most of these sorts here considered have been different from the sort which seeks to explain the movement of the apple to the ground. Scientific theory is one thing. Practitioners' theory is another, and legal theory is again something different. And all these three are different again from the theory of the children's game.

Theories and Cosmos-study

What now has this to do with the subject of our main concern? Simply this. As in the playing by children of their game, so in the conduct by the statesmen of the business of the world: the onlooker either does, or does not, have an insight into what is going on. And what is going on in the case of the statesmen is no mere matter of men in white standing about with others looking on. It is men, often in black, sitting around a table and doing things which have a significance in the light of the relevant theory—or rather, the theories.

Which theories? Two in particular. One of these is the orthodox theory determining the nature of the world-wide diplomatic set-up, and in particular the place within it of the element known as international law; and the other is the theory of that international law which occupies that vital place within it.

Of these two theories the first is logically pre-legal, for it concerns and accounts for the presence, in the picture, of the element known as law. The theory accounting in this way for the existence of law cannot itself be legal theory. What kind then is it? Some kind, let us recognise, of socio-cultural theory. But we can make our answer more precise than that. For we can call it the theory of diplomatics, diplomatic theory, if we like. It is not scientific theory like that concerning the apple. It is not practitioners' theory like that of the Commander-in-Chief. It is more like that of the children's game. For it is as if mankind had one morning responded to the suggestion: 'Let's play sovereign states.'

Why Play Ball?

It is because if that ever did happen it was rather long ago that we in our day, having never not been engaged in the game, may have failed to recognise it as a game; and failed therefore to recognise the theoretical, artificial, non-natural basis on which it has all been going on. But, if we would follow with intelligence the course of events, we would do well so to recognise it, and, if we did not choose to call it diplomatic theory, then at least we should decide what else we would wish to have it called. And similarly, in that domestic field within which courts of law and policemen have their place, the claims of law upon us have equally to be accounted for in terms not of fact, but of theory. That the law is binding upon us as citizens is true enough in the sense that it is a true statement of the orthodox theory, but only in that sense is it true. It is the orthodox formulation of a crucial point in the relevant pre-legal kind of socio-cultural theory, namely the theory of the constitution, without the sufficiently general acceptance of which the country could not function as it does, any more than the game can go on if the children no longer want to play.

Why Continue Playing Ball?

Why the children go on playing, why the country goes on functioning, and why the big world of diplomacy keeps moving on its traditional way—to these questions it is social psychology that must provide at least a large part of the answer. And the answer will to that extent be a matter of socio-psychological theory, analogous not to the legal, nor to the socio-cultural, but to the meteorological theories we have noticed before; but analogous only, be it noted, in as much as we have not in the social sciences quite as good reason as in the physical for assuming that the correct explanation, if we can find it, for what happens on one occasion and in one place is quite likely to serve for something similar having happened elsewhere at another time. Reasons why men do the same things now as formerly they did may not be the same reasons now as formerly, but this is not to say that theories of what they are doing will have changed; for what one does in the theory of the matter is one thing, one's reasons for doing it are another. One may of course theorise about one's reasons, but that again is a different story. We may all applaud on the theory that 'he's a jolly good fellow', though each with his own independent theory of what justifies the applause.

Why do the children keep on playing? Why does the country keep on functioning? People's reasons for going on doing the same things now may not be the same reasons now as formerly.

It is not as if we always were able to feel quite sure even of our own reasons for keeping on behaving as we do. Sometimes we find ourselves looking around for new ones, yesterday's reasons having ceased to carry with us the conviction that once they did.

The Secret of Collective Happiness?

A happy society is one in which men have, or at any rate believe themselves to have, excellent, or at any rate good, or at any rate adequate, reasons for going on doing the things that the powers that be are expecting them to be going on doing. The captain expects his team to remain with him on the field. They know this: but is that the only reason why they remain? Even if no longer enjoying themselves, do they not feel, and indeed believe, or even believe themselves to *know*, that it is 'up to' them to remain?

Not all law-abiding citizens greatly enjoy their role as citizens. Yet it is not simply out of fear of being brought to book should they transgress the law that they continue to obey it. Most men believe, or even believe themselves to *know*, that it is 'up to' them to do so.

Most people at Christmas time *feel*, at least, that it is up to them to enter into the spirit of the occasion. With some, the propriety of their so doing may be a matter of conviction. With some, a matter merely of convention. Even little Willy, as he so carefully hangs up his stocking for Santa Claus to fill, may nowadays be doing it with his tongue so to say in his cheek. Is he bound to reveal to his Daddy that he now no longer takes literally the orthodox doctrine of the occasion, but is content, as well in the general interest as so obviously in his own, to accept, as his Daddy apparently does, the assumed reality of a Santa Claus, as the methodological premise for a co-operative enterprise in the pursuance of which a good time should be had by all?

Old Men's Wisdom

The question is, Just *how* good a time could it be if in the having of it all were to be motivated by the same coldly calculating selfregard as little Willy? Is it enough that no single member of the family should be so outwardly antisocial as so to say to walk off the field? Must not some at least of the players be going on playing simply because they happen to like it? Must not some at least of the family be actually enjoying their Christmas? Must not some of them be sufficiently good citizens to be able to keep on as it were 'kidding' themselves that somehow they do at least half-believe in the reality of Santa Claus? No doubt, in the 'unconscious' of the harder-boiled among them, Freud's 'reality-principle' may be getting the better of that 'pleasure-principle' which would cling to the sweet old illusions of nursery days: but even the 'reality-principle' may deprecate the abandonment of a traditional ritual for which, even on strictly utilitarian principles, there may still be things to be said. The question however is, What becomes of the ritual if only on utilitarian grounds is anyone at all any longer taking part? There is a good deal of ritual in the collective living of the national life, just as there is in the collective observing of the family Christmas. In both cases there needs to be a general enough, and a generous enough, assent to the necessary half-dozen or so of shared assumptions. Not merely must most of the company join in singing 'For he's a jolly . . .', but some at least of them must look as if they meant it. And mean it indeed some if not most of them positively must. There is a mystique about nationhood, as there is about Christmas. And in the one case as in the other, mere mock-enthusiasm is, surely, not enough. There is a credal basis, a set of pre-requisite beliefs, social and political, if not also religious, for any successfully flourishing political system. Every living polity, from the most primitive to the most advanced, is dependent for its happiness on the continued acceptability, and prevalent acceptance, of its fundamental folklore. No portrayal, therefore, of things political will, if it means to be realistic, think to underplay the importance of myth. For the recognition of myth is not the same thing as its necessary repudiation. Little Willy need not cease to hang up his stocking. Some have used harsh names for what is required. The 'unmasking of ideologies' was Marx's idea. 'De-mythologising', in a different context, Bultmann's. Enough perhaps that we should ask, rather, from the adolescent political sceptic, that he re-evaluate, and with set intent strive to re-instate, the more socially and politically salutary of his myths. If the wise man is never too old to enjoy a Christmas party, is it in the young man a sign of wisdom to despise the symbols which to his romantically patriotic neighbour still mean so much?

The Nursing of Necessary Beliefs

What gives to folklore its mystic potency is its relation not to the reality-, but to the pleasure-, principle, in the psyche of those whose outlook it conditions. If people are to half-believe it, it may be indispensable that some of them feel anyhow half-inclined to. They must be emotionally pre-disposed, in respect of its veredicity, to give it the benefit of the doubt. Something thus depends on the inherent credibility of the goods and something on the credulity of the customer. Tell me that they are happy who believe in fairies and you have not thereby taught me to be happy, if alas I cannot possibly believe in fairies. As well might one congenitally deaf be exhorted to join a glee-club. Those who recommend religion as being good for the nerves do not make religious belief possible for the honest unbeliever. Mere playing at believing is not enough. And analogously, if everyone in the state were merely to be playing at belonging, paying mere lipservice to the national symbols, what sort of a state would it be? This is why, while 'propaganda' is, in Russia, provided for the sound-minded élite, attention is also given to 'agitation', for ensuring that deference to the national symbols shall not with the rank and file remain at the level of the lipservice which would not be enough.

At the moment when in Moscow in 1917 the Bolsheviks got control, the doctrines on which their new order would be erected were familiar to comparatively few. The fact that they are now more widely understood, and even more widely subscribed to, is not an accident. The question with them was not whether the young folk should be prepared beforehand for their role as citizens, but how. It would seem that, as was the practice in the medieval Church, to which Lenin had apparently given some study, there was accepted in Moscow the distinction between two levels of didactic presentation—the 'exoteric', aimed at the edification of the many (the undergraduates, as it were), and the 'esoteric', the austere quintessence of the matter, for consumption so to say at high table by the dons.

The Arts of the Possible

At high table level there will also, we may take it, be accepted a further important distinction: between the authentic, and the ostensible, methodologies of Soviet administrative, military and diplomatic practice. For if, in disposing of the content of their 'IN' tray, the Soviet leaders may profess themselves the people 'of a Book', it is hardly to be believed that they do in fact at all seriously rely on the sacred writings to prescribe for them a remedy for every social ailment which, as general practitioners, it may be incumbent on them empirically to treat. Nor, given that they are understood to see their overall problem so largely in terms of unremitting worldwide sociological strife, is it to be supposed that even at the level of general principles they would be any more content than were Engels and Lenin before them, to read their Clausewitz in anything short of the original.

Contrary to what might, by the 'undergraduates', be supposed, the 'code of the Politburo' does not assume that 'the Book' has all the answers or that practice must rest immediately upon 'the Book'. It means, on the contrary, that theory serves its purpose only as junior partner in the theory-and-practice firm. Which is of course the philosophy of all sensible men: life is an applied science only if the application of science is recognised as an art. What surgeon ever relied upon the theory of his craft to the disregard of that trained intuition which, as in a split second, tells him, in a novel situation, what novel thing to do. Afterwards, while the patient is recovering, he may theorise at leisure on why what he did was right. So doing, he will be bringing his theory up to date, obedient to the principle of the unity of theory and practice. On this analogy, the Marxists' unity-doctrine means simply the constant reformulation of theory to bring it abreast of the policy-changes demanded by the changing state of the global game. Experience first, explanation afterwards. The scientific theory is that of the observer and interpreter, the 'unity' doctrine that of the man of deeds.

The Opium of the Peoples' Democracies

At the exoteric level, dialectical materialism is not so much the answer to any particular questions as a standpoint for the outright rejection of all sorts of possible answers inconvenient to the régime. For the rejection in particular, of all so-called 'metaphysical' explanations of reality, and of anything that might point to the need for independent speculation, other than what is methodologically pertinent to natural-scientific research.

Point number-one in the Soviet system of official teachings is the remarkable notion that what is being so dogmatically presented has peculiarly the authority of science. Not only does Soviet society purport to be making the moral breakthrough into a climate not poisoned by such passions as still are endemic in the pre-revolutionary types of social order: it might almost be understood as claiming also to have outlived the era of scientific doubt. Though the answers be even now not yet all of them known, the process which should presently produce them would seem already to be well advanced. It is not systematically admitted that, not only is science essentially tentative in its conclusions, but there also must ever remain questions on which science is incompetent even in theory to provide or indeed even so much as to seek an answer. The allegedly scientific quality of the premises of the present system is a matter not so much of theory, whether scientific or philosophical, as simply of social myth. And, as such, it is both an influence in the movement of events and a clue to the direction in which they are heading. The myth is like the marching song, the burden of which is that the marchers, having in their hearts the assurance of ultimate victory, must keep right on to the end of the road!

But if the scientific irrefutability of Marxist-Leninist metaphysics (repeat metaphysics) is no better than an implausible myth, this does not mean either that it therefore must inevitably fail of its purpose, or that any alternative system, whether on a Western or any other model, could be based at bottom on anything other than myth. For such is the nature of the state.

At one time in the West the faith upon which the social order officially rested was still avowedly religious. Now, the logical status of the ultimate presuppositions is less unambiguously specified. In some countries everything rests on the supposedly self-authenticating validity of eighteenth-century conceptions of the rights of man as man.

Science may yet teach us how to meet the menace of messianic materialism, just as it may tell us how to land on the moon. But it cannot tell us whether or why we ought to want to land on the moon. Nor will it tell us why we should wish our Western civilisation to survive. But, since it equally cannot tell us why we shouldn't, it can be considered so to say as leaving to our system the benefit of the doubt. If others have seen themselves as chosen peoples, why should ours not be defended as a chosen 'camp'? Have we any less reason to see our cause as worthy than others purportedly have to feel themselves the protégés of History, with a capital 'h'?

CHAPTER XII

SECURUS JUDICAT . . .?

A Multi-purpose Adjective?

At the opening of a further chapter on the nature of 'moral' judgments, in this case of judgments collectively expressed, it may be helpful to remind ourselves with what a diversity of meanings we may use so familiar a word. A story may of course have a 'moral': and here we are dealing with a noun. We may speak too of a person's 'morals' (again a noun), meaning the standards reflected in his behaviour—in distinction from his 'moral code' (an adjective this time), meaning the standards to which he would subscribe as being in his view the 'right' ones. Of a person very badly behaved, we may, alternatively to speaking adversely of his morals, say simply that he hasn't any morals at all.

Not every story has a moral of any kind, and not every moral is a moral one! Here again we see the adjective, used as a synonym for 'edifying'; calculated, that is, to improve the character of one who takes the story, with its moral, to heart.

Sometimes we may equate 'moral' with 'ethical' ideas. But probably more often we differentiate, in one way or another, between them. We may for instance choose to use the latter term of those ideas which their holder would cherish no matter what others might say, the former of ideas asserted by society. The French, again, speak of *une personne morale*, meaning an entity endowed by law or custom with the imputed characteristics of a person of flesh and blood: the interesting thing to notice being that here there is no more admixture of ethical implications than there is in the description we may give of a possibility (e.g. in a horse race) as a 'moral' certainty. All that we in this case mean is that we would be prudent to proceed as if that were indeed quite certain which is in strictness not absolutely so. It is, we alternatively say, 'virtually' certain, the adverb 'virtually' having equally little ethical import.

The Moral Value of 'Moral' Weight

So far so good. As someone may sometime have said, We are *not* confused. Where our discussion begins to be tricky is where a touch of genuine doubt affects so to say the thinking of those who do not pause to think. Neat, we may find, are the abuses of ambiguity. We speak of a person's moral stature, and hence of his moral weight, the moral authority with which he speaks. We may speak of his as a moral influence, meaning a good one, although equally a man's moral influence might be bad—an *im*moral moral influence, we almost might say.

But if moral influence is, at least presumptively, wholesome, how about moral suasion and moral pressure? In other words, is it necessarily always morally right to yield to moral pressure, and morally wrong to resist it? For it is one thing to say: This, for the sake of a quiet life, we had better do; and quite another to say: This, for the sake of a quiet conscience . . . Even therefore when we do indeed give way to moral pressure, this may or may not be because we would feel it to be immoral or unethical to resist; our motive may be purely prudential. Compliance, as proverbially, with some people, honesty, may be preferred as being the 'best' policy—in which case there is nothing obviously very moral in the compliance.

Obvious meanwhile, indeed so obvious as hardly to deserve a mention, is the distinction between moral weight on the one hand and technical effectiveness on the other. In terms not of abstract justice but of constitutional doctrine, what Parliament says 'goes'. What Parliament enacts, that is, is technically decisive, and this irrespective of whether the voting be unanimous or by a majority of one. That something has been given the force of law tells us nothing as to its intrinsic moral rightness. If there is any presumption at all that Parliament's attitude is morally admirable this is because it may well have been affected by moral pressure from those whose motives, purposes and ideas are assumed to be moral. A large assumption, surely!

There is of course nothing to preclude, say, a newspaper, or a nobleman, or a nobody, from urging upon, say, the Irish

Parliament, the enacting of a certain law. If such urgings carried any weight at all in the matter that weight would be describable as moral. But what if similar urging had emanated say from the American State Department? In that case we might be inclined to call the pressure not merely moral but diplomatic. The weight of formal diplomatic pressure is a moral weight, and as such it may be important however slight its intrinsic moral value. Even supposing some eighty countries to have joined in the exercising of such pressure, that pressure would still in this same sense have been specifically diplomatic. It might of course in this case have been intrinsically more persuasive, not to say compulsive. But that is merely because the prudential ground for not ignoring it would have been stronger. But that, after all, is all.

Sed Victa Catoni?

A Parliament is a notional person to whom there is constitutionally, legally, and socially ascribed a standpoint of its own. On the notional level, Parliament has and exerts a will. What now of such a 'body' as the United Nations, or the General Assembly thereof? To these likewise there is, or is coming to be, ascribed the appropriate aptitude for thinking and for willing. And what the General Assembly has affirmed is no doubt widely accepted as reflecting what is conceived as being the standpoint of the United Nations. Not that the urging of the United Nations is quite in the same category as the concerted diplomatic pressure of a 'concert' of its member states. Enough that there equally here may be good prudential reasons for giving heed. Were those prudential reasons to become so cogent that states would be unlikely in practice to ignore them, we might speak of the United Nations as having acquired as it were the status of a 'moral' super-state. But even then it would remain debatable whether there need be anything morally wrong, as opposed to diplomatically rash, in rejecting the General Assembly's representations. Not, like an Act of Parliament, technically binding, they could, without formal impropriety, be treated as of little account. But their diplomatic weight might be 'virtually' irresistible, however morally ambiguous their content.

Suppose, for instance, an assembly dominated by totalitarian

states, whose resentment of the freedom of the British Press
should find expression in a *voeu* to the effect that Britain should
silence a certain paper. It will not be assumed that Britain
would relish such a situation: but the question is whether she
could with an easy public and official mind say about it just
what she thought or treat it exactly as she felt it deserved to be
treated. But were she, *per* almost *impossibile*, to defer to it,
would anyone think to admire her behaviour as *morally* right?
Happy the country so diplomatically strong that it never need
compromise its conscience by deferring, against its moral
convictions, to 'moral' pressure from abroad.

What Are Little Resolutions Made of?

The observer of international institutions should therefore
ask himself whether there is even *prima facie* anything particularly moral in bowing to diplomatic pressure, and on the other
hand whether sovereign states, by very virtue of their being
sovereign, are necessarily in a position to withstand it. If in
home affairs, for instance, a majority should allow itself to be
guided by envy, hatred or malice towards a minority, this might
well be an abuse of democratic authority but not a negation of
it. And diplomatic authority could comparably be abused.
Given the nature of the domestic political process, whether in
general or in particular countries, the motives with which
governments instruct their delegations on the stance they shall
adopt on particular draft resolutions may have little to do with
abstract morals. Even were one to take it that the feelings
of the man on the Clapham omnibus must be consistently
right, could one equally assume it of the aims of any given
group of governments? The truth is that men of experience
will know just what sort of weight to attach to particular
resolutions even of the General Assembly of the United
Nations.

The process of which fashionable opinion is a product is a
social one. The one of which General Assembly opinion is the
outcome is not. The two occur indeed on different planes.
The United Nations process is not social; it is diplomatic. Ex-
pressions of communal opinion proper may be not unlike what
a barometer does for the weather. But General Assembly
pronouncements are not quite like that. Suppose there to

be an issue on which there did exist in the world a consensus of feeling: your individual journalist, politician or poet might be at least as safely relied upon to find the words for it as might the General Assembly. After all, the question at the United Nations is not simply: What does mankind as a whole feel about this matter? Indeed there is, *at* the United Nations, strictly no such question at all: it is rather that a question presents itself in the capitals of the several member states. In each of these places the problem is: What instructions shall our delegates receive with respect to their speaking and voting, as well as their off-stage interchanges, on what shall be imputed to the General Assembly as its opinion on a certain point?

Synthetics Unlimited

Each delegation will have its own particular instructions. Proceedings, perhaps of inordinate complexity, will occur. Though many may, as poets or publicists, have views on what humanity is feeling, no wording that any of these might favour need ever be voted on at all. What emerges is simply that formula which secures the votes of enough of the variously instructed delegations. This is not of course to say that the resultant will necessarily not accord with any such opinion as may be tending to prevail throughout the planet: only it may be rather in the nature of an accident whether it does so or not.

Indeed, even if planetary opinion were something readily ascertainable, it would not necessarily be always right. Nor is there likely very often to exist any kind of a planetary opinion. Even a poet may be hard put to it to know what 'the world' is thinking; and the chances are that this is partly because 'the world' as such is so little given to thinking, as a rule. Meanwhile the opinion of the General Assembly is, essentially, a synthetic achievement, whose importance, diplomatically, may admittedly be vast, but whose moral status is a different matter, particularly if it affects to have the *imprimatur* of the moral conscience of all good men and true. The business of 'voting-power politics' need not be stigmatised as sordid: it is enough to insist that its motivations are apt to be mixed. Its techniques and criteria are a study in themselves. And the interests which it may be thought to further are perhaps best understood by those, its older practitioners, who have had time to observe the after effects of their own best-intentioned past moves in the game.

Pious Hope

Meanwhile it may be that the very presence of a mechanism popularly believed to mirror world opinion will help to inaugurate an era in which the world may more often have an opinion of its own. Before the General Assembly comes to voting on what is recognised to be a point of law, some at any rate of its members are wont to consult their lawyers. So, someday perhaps, before delivering, as it were, the verdict of Humanity, the General Assembly may itself think to seek the opinion of persons, whether laymen, philosophers, or poets, who should know their Humanity better than those whose minds are ever engrossed in the manoeuvrings of international chess! And even then it should still be open to a brave man to demonstrate his integrity by sticking to a judgment of his own.

The A-septic Formulation

Now it need not be asked of the social scientist that he accept socially the role and the risks of a 'Daniel', by daring to pronounce himself unfashionably on moral issues. If he does so, it will be in his quality not as a scientist but as a citizen. Nor need he be asked no longer to glory in his prejudices, or to cease believing in their rightness. But what can, and indeed must, be asked of him, if it is a social scientist that he wants to call himself, is that he make it his concern, independently of his prejudices and of the fashion in his social milieu, to detach his mind, where appropriate, from all except the struggle to see squarely, for his own illumination, those issues which should in the objective nature of a situation present themselves to the ideally disinterested inquirer. It is not a matter of his avoiding taking sides: but rather of his viewing a question *as if* he had not cause to do so. It is a matter too of recognising in his private heart where, if he happened to be a Daniel, he might now be having to stand. Should he find even this too difficult an effort, let him try at least to see why. And let him confess that his failure to do it is part of a wider failure to see the situation as it is.

There's Sanctity in Numbers?

This advice particularly applies to his assessing of the status of a United Nations resolution. He may know what he feels about the matter at issue. He may also have noticed what it is the fashion to be saying about it. But what he may not find so easy is to situate the question in the setting in which it can be realistically faced. Man's ideas of right and wrong apparently began by being applied, if they did not indeed originate, in his experience of an environment where along with others like himself he was subject to social control. At the primary, human level, society is a reality, and society's standpoint, the communal standpoint, as we have been calling it, is a factor to be taken as given. If ostensibly for the voicing of society's standpoint there is a special social mechanism, this will no doubt be judged by whether that is what it seems to do. Newspapers for example may be seen as rivals for recognition as speakers for the communal point of view.

But at the global level and on the world-wide scale there is as yet no such society. Seldom would it be possible with any plausibility for a newspaper to project, so to say, its own opinion as expressive of a standpoint at once communal and universal too. Seldom is there on a global scale any such opinion as it would be Daniel-like for an individual to gainsay. But even were it otherwise, the question would present itself, no less here than in a strictly domestic setting, whether the prevalent opinion, merely *qua* prevalent, was necessarily to be rated above the independent judgment of a Daniel. Is fashion merely fashion if local, but morally mandatory if flourishing on a wide enough scale?

There is at any rate a clear enough distinction between asking: What do I see? and: What do I do about it? When, in a moment of exaltation, Stephen Decatur cried 'My country, right or wrong', that is not all that he is said to have said. He was engaged at the time in proposing a toast to the land of his allegiance. He did not even say he would support his country when her course was wrong. He said indeed, 'May she ever be right' and thereby admitted by implication that she might sometimes not be. He thus was denying neither the existence of international morality, nor its authority for his country.

To the question: Were my country wrong, what would I do about it? he does not appear to have addressed his mind.

It is indeed almost trivial to observe that, though might be allowed to triumph, as if tantamount to right, this does not entitle us to defer to it as right. The distinction persists in truth even if blurred in prudent practice. Might, in its courtly uniform as diplomatic influence, may secure the passage of a resolution in New York. This merely of itself can hardly render the resolution right.

Or Figs of Thistles?

Let then the student of international institutions at least perceive that it is the diplomatic rather than the intrinsic moral authority of the United Nations that should engage his interest, and that, even if pressure of a diplomatic or quasi-diplomatic nature had got to be referred to as 'moral', this could not mean that there need necessarily be anything other than moral in resisting it. Let him confront squarely the following general issue. Given that the state is an organisation for safeguarding the interests of a segment, but only of a segment, of humanity, is it wrong for those in whose hands is the responsibility for the affairs of a state to accept those interests as the criterion of what they are to agree to and to do? And if his answer be No, not wrong, then how much moral weight will he personally attach to demands made upon such persons, contrary to those interests as they well may see them, by others who have not their necessity to be looking at such issues from that particular point of view? Does anyone with his social eyes open really expect it of a trade union that in times of industrial trouble it will put its country's interests first? No one calls upon a Church to behave like a secular organisation. Can then the state, conversely, be expected to behave like a Church? Is there any logically sustainable reason why the feelings of humanity should be taken as the test of political rightness in the conduct of the affairs of a state? And does a particular suggestion become intrinsically any more morally imperative if instead of being made to one country by another country or by a number of others it is made to one country in the form of a resolution passed by a two-thirds majority vote of the United Nations? What one government shall say to another and what it shall instruct its delegates to vote for are equally matters of policy, the ethical aspects of which are neither more nor less primary than they are in the determining of any other line. There are after all more ingredients in the making of policy than are found in the writings even of the dons.

The importance of General Assembly resolutions lies less, however, in their intrinsic moral credentials than in their extrinsic moral weight. Basically inequitable as their evaluations may be, it may even yet cease to be diplomatically worth the candle to call their propriety in question. In that event they could become, as an instrument for the influencing of state behaviour, hardly less effective than the pressure of a major sovereign state.

Why not Worth the Candle?

'All my life,' writes de Gaulle, 'I have created for myself (je me suis fait . . .) a certain idea of La France.' He might it is true have said the same of La Grande Bretagne or Les États Unis. But we know that it is in his idea of La France that there must be sought the mainspring of his career. We all have our 'certain' ideas of our own and of other countries. The state of the ideas, and of the image, of politically conscious and active people throughout the world in regard to any particular country is at any particular moment as much a historical fact as is the state of that country's finances. 'Who steals my purse steals trash. . . . But he who filches from me my good name steals that which . . . makes me poor indeed.' Irrational as it may be, there seems reason to suppose that what happens when the General Assembly discusses French affairs has its impact upon the ideas and the image which people generally may have of La France. And he who filches from her her good name. . . .

Should individuals generally come to hold a poor opinion of France, this prevalent poor opinion might presently have as its offspring a world *communal* opinion, whose birth would make France poorer still.

The Myth in the Making

What is technically important is important in virtue of the significance assigned to it by relevant rules of interpretation.

What is morally important is such in virtue of the weight accorded to it by the public. It so happens that people may now be coming to attach a certain importance to what occurs in the General Assembly. For the observer, what happens there will thus come to have importance both as an index of the trend of official policy in the several countries on a particular matter, and also as a factor to be reckoned with for the influence it may have upon the state of public feeling in regard thereto.

When 'Ernie', the winner-picking machine, produces a certain combination of figures, the technical effect may be to render wealthy some Premium Bond holder previously poor. It is a technical effect, but unmistakable and beyond debate. The same machine producing in other conditions the same combination of figures might have no technical consequences at all, leaving everyone neither richer nor poorer than before. Resolutions of the General Assembly have comparably no legal effect. The legal position of all concerned remains unaffected either way. And a single vote cast differently might technically have made the difference between adoption and non-adoption of the text. It is tempting, but insufficient, to say that in the circumstances that very little difference could make very little difference. For why then the excitement with which men await the results of such a vote?

Though there be no such thing as world opinion, or even United Nations opinion, both these factors may by many a given individual be conceived of as if given. Existent notionally only, they may be conceived of as if actually there. And if a particular numerical outcome of a particular process is by a particular individual understood as reflective of a world opinion which he conceives of as existent, it may have some effect upon his actually existent personal opinion as an individual.

When a vote is taken, the connoisseur will appreciate that the import of the event for the undiscerning and its import for him may not be the same, and that its import for the undiscerning is itself an element relevant for his evaluating, as a connoisseur, of its import for him. Though its technical significance be nil and he know that it is nil, nevertheless, if the undiscerning believe, or purport to believe, that it is great, then its moral significance, even for the connoisseur, ceases to be nil. This even if notoriously the passage of the resolution was due simply to the abstention from voting, or the absence, on grounds unrelated to the merits of the matter, of some who, if participating, would assuredly have voted No.

As a calculating machine emits answers which may be treated, and even thought of, as if resulting from an actual calculation, so do United Nations procedures produce formulations which may come to be conceived of as if the results of a judging, a judging by the organisation, itself a reflection of a judging conceived of as a judging by the world. What matters here is not how things perceivably are, but in what way they come to be conceived of. This requires that the world come, by the world, to be conceived of as having a mind, a standpoint, and a scale of values to which issues may be referred.

Why then is it already considered to make so great a difference whether France's policy in say Algeria is, at the United Nations, condemned, or condoned, be it only by a majority of one? Is it not because already there is coming to be accepted officially, and by many even official people assimilated as part of their conception of social reality, the image of the General Assembly as voicing the judgment of all the world, even though in so arbitrarily artificial a way? Not only is there an official awareness of how the voting figures may be used in the propaganda war. It is rather that the mystique of communal opinion and communal judgment might seem to be seeping into official thinking on this theme. On the potential historic importance of such a development there is perhaps no need to dwell.

CHAPTER XIII

SORTS OF GAMES

Clubs of a Kind

If then the functioning of the United Nations is of such potential importance, how in the world, as we know it, has this remarkable thing come to be?

In its endeavour to assist the reader in his private conceptualising of the existing global social order, this discussion, as he will certainly have noticed, has leaned heavily upon the arm of friendly metaphor. For the sterner sort of critic the metaphor is always an easy target. At this immediate point for instance he has merely to remark that essay-dissecting is one thing and target-shooting another: with which objection he scores of course a bull's eye, holing out, as it were, in one!

It is at any rate too late at this stage to renounce this particular aid. After all, there are other such everyday devices—fire, for instance, and aspirin, and the scooter—which are safe only if availed of with common sense and moderation. One has to live, and communicate, dangerously, to find any fulfilment at all.

Granted that any given metaphor, and all analogies, if accepted without realism and restraint, may lead the innocent astray. One remedy is not to eschew them altogether but to multiply them sufficiently to leave none with a monopoly of the field. In the present chapter for instance, besides the now accustomed figure of the game, reliance will perhaps in equal measure be put upon the club, and maybe also, if in lesser measure, on the drama. Each of these several analogies, it will be noticed, implies the willingness of a plurality of independently self-determining participants to maintain in concert a certain sort of system in being as a 'going' concern; going, moreover, on the basis of a necessary corpus of shared dogmatic affirmations. On the status, moreover, of these necessary dogmatic affirmations there is, in the case we are considering, the case namely of our social cosmos—and indeed there can be—no debate. For it is of the essence of any orthodox dogma that its status—*qua* orthodox—is treated as beyond debate. (On their interpretation, as distinct from their status, there may indeed be debate, but that is another question.)

The 'club' analogy has for the present chapter its special attractions—in suggesting, for instance, not too much about common purposes, as distinct from a mere common preference for having, rather than not having, such a rendezvous for their regular consorting with each other. The 'game' analogy has by contrast the merit of suggesting something more specifically purposive, a shade more contrived and artificial, a bit more dependent upon the disposition and capacity, of those involved, for the enactment of a role; their aptitude, that is, for doing the 'stuff' required of them by the given occasion. It implies their disposition to make the appropriate gestures, to express the accustomed sentiments, to observe the established rituals. About an unfamiliar game almost the first question to be asked is, What is the point? With respect to a mere club there is by contrast less need for the visitor-from-Mars to be inquiring what exactly is the point, the big idea, the rationale, of the business. Though there are clubs and clubs, the general point in having clubs is no particular mystery.

Games of Sorts

With games it is otherwise. There are games, and there are games. Only by discovering the point of the particular game in progress can the newcomer hope to follow intelligently the progress of that particular game. And if this is true of the playing of a game, how much truer of the acting of a play. (In *Hamlet*, itself a play, there occurs incidentally the playing of a play. A play within a play. Why not?—only it does need explaining. For, if there can be a playing at living, why should there not be a playing at playing at living?) All these analogies may in this chapter be with advantage kept in kind.

Sub-world Within a World

Actually it is this analogy of the game that seems at first sight the more helpfully pertinent for the appreciating of what, at a meeting, say, of N.A.T.O. or of the I.L.O. or of the

U.N.O., everything is all about. As, during a game in progress, what one has is a kind of sub-civilisation, with a specific ethos, unlike that developed in the playing of any other game that ever was, so, in the functioning of any of these several organisations, there develops a kind of miniature civilised world in which the indigenous peoples are pretty well at home, but where, in the absence of a guide, a visitor from Mars must needs feel lost.

Moral Conscripts

And yet, even in considering such a set-up as now exists in New York, it is well not to lose sight of that other analogy, the analogy of the club. For, whereas there will be some such organisations which states feel diplomatically at liberty to join or not to join at will, others there may be which, as living inescapably within the given milieu, the social cosmos of the day, they may not feel effectively free *not* to want to join. As, on a liner at sea, the initially least enthusiastic passengers may presently find themselves joining willy-nilly in the organised deck-sports, so in the international society there may be started enterprises 'on' which from the outset most states may feel that they had better be 'in'. The psychology of their participation is almost self-explanatory. We many of us belong, do we not, to societies which, if they cost us little beyond our annual dues, cannot be seen to bring us personally very much that we could not easily have done without?

In such cases the question for consideration is not: Whence the membership, but: What the originating idea? There surely must have been some point in starting this particular game, over and above the fact that enough potential players were willing for a game of some sort or other to be played.

About the origins in general of international organisations, there is comparatively little that can usefully be said. Of the few such significant generalisations the most obvious seems to be that, when once those persons who matter have in common hit upon the particular game that is to be played, the others will behave in the main as if this particular game were for their purposes as suitable as any other. In the drawing-room at a Christmas party it is the master of ceremonies who ordinarily decides what game shall next be played, and it is the mark of a well-conducted guest that he forthwith discovers that there is nothing he would rather be doing than playing precisely that. (One is reminded of the old revolutionary doctrine of consciousness-before-spontaneity!) The school, moreover, in which the children are told to do just what they choose is not certain to be a happy one. How can they know what they want to play if they haven't been told what to play?

The Dumbarton Oaks Conference met in 1944 in order that on an appropriate occasion the generality of those already members of the United Nations, an association formed in 1942 for the winning of the war, might be told in all but minor details what game in the post-war period they would all be wanting to play. And somewhat the same task had been performed in 1919 by the Covenant-drafting committee, for whose members incidentally Woodrow Wilson and others had very largely done the thing already in advance.

Minority Rule

A majority of the United States Senate had in 1920 voted in favour of treaty-ratification, and with it of United States membership of the League. But it was not quite the needed majority, of two thirds. Had it then been with certainty predictable that the Senate's decision would never be reversed it seems more than possible that the experiment might, there and then, have been abandoned out of hand. But who could tell? The vacant American seat was always ready, and, while attitudes in Geneva were often affected by a desire not to embarrass those who, in Washington, were working to get it filled, processes in Geneva were also affected by the need to adapt the playing of the game to the absence of that most important of those who had been expected to be players. Had it been a game originally devised to be played by the others only, it is hardly conceivable that the rules would have been worded exactly as they were.[1]

The Morning After

Having done in this way what in the first place they might never wittingly have elected to do, it was now perhaps inevit-

[1] Nor of course would the Treaty framework have been constructed as it was had not the continued presence of Wilson's country as its guarantor been by all concerned assumed as virtually foreordained.

able that the players should presently be engaged in re-interpreting what it was that they had done. They must not appear to have promised too much more than in the altered conditions they could now be hoping to fulfil. If their words could be given a new meaning—and who in this matter was to say them nay, for was it not their game, and who but they, the players, were to say what their rules were to be understood to mean?—the different meaning would in effect be substituted for the one to which they no longer could realistically subscribe. Throughout the history of league-of-nations number-one, a debate was to continue on what the Covenant should be taken as requiring, concurrently with a debate on what was to be substituted in its place. But there was now no Woodrow Wilson present, and, the players having each his own ideas, the game went disconsolately on with no referee, and with rules which the players were frankly unwilling any longer to understand *au pied de la lettre*.

The Undesirability of a Winding-up

What will in such conditions have accounted for that measure of success which was nevertheless to be achieved was probably less the foresight of the draftsmen of 1919, for they had been far from contemplating these conditions that were to supervene, but rather the prevalence, among the tone-setting élite of the membership, of the impression that in the changed conditions the continuation of the game was probably a less unfortunate alternative than its formal abandonment, at any particular juncture, would have been. Many a couple, though having come to repent them of their marriage, have forborne to think of a divorce. (Time tomorrow for a divorce if we should still be wanting one then.) What was virtually certain was that, once abandoned, the game could never have been resumed, unless in the sufficiently exceptional circumstances of the ending of another universal war. And incidentally it seems at the diplomatic level to be almost a kind of 'law' that, when once there has got started something which, unless formally objected to, is able to recharge its own batteries and generate its own propellant, the thing takes on as it were a life, even a potential immortality, of its own.

The Alternative: a Watering-down

Woodrow Wilson, the moment the Covenant-drafting Committee had completed its task, declared, perhaps a shade prematurely, that 'a living thing' was born. Any new organ may be called a living thing, but with some such things it is less invidious than it is with others formally to propose their winding up. Not until the United Nations was itself a going concern did the self-liquidation of league-of-nations number-one become inevitable. Meanwhile there had been a fair amount of what some have come to call the *de facto* revision of the Covenant: meaning by this a *de facto* supplementation, for a distinction should submittedly be recognised between mere reinterpretations of the wording, and developments accepted in admitted disregard thereof. No one could well pretend that the announcement by so many members in 1936 that their fulfilling of their obligations would thenceforth be treated by them as a matter for their free discretion was merely yet a new way of interpreting the Covenant's unequivocal terms.

The Non-Security Organisation

The story of league number-two has been different. The perspicacity of Brierly's famous comment—that not only, like the Covenant, might the Charter not work, but that, unlike the Covenant, it *could* not work—has amply been confirmed. Yet the club lives irrepressibly on. What this seems to suggest is that why the Charter originally came into being will really have been because the states judged it propitious to have a club of some sort, and that on this point they do not happen since then to have changed their view. It almost is as if the constitution of the United Nations had existed rather in the minds of those who had the working of it than in the wording of a text. In both cases what the world was given was not an organisation only, nor an association only, but a club.

In its character as a security game, the United Nations has hardly yet become a going concern. Assume that there are different kinds of polo. Why don't you boys play polo? Answer: (*a*) Because we all like different kinds of it, and (*b*) because all kinds of it are played on ponies, and we haven't any ponies. The United Nations Charter presupposed something, and it anticipated something. Of neither of these two postulated somethings was it able to be certain. For neither was it able itself to provide. And neither of them was to materialise. This contributes to explaining why the Charter has not been working according to its verbal plan. Presupposed was an unattainable concurrence among the boys with respect to which polo they should play. Anticipated was an unattainable availability of the indispensable mounts. No ponies, no polo. No armed forces, no armed force. The Charter did not itself give to the Security Council those forces which, if it was to function as foreseen, it would require. It merely assumed that those forces would be forthcoming. They have not been. Nor in any case has there existed among the élite the requisite unanimity on the uses to which the forces, had they been there, would have been put. Yet the club still exists, the 'town meeting of the world' still meets. Issues are debated, arguments sifted, and sometimes an approximation to some sort of a consensus is found to emerge. Could the club require any better justification than that? A better justification it is not at any rate likely to show. 'Jaw jaw,' says Sir Winston, 'is better than war war.'

The Bones of the Matter

What the reader will do well to recollect is that, whereas men when they organise for a purpose commonly have indeed a common purpose for which likemindedly to labour, the league-of-nations experiments, both of them, were launched within a difficult world, precisely for the purpose of rendering less impossible the peaceful co-existence of those whose purposes were far from certain to be readily harmonisable and whose mistrust of one another was unlikely to be much affected by their common commitment to participation in a game.

Ordinarily, in a game, it is as if the players were interested in their game, their whole game, and nothing but their game. Far otherwise is it when on the stage of the diplomatic theatre the members of international society are drawn by historical circumstances into the playing of a play within a play. For an understanding of the way things happen, it may then be less important to note what the book appears to call for than to divine with what reserves particular players must be suspected of originally having joined in the writing and the playing, as so worded, of the drama. It may equally be necessary to note the changed conditions in which a game which had started under a bright blue sky has been continued into a period of gathering storm. And condition number-one, with league number-one, had been the hoped-for accession of member number-one, an accession the prospect of which was steadily to dwindle as the years went by.

The Party Pattern

It is pertinent here to consider further what happens at a party. It can hardly be said that at Christmas the involvement of the guests in the playing of a particular game is necessarily a sign of their having in that participation any fervently entertained common purpose, beyond the purpose of supporting their hostess in her disposition to keep the party moving as a successfully going concern. All, she hopes, will be able subsequently to recollect that a good time was had by all. Not perhaps by each and all individually, but collectively by all.

In 1919 there was indeed an identifiable host, President Wilson, who in effect acted as his own master of ceremonies. And those at the party comported themselves as well nigh perfect guests. In 1945 the position was broadly similar, with the difference, however, that the host himself was by the hand of death prevented from being there. But that was not the only difference. Further differences lay in the nature of the game in prospect, and, also, in the identity and the mood of those volunteering to play.

Of the 1919 experiment it can be said that the object of the exercise was rather readily specifiable, and that the general willingness to pursue it was not in any obvious doubt. In 1945, by contrast, the picture was in both these respects less clear.

At Christmas the guests might reflect: We knew what we would be in for. She invited us: and we need not have come. As in 1919, so again in 1945, the corresponding thought would by contrast have been: History put us where we are. We had no effective option. What we may be in for we do not precisely know. We must at least do whatever we can in advance to protect ourselves from various disagreeable possibilities. And, for the rest, we must wear the social masks of happy guests, and wait and see.

Other Times Other Games

There had in 1919 been many conceptions in the air on the possible character of a possible post-war game. But, the host having so to say the whip hand and clear enough notions of his own, a clear enough programme emerged. Malcontents, if any, will have kept their disappointment to themselves. The key idea was the one which Wilson had accepted from the British Phillimore Committee, having as the core of it a procedure for the attempted peaceful settlement of certain sorts of dispute. At Dumbarton Oaks in 1945 it was at first not obvious that the syndicate of architects had had the pacific settlement *motif* vividly in mind at all. Something relatively specific on that point had to be worked in almost as an afterthought at San Francisco. In 1919 the keynote had been the idea of Philip sober arranging for the restraining of Philip drunk. Supposing one of us should so far forget himself as to . . ., what shall the others of us undertake in that case to do? Whereas in 1945 it had rather been: Supposing one of *them* . . ., with very little stressing of the supposing-one-of-us. A game having the emphasis on this latter theme might not have got going at all. Guests might have recollected that they had a long way to travel before getting home through the snow.

While therefore, as being both of them games, those of 1919 and 1945 are deserving of consideration, comparatively, together, this had better not be done with any too confident expectation of finding that the rules, the setting, the preoccupations of the players, or the mood of the admiring crowd will on the two occasions have been nearly akin. For the fact is that they differed rather radically in all these respects.

Doctrinal Sine qua non

One important, nay indispensable, prerequisite was, however, in each case given. The floor on which the players were to assemble was well and truly laid. If anyone wishes to question the persisting importance in the world of today of the system of international law, let him consider how otherwise than in terms of their common subjection to the standard of that system such a mixed assortment of guests could ever have been assembled for the playing of any game at all. Who would ever resort, as do so many, to a race-meeting save on the safe enough assumption that the procedures will be as usual and that as usual few if any of the bookies will slither away, with the stakes, through the crowd? As the assumptions behind a race-meeting are found in practice to hold good, so are those with respect to the ostensible submission of sovereign states to the expectations of international law. Each, when entering, in proper legal form, into the playing of the new kind of game, could posit with quite sufficient confidence that this, whatever its form, would by others also be played on the whole in compliance with the rules—as interpreted, that is, by themselves. For it is one thing to have one's own peculiar way of interpreting one's commitments (and all states tend to do that): it is another thing to deny, or to repudiate out of hand those commitments (and this states will seldom or never be known to do).

Laws as Uniformities versus Laws as Norms

The game within the game: it is with the aid of this analogy that the quality whether of the Geneva process or of the one in New York may thus be conveyed. In common the two have beneath them the firmness, and the artificiality, of the drawing-room floor. This floor is to be seen, not in the degree of faithfulness wherewith states discharge their international duties, but in the consistency with which they profess to be taking them seriously—as seriously indeed as they look to others to fulfil their obligations to them. Some people sometimes appear to have difficulty in thinking of law as binding, given the way it is broken, on occasion, by those whom it purports to bind. Such people overlook the most elementary point: namely, that only by those on whom it indeed is binding is it logical to speak of a law's getting broken at all. If the so-called 'laws' of physical nature are thought of as unbreakable this is because in principle they are simply statements to whose validity no clear exception has so far been observed. In principle they are summary reports on past experience, and if rendered obsolete by new experience may be replaced by new reports. By contrast, norms of conduct are statements of what ought to be done, rather than of what invariably has been done. The doing of what ought not to be done is a breaking of the rule, and not a negating of its status as something that binds. That international law is binding no more presupposes that states are unable to break it, than the existence of the criminal law implies the impossibility of crime.

A Distinction with Indeed a Difference

Just as man has always that freedom in the abuse of which he may sin, so states have that sovereignty in the exercise of which they are ever technically in a position to contravene the law. The question is not: Why do they sometimes do it? but: Why do they not do it more often? And to this the answer partly is that the field of their still unaffected legal freedom is still so wide. Construing for themselves such limitations upon their legal liberty as, in entering into a game, they will admittedly have accepted, they are under relatively little temptation to do what even their own tame jurists—whom they will normally have consulted in advance—will be at a loss to defend as being within an arguable interpretation of the rules.

Between, however, the respectable member of domestic society on the one hand and of international society on the other, the difference is that, while both alike may pose as law-abiding, the latter need defer to no third-party judgment on the validity of his pose. Not, that is, unless by his own act he has agreed freely in advance to accept the compulsory adjudication of any such issue should it arise. Neither in 1919 nor in 1945 was such an agreement in advance made a condition for participation in the proposed new game. The Statute of the Hague Court, whether in its earlier or its present-day form, is rather in the nature of a convenience at the players' disposal than a denial in principle of the primordial freedom of each to proceed upon his personal understanding of what it is that he has promised not to do. It is by his diplomatic relationships, and by his concern for what folks might say, that a player is inhibited, rather than by any prospect of an adverse verdict of a referee.

It is remarkable what doubts and disputations may arise on ostensibly technical points during the playing of a game without a referee, especially if the rules are loosely worded. If the rules have themselves been the embodiment of a compromise between opposing ideas as to what they should say, the opening for this is all the greater. And, if not all the preferences of the relevant 'Woodrow Wilson' have been generally shared by the rest of the rule-makers, some of these having reservations on even the very nature of the game, the seeds will from the first have been sown for some wrangles in the time to come. And this is what may be considered to have happened with both of the league-of-nations games, to the disenchantment of those who had chosen to believe that every word in the founding document could only have meant what they, in their simplicity, had privately supposed that it did. To the disappointment also of those who, though not up to understanding the realities of the game, had given their enthusiasm to a simplified alternative, an image of their own creating, a figment of their wishful mind.

Scientific Angst

Social and diplomatic processes are not all of them self-explaining. And the interplay of myth and reality, of theory and fact, of form and substance, in the logic of their movement, puts them beyond the comprehension of anyone diffident with respect to the analysing of the hallowed or obscure. And for all that, or, probably even thanks to that, they perceptibly work. But would they equally do so were they more generally understood? Who knows? To publish the secret of their functioning might even be—might it not?—to bring them to a halt. In short, the social scientist is not so altogether different in his moral predicament from his counterpart on the natural sciences side. Who knows but what the success of his humble inquiries may bode for humanity more of evil than of good? Folklore, if by him identified as folklore, might no longer serve so efficaciously as folklore. Myth, recognised as myth, might no longer remain dynamically alive as myth.

All, perhaps, that one here can say is that, thus far at any rate, man the mystic has had little apparent difficulty in defending his inheritance against the nihilists. Or, if anyone prefers it, the pleasure-principle in the collective psyche continues to hold the reality-principle effectively enough at bay. Anyway, the social cosmologist's immediate concern is not to foretell the future, but simply to shed light on what is occurring now.

The Gentlemen and the Players

It is probably true of any on-going process of large-scale social collaboration that it profits by the active self-involvement of some, possibly many, who themselves may yet not fully understand it. Consult your typical bureaucrat on the staff of any international organisation. Ask him whether the delegates to whom he pays such studied deference are in general particularly knowledgeable regarding the organisation as such. Only superficially can the processes of world-scale co-operation be said to mirror those, in any country, on the domestic level. Yet the teamwork commonly obtained from the national representatives would be less easy to secure were they not somehow beguiled into feeling themselves more or less as if at home. Each probably tends to construe such fragment of the proceedings as he may happen to witness in terms of his own domestic experience. The full reality of what has happened, when in say New York a contested resolution 'gets through', is likely to be so different from the full reality of anything that happens in any parochial setting that the more self-explanatory the newcomer thinks he has found it the less likely is he to have fathomed what at bottom it was all about. But officialdom as a whole is presumably sufficiently in the picture, and privy to what is afoot. The babes in the international kindergarten[1] are not all of them babes in the wood.

When the resolution is adopted, this is the resultant of the concurrent manifestings of attitude of a plurality of governments. Officially—in terms, that is, of the doctrine of the matter—a judgment, or a hope, or a decision, gets imputed to the entity hypostatically posited as the seat and bearer of that will to which expression is being given in the wording so endorsed.

The official theory: this is what, were the functionaries mere babes in the wood, must presumably be serving, with them, like a folklore—such a built-in belief-system, namely, as might suffice to sustain and safeguard the organisation's continuance as a going concern. Folklore, it was however noted,

[1] It was Sir Robert Borden, veteran Canadian statesman as he was, who, in an imperishable dictum, offered from the Assembly rostrum, depicted the Geneva milieu as 'the kindergarten of peace'. What profounder comment was ever uttered on those endeavours?

might lose its potency as folklore proper if, as folklore, it was generally seen through. What, then, if it had never even initially had the status of folklore proper—but only that of a pseudo-mythology officially entertained? What then, indeed? The fact at all events is that the U.N.O. is there already, and palpably a going concern. The explanation? Perhaps one will have to reply that, at the sophisticated, world-aware, diplomatic, level, as opposed to the primitively social, the prerequisites, for a 'going', need not be—nay, cannot be—quite the same. Perhaps, in short, it is after all not so much to man the believer (*homo credens*) as to man the make-believer (*homo ludens*) that we shall do best to be looking, to keep the fuel flowing and the lights aglow, even through the heaviest of the peak periods, periods of spreading doubt and disillusionment, and of mounting stress and strain.

For skilled and successful playing of what we have seen to be a game within a game it is best to be dependent on those who know it for a game, and themselves for players.

CHAPTER XIV

WHERE, FROM HERE?

The Hazards of a Game

Man, the inventor of games—games, in the course of some of which he is apt to get hurt. Man, the inventor also of machines, in serving which, supposedly in service to himself, he is apt, as Marx and others have noticed, to become, in effect, a slave. And in a sense the whole of his modern civilisation is his creation, his invention, his machine.

Physical machinery. Social machinery. What else, but this latter, is the state? And what else the family of states? The question is, asked a famous character, Who is master?

Of ordinary, recreational games it is a merit that, ordinarily at any rate, one is not obliged to play them. One is not obliged to run the risk of hurting, and getting hurt. But given that triumph of man's inventiveness, that machine to dwarf all other machines, the system of sovereign states, and given the nature of the game in which it involves willy-nilly its inventor, what escape has he from the risk of getting hurt, and in our day very severely? For it is in the very logic of the game of let's-play-states that occasions must from time to time occur when the risk of which we have been thinking grows great indeed.

Man, like the grass of the field, does not long endure. But the states? Some do: some don't. Enough that they may, as may their neighbour states. Old friends, sometimes, those neighbours: sometimes not. And it is to the image, the conventional image, of conflict as occurring between those social machines, those mere hypostatised abstractions, the states, that we are constrained to attribute a major apparent impediment to the coming of peace among men. Tomorrow's generation, yet unborn, are, we may fear, foredoomed to find themselves, as we have been, grouped together in our various camps, each with its possible dossier of old scores to work off against another. And this, it would seem, simply because the bygone encounters of men with men, now all of them dead, were notionally the clashings with each other of states which still are just as much alive, or just as little dead, as ever, and one anothers' distrustful neighbours still. Though this prospect may seem grotesque, it is hard to know how it might be conjured away. The game of let's-play-states is still in progress. As a going concern, it is as insistent a factor as anything in our socio-cultural environment. Yet this, as we know, does not serve to put the big protagonists, the sovereign states, whose given-ness the process presupposes, out of the realm of the merely notional into that of the sensibly real. It is in the order of the intelligibles, apprehensible to the imagination and not the eye, that the states maintain their influential presence. And pursue their dangerous play. Intelligibles? What exactly is it that we so imagine? What, *qua* 'sovereign', *are* these sovereign states?

Why 'Sovereign'?

Why 'sovereign'? Is this an inquiry into the uses of a word, or, is it an investigation into the nature of social reality, of social arrangements in the social universe in its contemporary condition? The latter, not the former, surely.

It is in the nature of any social organisation to reveal upon inspection a theoretical 'structure', its 'constitution' as this may be called. And it is thanks to its kind of constitution that a state is technically classable as a sovereign state. For the 'person' of international society is typically a sovereign state, and this by the nature of its constitution.

An island's accessibility from a nearby continent may so improve that we may tend to forget that it is any longer an island. Reaching it by subway, or by rail across a bridge, we may mistake it for a part of the mainland. But its technical insularity will remain unimpaired, not being a matter of relative practical inaccessibility. Though linked with the mainland by a bridge, an island it still will be.

If by definition war were a relation conceivable only between islands, the end of insularity would presumably mean the end of war. And in the same way, admittedly, were there no more sovereign states, there would be no more wars between sovereign states. But, as it is, what we still have is a world of sovereign states. And still, alas, the possibility—however 'unthinkable'—of war.

Avenues of Escape?

Such then is the formal nature of the social cosmos as we see it in mid-century. Not always was it so. And it is scarcely conceivable that it will never again be otherwise. But what also is hard to conceive is just how in practice a radical change in it could ever come about. What would in theory be the possible ways? One may think of several. First, world war. But who would opt for that, particularly since, as Mr. Neville Chamberlain perceived in 1938, none can ever today foresee the state of the world on the morrow of tomorrow's war. Federation? True again. That, in theory, is likewise an obvious possibility. And there must have been many, among them able men, who, though without the Archimedean point from which to operate, will have exhausted themselves in strivings to bring world federation into sight. Given the need of effort for the advancement of other less utopian aims, this was perhaps a misemployment of resources. Next suggestion: the 'erosion' of sovereignty, bit by bit. When scrutinised, however, this idea seems to mean nothing more than the accepting by sovereign states of so many further formal limitations upon what remains of their formal freedom. Such limitations are numerous already, even with things as they are. There simply would come to be more of them. That is no proposal for changing fundamentally the existing order, but merely for making it different in its detail. It might well be the better for that. No one need quarrel with that, as an idea.

But now, another suggestion, not always very precisely put: the 'strengthening' of international law. With this one need have no quarrel either, or not until somebody has first explained what it is expected to entail. Here again, so far from representing an essential change, all that would appear to be envisaged is a reaffirming of that sovereignty with which the legal order is all of a piece. What is essentially a system of law *for* sovereigns, being premised upon their very sovereignty, does not, by the fact of being strengthened, put in jeopardy the sovereignties which are the dogmatic basis for its very existence. Not, at any rate, in logic. For a consolidating of the law, and so of the sovereign statehoods which the law assumes, is in no sense logically a threat to the system of relationships which they sustain.

If therefore sovereignty is ever to be dispensed with, this will hardly be accomplished through a 'strengthening' of international law. And yet, how else?

A Sinister System?

It might in these circumstances be germane to consider whether the sovereignty system, since we see as yet no obvious end to it, has, after all, been wholly a misfortune. What without it would the position in Europe have been? What in the world as a whole?

A theorist, reflecting on Europe's chequered past, was heard to deplore two causes, as he deemed them, of untold human misery. One was the power of religion, responsible, no doubt, for the religious wars. The other, the dissolution of the early Empire into so many potentially warring states. He was entitled to his feelings. And yet, one asks: How except by a multiplicity of independent entities within an established Christian tradition could our present framework have been created for even the beginnings of an orderly co-existence? Had not Christendom fallen asunder into separate polities, how could it ever have been required to develop its basis for the doing of business between the resulting units, that basis which in our day serves the needs of polities in every part of the planet? The world-wide system of the present is the European system of the past, bequeathed by a never too brotherly company of fellow-Christian princes to their variegated successors, their not even human successors, indeed, since it is those abstractions, the 'countries' members of the 'international family', that are now with at least an affectation of punctilio observing the time-honoured western form of the family way of life. And had those princes loved each other better, who knows but what they might never have required such a paraphernalia of procedures, whose very artificiality we now may value as perhaps its principal merit. Except in the terms of such artificial diplomacy, it might in cold-war conditions have been difficult to do effective business at all. On the other hand, but for their commitment to their ostensible belief in a human brotherhood under God, how could the princes ever have been led so readily to acknowledge any theoretical limitations at all upon their formal freedom to act in just whatever way they chose?

Modern man might indeed be more grateful than he commonly shows himself for the structure of international society as established by his forebears. It is odd how nearly we take it all for granted, as if a very part of the natural order. It is odd how little we perceive what it means. For what more dependable causeway could we have been given for a relatively sure-footed eventual advance into what might yet be an endurable future? It is perhaps fortunate after all that, though states may come and states may go, the system remains.

Could not Anything be Worse?

Meanwhile the states, it is true, may go. Men have supposed that the species of animate nature were created *de novo* and immutable. Evolution has shattered that conception. Men may likewise have believed that the states were incapable of change. Yet, as H. G. Wells, of the nations, hyperbolically remarked: 'They come and go like the shapes of clouds.' The question however is not: Could even the structure of international society also some day disappear? Rather might we ask: Have we sufficient reason for desiring that it do so, seeing we have no assurance of what would take its place? What such assurance could we hope for? And incidentally, what revolution, after having run its course, has left things as its sponsors would have hoped to see them?

We had better perhaps return now to the existing set-up, which we may not always have sufficiently understood. For instance, are the nations, in particular, all that at the social level we need consider?

One Solidarity Among Others

Without its moral solidarity—a relative and unstable factor even, if not especially, in times of strain—the nation would be effectively nothing. What makes of nationalism a social force is the fact that people feel it, and are moved by it to do things.

The point is that, as working through the heart, it operates in competition with solidarity-principles of every other kind—relative, and fluctuating, as their manifestations likewise are. An assessment of the state of things political requires a weighing of the several sorts of solidarity in play and a judgment as to which of these will prevail over which. Of this, there was an instance in 1914 when to Lenin's disillusionment the German Social Democrat deputies gave support to the Kaiser's war. Which solidarities other than the nationalisms command acknowledgment in the world today? Old-style Chinese anti-foreignism? Probably yes. Free trade-unionism? Not very effectively. Arab anti-Zionism? Obviously. Africanism? Potentially. Pan-Islam? Doubtfully. Anti-colonialism? Emphatically.

All these serve in their varying degrees to complicate in one context or another the picture of a world merely of rival national sovereign states. And these are examples only of the most positive, militant, aggressive solidarities. There are also some that come to their fullest self-awareness only in the presence of a real or suspected threat.

At the diplomatic, sovereign-states level, the social cosmos, mercifully for those who require to take their bearings in it, is as simple, almost, as the chessboard. But at the social level its complexity baffles description. Ultimately all behaving—like all thinking, feeling and willing—is that of individuals; but, effectively, as we have been seeing, much of the most important part of it is that of political movements, professional organisations, and other social wholes. Once a given sub-public feels its identity as the holder of a standpoint peculiar to itself, the several sorts of status which we identified in Chapter VIII become available to whatever opinion this may prescribe. And here again, even though the given opinion is not institutionalised, as happens in an organised group, yet, when once it has become communal and not merely prevalent among the sub-public in question, it seems to become relatively proof against appeals to the broader interest of the community as a whole.

A social cosmology which was inattentive to the social as distinct from the diplomatic level of human experience would thus be unworthy of its name. For we meet at the social level with so many more historically important solidarities than have their expression through the mouths of sovereign states. *Quot homines tot sententiae*, they say. One might modify this into something on the relation of solidarities to the mentalities that they respectively encourage and display. Public opinion, madam? To which public would you like to listen?

A Choice of Keys to History

It was because solidarities were of so many sorts that Karl Marx could be charged with oversimplification. It was, he affected to think, as if nothing very much had fundamentally mattered in history beyond the struggle of class with class. This implied not only that individuals, and collectivities other than class, were relatively insignificant, but that the diplomatic, as opposed to the social, level of the cosmos could also be safely understressed. For the deeper explanation of what had happened diplomatically was to be found in what had happened in the struggle of class with class. This was an ideologically distorted reading of facts of which the social cosmologist is unlikely to take so simplified a view. For economic interest is not the only key to history. And if men's ruling aspirations are recognised as orientated to more than to economic interests only, then it is in their culture that the key may more truly lie. The distinctive elements in a culture are beliefs, which need have no rational basis. It is the myths rather than the realistic calculations that are the core of any culture. And before beginning to speak of a need to clear our minds of myth, we might do well to look more closely at the role which myth has perennially played in the affairs of men. Whence, in particular, does a modern community derive its basic beliefs?

Reality, as primitive man took his knowledge of it, is said to have seemed, so to say, all of a piece. To many of the distinctions now commonplace with us he was not at first alive: those, for instance, between the natural and the supernatural, between the material and the spiritual, between the religious and the secular, between knowledge and belief. Modern man, when puzzled, is not easily put off with less than a scientific explanation. Primitive man, not having articulated his distinctions between the sorts of explanation, or that between wishful and critical thought, was rather more receptive than we moderns may suppose ourselves to be, of myth. As authority is nothing unless it is deferred to, so myth is very little unless it is believed. Primitive man was more prone to believe the unproven than we are. Or so we are prone to believe.

Now on spiritual reality, as we think of it, science, as we understand it, can have little to say. In giving expression to his sense of the spiritual, man has always had recourse to myth. And, where politics and religion are as yet interfused, the belief system wherewith man puts meaning into both his religious observances and his political forms, is a single system, the boundary between these two orders of experience having not yet been consciously drawn.

Maturity and the Myth

But life moves on. There comes the age of reason, the Enlightenment, the 'dawn'. The mists of superstition are dispelled. The bond between politics and religion is dissolved. Heir, as he now finds himself, no longer just to one belief system but to two, man rejoices, in his modern *hubris*, to set religious myth aside. Henceforth no longer will he think as a child. No longer will man, the sceptic, believe where he has not proved. The statistician's tables, the historian's footnotes, the logician's reasoning, the engineer's exactness—these only will he serve. If he is in any sense to remain a man of faith, his faith will be a faith in the rejection of faith.

All this, however, is somewhat of an exaggeration. For we were after all thinking only of modern man's rejection of religion. What has become of his other beliefs? Has he equally dispensed with them? Is he now, as *The Times* has described poor Camus, 'the man who walked alone', who never 'committed himself to a creed either religious or political'? Watch him, and judge whether he has lost his political concern, his political convictions, his political creed. How is he to square a continued attachment to his cherished ideals with his pose as the believer in nothing that is not proved? At what point does he claim, modern-minded though he be, to have dispensed with myth for the validating of a political line?

We may speculate about whether, and how, life would any longer be possible, were men in general to have outgrown their addiction to myth, their disposition to allow their 'ought' to do duty for an 'is', to assimilate their 'I feel certain' to a 'We are certain'. But of political life in such conditions we have had no experience as yet. It is perhaps, theoretically, not impossible that social co-existence might continue on the basis of mere universally accepted conventions, everyone in effect being pledged to behave *as if* believing in certain suitable sets of words. Then indeed would social co-existence be in the nature of a game—in somewhat the same sense as diplomatic co-existence will always have to be, if to be lastingly feasible at all. As things are, however, the student of actual societies needs still to inquire into the beliefs by which men live, the values which, being for them values indeed, are cherished as if values objectively and *per se*.

Except . . . as Little Children

Religious dogma is not in principle open to rational validation. It need not seem surprising therefore if the holders of one set of religious beliefs find the tenets of some other religion absurd. That this is so with religious beliefs will presumably be accepted. But of political dogmas it somehow looks less true. Men commonly seem less disposed to accept as inevitable the incompatibility of different political belief-systems. On the one hand they tend to suppose that their own positions are grounded in reason and the real: and they are on the other hand inclined to be scornful of views which they themselves do not happen to share. It is almost expected of others that they be sensible, not just sentimental, in matters political. In a scientific era, so it is implied, men should no longer be as children, believing in Father Christmas, or in the superiority of the Aryans, or in the supremacy of the general will. But why not, you ask, the general will? That surely is still an 'absolute'? Surely it still is all right about that? Yet, what is the status of the general will, nay, its very existence, except as matter of dogma? Is it merely as a methodological expedient, a conventional gimmick, that men in a throbbing democracy subscribe to the enthronement of the general will? Have men, in democracies, no longer any faith, not even in the all-rightness, and therefore in the rightness, of democracy?

As experienced at all events up to now, political systems have certainly not dispensed with myth. Where they vary is in the measure in which their myths can be left to themselves. There is a process known as the building of a nation. The nation, if it is to stand in stormy weather, requires a frame of steel or other such stable component. This need the myths supply. If deeply enough entrenched in the groundwork of the collective soul they may demand little attention. (The inevitability of the monarchy is with some Englishmen still a bit like that.) But when, by contrast, a nation is as yet in the nursery, it may still be the better for a hearing of nursery tales. For this is the stage when the national self-image is not yet fully established in the public mind. (The young American may still need reminding to salute the Stars and Stripes, and to name with bated breath the Monroe Doctrine.) It is the stage when with the advent of fascism there had to be opened in Milan a school—not, one hopes, a Sunday school—of 'fascist mysticism'. How easy, in a land whose last 'revolution' was in 1688 and then perhaps not strictly that at all, to smile at the puerilities of the inventors-to-order of national emblems, symbols, origins, traits. The point is that, without political order, men might still be existing as in the jungle; that political order depends upon the prevalent presupposing of what cannot be proved; and that the unprovables fundamental to one system need not look very sensible to the fledglings of another—or those of any of them to the social cosmologist as such. For political man is not merely man the sceptic: he is essentially still, as in his beginnings, the mystic. It is by their mythologies, their bodies of folklore, their cultural infrastructure, their inherited creeds, that societies spiritually live, and it is by them that they are most typically marked off from one another. The social cosmos is a multi-cultural world, a mosaic of belief systems, a jungle, after all—of luxuriant myths.

Lines of Cultural Cleavage

No thoroughgoing agnostic can expect fully to understand a war between rival faiths. Of religious feeling, while some people have more, some have less, and some, it might seem, have none. And what thus is true of religious values is true also of those that we relate to culture. Let Welshmen tell us, since they alone can know, what Welshness means to them, and how much to them it really matters whether they are or are not permitted to pass it on unsterilised to their young, meaning here such a nexus of feelings, beliefs and valuations as gives its essence to what is called a way of life. Would Welshmen fight for their way of life? One suspects that they might. Would the ex-Austrians of the South Tyrol? Surely, had they the chance. Would the settler element in Algeria? Presumably. Or the Turkish element in Cyprus? Or the French Canadians? The key to domestic peace, the basis for co-existence, in the situations here referred to is commonly the rendering of respect, if not of understanding, to prejudices, preconceptions, predilections, the reasons for which are rather of the heart than of the head. As there are those who simply cannot comprehend religion, there may be many who have little sense of what, to others, their culture, its preservation unimpaired, and its perpetuation by transmission to the young can mean. And lines of cultural cleavage are not invariably those on the political map. Nor are they necessarily geographical lines at all. Two cultures may be intermingled in a single habitat, as in Palestine for instance, at least until partition, were those of Arab and Jew. And the habitat may of course have the function of a melting pot. But not necessarily. In London alone there may co-exist many cultural systems, each vitally and sensitively self-aware, but none a serious menace to another or frustrated by the political framework within which together they thrive.

What renders the factor of cultural self-concern so apt to be under-rated, or overlooked, is the frequency with which it can figure in what, in appearance, is a racial guise. Whether Hindus and Muslims may be said to differ significantly in point of race may matter little. Or, in colour either. In culture they remain apart. And the world knows what—including blood—has flowed from that.

Where, however, there are distinctive physical traits, concern for cultural survival may look, and become, like the prejudice of race. Those policies for example in South Africa wherein is presently reflected the collective self-concern of the Afrikaner people are apt to be referred to abroad as if specifically 'racial'. Yet it was not, after all, a colour-difference that set them against the 'invading' Uitlanders in 1899. Then, as today, they were unwilling to have their distinctive group-personality crushed by the weight of a culture not their own. What the fathers then fought to preserve their sons hold precious now. There is not necessarily very much rational basis for such a stand.

Varieties of One-ness

In their analysing of the familiar forms of social organisation, sociologists have made a distinction, fundamental in its nature, between solidarities, such as the tribal, which can be thought of as primordial and so in a sense natural, being directly derivative from the socially gregarious, or gregariously social, nature of man, and those, on the other hand, such as the 'body corporate', which, being based upon agreement, are by contrast artificial, conventional, non-natural, contrived. If to the former there be given their German name of *Gemeinschaft*, the latter may, in contradistinction, be termed *Gesellschaft*. This needs no elaborating here. What brings it however into this discussion is a suggestion that international society be seen in similar terms. What in practice this has meant is that, international society at the present time being so palpably *not* a *Gemeinschaft*, a *Gesellschaft* it therefore is taken to be. And the goal to be envisaged by rightminded men in their constructive thinking on the problems of human advancement is prefigured as the gradual transmutation of the global *Gesellschaft* of today into the global *Gemeinschaft* of an eventual tomorrow.

The idea is intriguing, and few seem to have voiced about it any theoretical doubt. Yet challenged it can be: especially if looked at in the context of the social cosmos as we have been trying to see it. The body corporate is typically an institution of domestic law. It is an artificial drawing together of persons all having already in common a relationship to the over-arching constitutional order. As members of a national society they are already in principle a *Gemeinschaft*: for their national community is not due to a contractual coming together. And it is within, and as between members of, the pre-existing national *Gemeinschaft* that the contractual arrangement, the contrived *Gesellschaft*, is brought into being.

The international society, by contrast, was never the body corporate. And yet, very true, it is not the *Gemeinschaft* either.

However, and here is the crux, it *corresponds* in the field of multi-sovereign-state co-existence, to the 'family', the *Gemeinschaft*, as we meet it in the ordinary experience of fleshly men.

Community and Community

If now the international society is more validly to be thought of not as a *Gesellschaft*, and not as a *Gemeinschaft* either—but as a *tertium quid*, namely a quasi-*Gemeinschaft*: what are we to desire? Should it be our aim to see our mere quasi-*Gemeinschaft* (for that surely is what it is) transmuted into the true *Gemeinschaft*, the veritable community, of sovereign states, of an imagined better tomorrow? Submittedly not; for the international society is indeed strictly and in its essence a quasi-, and not a true, *Gemeinschaft*; and this not by reason of any rudimentariness in its current state of development, but simply because it has its very existence in what is not a true, but a quasi-, kind of world. It exists, does it not, in a notional world, peopled by notional personalities: and out of such material what more could there be built than a notional community, a quasi-community at the most? And that, it has just been contended, is what we already have today.

No. If anything is to supersede the sovereign states system and, perhaps, to serve us better, it is unlikely to be formed of just those selfsame states: rather will it develop out of something which, along with them, already is present upon the historical scene. Within, beneath, alongside, behind and transcending, the notional society of states, there exists, and for some purposes fairly effectively, the nascent society of all mankind. That it is not yet very effectively a community may be conceded: but that potentially it is in very truth a community should be apparent as well.

The Social and the Constitutional Levels

As, in Switzerland, along with the political society of men, there flourishes the national community of men and of women as well, so globally, along with the diplomatic quasi-community of states there is emerging the true, social, community, the living world-tribe of human flesh and blood. As, when the Swiss women concert their efforts, they do it, so to say, in an extra-constitutional medium, so, when for a thousand different purposes men get together on a world-wide scale, this too is an extra-constitutional manifestation.

It is their sense of solidarity, and not the requirements of the political order, that brings the Swiss women together. With the dawning of a similar sense, among, say, the athletes, or the writers, or the Rotarians of the world, there is given a further living sinew in the body social of humanity-as-one.

Even assuming then that at the notional level the states, as states, must at best remain a mere quasi-community to the last, there yet is in principle nothing to preclude the emergence, at the *de facto* social level, of a true, strongly-grounded, exuberant community of mankind. This of course could hardly be caused to come about by any mere stroke of a pen. But that is not to say that nothing relevant to its emergence is being currently done. In what way relevant? Of those who desiderate a 'strengthening' of international law, some may in fact be essentially thinking merely of that detailed elaborating of the law's provisions which is going on all the time. By and by, when the dream of a true community has found fulfilment on the level of global social co-existence, it may be possible in retrospect to honour that part which the jurists— 'on tap', but never 'on top'—will have played in bringing it down to earth. In his recent *The Common Law of Mankind*, C. W. Jenks has looked to an impending 'transformation', of the international law which has traditionally been that between the states, into the 'common law' of a world community. He certainly already can point to an array of dispositions congenial to his line of thought. When once it is effectively in existence, the true world community will doubtless have indeed its common law. And the corpus of that law may well retain in point of content much that is reminiscent of our international law of today. In principle however it will *not* be merely a modified form of that traditional system; rather will a new-fangled system have emerged to take that system's place. The new-fangled system will be the law of a single world society; not that of a single quasi-society composed of sovereign states.

What is at issue is not a question of substantive content— but of technical status. In point of status the law that we have is still the law, not of a community, of men, but, as for centuries past, of a quasi-community, of states. Whereas, if the evidence for the existence of a true world-community had suitably to be looked for in the content, not the status, of its law, then indeed might we be proclaiming that community as either already in being or on the verge of coming to be. But so long as the law remains, as hitherto, the law, technically and therefore basically, of the traditional quasi-community of sovereign states, its content, however forwardlookingly inspired, is simply neither here nor there. That content, influenced in its development by men of vision, may certainly play its important part, in reflecting, and so assisting, the progress of world society towards its goal. But it is in the realm of social reality that the movement must proceed and the goal be achieved: it can not be accomplished, it can at most be reflected, in the world of law.

Existential Unification

Some day there thus may yet be seen the true *Gemeinschaft* of all the human race. The sign of its advent will be not merely the fact that somebody somewhere is affecting to say things in its name. Rather will it be that when, on some matter of universal moment, some single opinion has in fact become prevalent on a universal scale, there will, as if instinctively, be allowed to such opinion that peculiar, semi-mystical, prestige which belongs to what is not merely prevalent but communal as well. Doubtless there are not many matters as yet on which mankind is anywhere near to having found such a communal view. But it is too soon to conclude that even for those already living it must necessarily for ever remain a dream. A child, a singer—or even, dare one whisper it, a charismatic leader—emitting on a world-wide TV hook-up the appropriate sounds, with congenial gestures, at the critical moment, might even tomorrow voice a judgment, with an air of inevitability, as on man's collective behalf—and not be figuratively shouted down. And what once had so happened, might happen again. Then, the possibility of all humanity sharing a 'mind', and of expression being found for it, having, like the possibility it now seems of space-travel, become an item in the image by which men live, things could never again seem quite the same. The lilies, as artificial-looking and as ornamental as always, would still be each rooted in its original pond: but the flood of human fellowship would all the while be imperilling the separate identities of the ponds. True, the flood might momentarily subside, but it would hardly be forgotten, even by the lilies. The forces which had brought the first one might bring another flood, more lasting, by and by.

If the women of Switzerland can feel and speak together, why not the women of the world? No need here for new constitutional forms. Community is not something to be deduced from words on paper. Its roots are in sentiment, not convention, and its seat is in the psyche of those whose moods become the public tone. It is to the science of social psychology that we might logically look for light on how all this might come to pass. What, one wonders, within its customary horizons, would this science presently find itself able to say? Not perhaps, within its heretofore customary horizons, very much, as yet.

The Wanted Image

The sign of the coming of world community would not be mysterious: merely, the spread of a conviction that it indeed had come—a conviction at first prevalently, but eventually also communally, entertained. And as footing so to say for the myth—or as conceptual bone for the emotional body—there would be that symbolic image which Kenneth Boulding would ask for, as something that could 'unite us all'. The rise of community whether global or national is a development at the level of the unconscious—and not as yet very well understood.

But all this of course concerns the future, and not the world we know. Meanwhile some fair examples, even today, of what may be accomplished by the provision of new symbols, for the fostering of new feelings, are becoming available, under the 'sign', as they say, of 'supra-nationalism' in the less-than-universal context of Western Europe.

Today, in a changing world, the peoples of France and of Western Germany are finding in terms of partnership possibilities which a generation ago were at best but a utopian vision. Enduring and reasonably endurable co-existence has not as its condition the radical elimination of tensions, for of that, this side the grave, men in society can have but little hope. What it does require is an appropriate approach, between states and peoples, in their dealings with one another. On the one hand, a kind of formal correctitude, a degree of mutual self-restraint, a growth of gentle manners. On the other, a measure of understanding, born of an appreciation of individuality, each seeing the other as significantly unique.

The world of many sovereignties, each equally tolerant, equally heedful, of the cultural idiosyncrasies of every other, is a 'possible' world—'possible' here being used in the philosophers' sense, as of something which in principle *could* exist, whether or not it does—a conceivable world, in short. One must at least not abandon hope that events might yet give us such a world. It would be a world in which standards of moderation and self-restraint had become accepted, as by common consent, in the uses made by states not of their power only but of their influence also. Only in certain conditions, however, could it conceivably be achieved: one of these being presumably that the peoples had ceased to have cause to suspect one another of working for one another's destruction. And it is not of course on other governments only that the influence of governments is employed.

CHAPTER XV

INFLUENCE AND IMMUNITY

The Spider and the Cat

To have pointed to the element of influence, with the profusion of its manifestations, is to have focused upon what gives its distinctiveness to Diplomatics as a branch of study. Influence, as someone well said long ago, is *not* government. And Political Science, at least as heretofore developed, has centred essentially upon the governmental process. International Relations (*alias* Diplomatics), its neighbour discipline, presupposes indeed a quasi-social coexistence of 'governed' countries. But its own peculiar concern is with the special nature of one special mode of social co-existence, marked by the absence, even in principle, of any inclusive system of governmental arrangements, any over-arching framework, that is, of formal authority. On the universal, world-wide, scale it is essentially as influence, and not as institutionalised authority, that power, for instance, has its impact on affairs.

As Political Science (*alias* Public Administration *alias* Government) is *par excellence* about government, so is Diplomatics characteristically about influence. Sister topics, neighbour disciplines. It might, on the face of it, seem a useful arrangement if every student of politics officially a specialiser in either of these two subjects could be in a position to pursue along with it, as an 'underpinner', the other. For the connoisseur-in-the-making of international relationships it would be scarcely less inopportune to eschew the study of government than it so patently would be to forgo the study of international law.

How then may one analytically differentiate between government and influence? Crudely, and far too innocently, one might think to put the point as follows. Government is what you give them when you have them where you want them:

influence comes in when, not having them where you want them, you can, at most, endeavour to get them to want you to have them where you want them. Overdrawn illustrations are: on the one hand, the cat with a mouse and, on the other, the spider on the watch for a fly.

All of which however is of course oversimplified to the point of caricature. On the one hand, the truth is that government, as political scientists are accustomed to understanding it, is far from being merely a matter of the pushing of people around. And, on the other hand, so far from being the *differentia* of diplomacy, influence, alike in all the affairs of human kind, is more ubiquitous even than speech. One has only to think of salesmanship, gospel-preaching, barracking, courtship, fly-fishing, to perceive that to define a subject as having for its subject-matter the manifestations of influence would be as intemperate (while at the same time just as inhibiting) as it would be to define another subject as simply the study, in its various forms, of power.

Sorts of Social Worlds

What differentiates Diplomatics from Government is the difference between the milieux within which by these respective subjects the element of influence is studied. Whereas in the latter case there is presupposed as its context a functioning governmental system, in the former there distinctively is not. The arrangements in relation to which influence is employed are in the one case governmental, in the other inter-governmental. The relationships, the problems, the possibilities, belong in the two cases to different institutional levels, different social worlds. And one has only to look again at the examples given above of sorts of situation, to see that the techniques invoked for the exercise of influence may be as dissimilar in many respects as they may, it is true, be similar in some. All's fair, they say, in love and war: yet there are *ruses de guerre* for which a suitor might with difficulty be forgiven.

Between the techniques of little Johnnie negotiating at the tea table for a second slice of cake, and those of a Big Bill Thompson canvassing in Chicago for re-election to the mayoralty, there may be things in common. But electioneering has in particular the quality of a dual approach. It is hardly less concerned with dissuading the marginal elector from voting for another than with persuading him to vote for oneself. Now it will be seen that at the extra-domestic level, in the field, that is, of international politics, there may well, as they say, be more 'future' in suborning one's opponent's supporters than in attracting supporters of one's own. And one is tempted to suggest that in international 'electioneering', as practised by say an Eisenhower or a Khrushchev when he goes abroad, more's fair than on the home front, though still perhaps less than in love and war. But what in reality is the limiting factor, on unfairness, in canvassing techniques, at either level? Is it the conscientious scruples of the candidate? Or is it the amount that the market will absorb? Bad sportsmanship at either level is only too liable to drive out good, if only it be not *too* bad. And 'too' bad, here, is alas liable to mean too bad to be got away with.

The Good, the Better, and the Bad

It is easier to see the excuses for the occasional lapse from perfect candour when the sleight-of-hand is being successfully practised by those on 'our' side than on 'theirs'. And if the leaders in an advanced democracy give the impression of being less unscrupulous than some of those in a totalitarian camp, it may be partly because the less scrupulous types are perhaps rather less likely to become the leaders in a democracy sufficiently advanced. But in a country of little political experience there is an unfortunate likelihood that he who does not stoop to conquer may be conquered by those who will stoop to no matter what. That is why we may wish on the whole that the newer 'democracies' were more sophisticated, more discriminating, more mature. (It is no use inveighing against those who exploit the gullibility of a public if the certainty is that, were they not to do it, others would.) And that also is why we may wish on the whole that the relative maturity, political literacy, and awareness of what everything is all about, could in the case of the older democracies be at least as evident in matters of international, as of domestic, affairs. For the perils of political illiteracy are not less in the one sphere than in the other.

For though literacy may not of itself preclude apathy, the

effective vigilance which liberty requires might be difficult to maintain without it. And even under the extremest form of autocracy there is a residual freedom in the spirit of man; and hence probably a greater dependence upon the element of influence than on the crude pushing of people around. Meanwhile, apart from this, there are three further sorts of government, two being a governing of others, the third the governing of self. Colonial administration, or, as some may still prefer to call it, imperial rule, has not nowadays a sympathetic press. However good it be, it is, as if by definition, less good than is self-government, however bad. Nor is colonial administration necessarily even good. But whether government be bad, or good, or better, the element of influence, employed in the locally-productive forms and subject to the locally-operative limitations, is as characteristic in the contexts of government as in those of diplomacy. Since, however, this essay is not a treatise on government, it is specifically to influence, and to the conditions in which, internationally, this is exerted and competed for, that our further inquiry will relate.

Code-words for Co-operation

At the opera, incognito in the stalls, there sat a famous fiddler. Of a sudden there came the cry of 'FIRE!' All, in a rush, started for the exits. Surely somebody was going to get hurt. But no. Seizing from one in the orchestra a fiddle, the virtuoso began to play. As by magic, the confusion ended. Within seconds all were motionless, entranced by the wonder of his playing. The situation was saved. Panic was averted. But alas they all perished in the flames.

Listening, in the war, to pep talks, few who had heard it can not have been reminded of that story. But did they therefore cease to heed? Not if they knew what they were at. Full well they knew what the talking was for. Why does the pugilist, during training, so often mutter: 'I shall win!'? Why, before elections, do parties proclaim their assurance of success? The function of the pep talk is not merely to reiterate an axiom, but to recall the *motif* of that composition in the rendering of which all are glad to be reminded of their part.

No one in a well-commanded army queries the orders for the

day. No player thinks to question the decisions of his captain. Strength is what is wanted. Unity is strength. Unity in action postulates unity in idea, in conception. 'You understand, young man? In our emporium the customer is always right.' Such is the doctrine by which a successful salesmanship will be informed. The whips are on: let no backbencher have opinions of his own: leastways not overtly. Heresy to the stake. Deviation to the salt mines. 'If the missus says it's black, it's black!'

But *is* it? Don't customers *ever* err? *Is* the emperor clad? *Is* everything that serves the revolution *eo ipso* right? *Aren't* we downhearted?

Effective behaviour in politics is concerted, harmonised, collective, 'team' behaviour. Of this the ideal model is the racing crew. As to who shall set the time, there will be no contention, any more than in the case of musicians with a conductor. The conductor is the typical master of ceremonies. The instrumentalist is the teamsman. What in politics is solidarity, in games is the spirit of the team. The good party member is the teamsman if not in inward feelings then at least in word and deed. Conformity in politics may flow from teamsmanship, or conviction, or coercion: or, perhaps we should nowadays add, from manipulation. In the West the opportunity for such coercion is virtually non-existent, the need for such conviction relatively small, the scope for such manipulation greater perhaps than we may like to believe; but teamsmanship is almost universally the big idea. Men know which side they are on and who is captain. Like the conductor of the orchestra, who is the executant of a programme not of his composing, so the 'leader' in politics may affect to be merely the instrument of a purpose greater than his own. Meanwhile that participational response from others which alone makes his leadership a possibility is at any given moment just an empirical fact.

Modes of Leadership

If there should have seemed to be anything over-curious about the distinction earlier elaborated between communal, and prevalent, opinion, it should at least be conceded that it is not strictly new. The theories on which old-style Marxist conspirators prepared to meet their opportunity when it should come turned partly on this very distinction, differently though they may have expressed it. Where we here have written of communal, as opposed to prevalent, opinion, they, those theoreticians of revolution, would speak of 'consciousness' as opposed to 'spontaneity'. It would be of little use, they some of them judged, to wait for the masses to rise against their rulers, or, rising, to know what to do. Leadership must, when the time was ripe, be given, and consciousness engendered, from the top. And where in the wide, wide world today is muscovite subversion looking solely to the many? How about those cadres, Moscow-groomed? If Communism comes tomorrow, in what countries will this be on a popular vote?

Meanwhile that process known officially as 'agitation', as opposed to 'propaganda', is perpetually on the go, not so much for the instruction of the intelligent as for the anticipatory softening up of the unfortified popular mind, and the fanning of every flicker of potential discontent, wherever those spreading tentacles can get to—which nowadays means virtually throughout the world.

Making Friends and Influencing . . .

What in general are politics in the free world all about? What is the essence of a general election? A sort of sublimated civil war, is it not, between positions important mainly as being widely enough shared? It is a competition in the attempted winning away, by either side, of the less fanatical adherents of the other. Deviationism, heresy, non-conformity, non-docility, Durkheimian *anomie*, disarray—these are what 'we' shall be wishing to see among 'their' supporters, and they among ours. What in one light appears as the 'disease' of orthodoxy is the health of monolithic homogeneity when viewed in another. The art of the leader is to dictate and control: to be composer and conductor, while posturing as merely a leader and nothing more. Nasserism has to present itself as Arabism, Hitlerism as nationalism, Kremlinism as Leninism, Maoism as anti-imperialism. Carrots, sticks, slogans, incantations—many are the means whereby people's participation is brought about in the pursuit of purposes not immediately their own.

Diplomacy, more now than ever in the old days of the

'gentleman's' wars or of the fields of cloth of gold, is similarly a competition for influence. We speak, say, or at one time we could, of Britain's 'position' in the Middle East, meaning her influence in those parts. To reduce absolutely an opponent's influence-quantum is to add, relatively, to one's own. As the bedside portable fades out, the sound becomes the more perceptible of the set next door. Now is the opportunity for the set next door to smear what the portable had been praising.

It's All in the Day's Work, for Somebody

The competition for influence may be seen as an aspect of the ever-shifting world-wide balance of sympathies. Somewhere at this moment, for instance, there will presumably be busy the organisers, on a suitable scale, of a momentous operation: the setting of the West against the West. Reconnaissance for this purpose includes the spotting of ambivalencies. That means, in particular, uncovering the shadow-side of every perishable relationship of mutual esteem. No doubt George III was never typically English. But the Americans, having fought against England, long continued to find a sense of fulfilment in the twisting of a long since repentant lion's tail. In a later age they favoured a league of nations. But, having narrowly failed to vote themselves into one, they had thenceforth to keep on seeing how wise they must surely so have been. What a positive psycho-diplomacy will nowadays be doing is to spot and to exploit any comparable relationships of a qualified love, feeding the qualifications at the expense of the love.

They Must Educate Our Masters?

There are of course many differences between the so-called 'free' countries and those within the other camp. In each there are the decision-making élite and the public-at-large. But between these the relation is not in the two cases the same. Of two things an Eisenhower is well aware: that he must avoid doing what he could not hope to justify in the eyes of his public, and, that the judgment of his public is not going to be affected by him alone. A Khrushchev by contrast can count upon his public at least not to advertise any dangerous new insights that a distinguished visitor may have managed to wash into their brains.

The American régime, as being a democratic one, is like the parson with an active-minded flock. It is from his pulpit that he strives to keep them on the strait and narrow roadway. When outside, they cannot, by him, be prevented from attending to the atheist at the corner. But need he lend the man his pulpit? When a luncheon-guest at the Waldorf Astoria, Mr. K. is as it were a visiting preacher in the democratic parish church. Disarray: that is the word. It is this that totalitarian cordiality is so naturally concerned to be promoting within the democratic camp. And it is from this that within their own camp the monopolisers of the communications media are so anxious to preserve the public mind. And the care with which they so preserve it is itself an index of their respect for the efficiency of the washing-machine as a weapon of sociological war.

When Vyshinsky said: 'We shall win the world with our ideas', what he may well have meant was: 'The world becomes our captive when its trust is sufficiently eroded in what it has been getting from you.' Not 'our ideas', but 'their dubieties', his words might well have been.

Yes, but 'our ideas' also: and especially also 'our' neatly-timed achievements. In effect, the members of international society are on the TV screen all the time. Throughout the year, throughout the world, politicians, publicists and people generally are continually revising their impressions of at least the better known to them, be it only by repute, of the members of the society of states. Like candidates nursing constituencies, the states are forever posturing for the improvement of their 'image' in the minds of those whose ill-will they must wish to temper, even if their affection they cannot hope to win. To enjoy an exceptional prestige, to be in good standing, to have a following, are desiderata that no contestant in the arena either of politics or of diplomatics can afford not to entertain. 'Look to your moat' it used to be said. 'Look to your image' is the more up-to-date idea.

Disparity of Esteem

'I like a man,' sang Sir Harry Lauder, 'who *is* a man.' And his touchstone of man-ness was not the one accepted for birth certificate purposes. His touchstone was that of capacity—

the capacity, specifically, for convivial participation. All men may be equal but all are not equally men! (Witness the traditional rating of diners-out in terms of bottles, one or more than one, of port!)

And so it is with states. They vary not in formal status. Their sovereignty is unqualified and as uniform as is the humanity, biologically speaking, of men. Yet one state differs from another in political magnitude—by whatever yardstick tested.

As Lauder held not all his fellow-revellers in equal esteem— neither does the state its fellow-states. While a country's status remains incontestable, its standing may fluctuate almost from hour to hour. And its standing is conditioned by its stature. In contrast with its physical analogue—which he can do so proverbially little, by taking thought, to enhance—to his moral stature a man, by taking opportunities, may add from day to day. Similarly to its stature—moral, political, diplomatic—a state may add, and no state ever lightly neglects an opportunity to do so.

And perhaps because diplomatic stature is so tied in with strategic capability, it is of 'powers', rather than of countries or of states, that we tend in our historiography to talk. We speak, that is, not of power merely, but of powers, and powers unequally graded. Graded in terms of what? Of their sheer strength? No, not of their sheer strength, but rather of their stature, and hence of their standing. The great power is the power great in standing, great in the eyes of other states. It is the power deferred to as great. And similarly for the near-great, the middle and the small.

I heed, a diplomatic Lauder might say, a state which *is* a state —with a capacity for diplomatic participation.

So even the states are not states merely. They are 'powers', and, though equally powers, not all of equal power. Through the lens, that is, of dynamics, as distinct from formal structure, it is not simply a system of states. And, while states have status, powers have stature and standing and strength. The binocularity which avails itself of both the lenses at once has its relevance to the appreciation of much else in social experience besides the mutual dealings of states. And much of this 'much else' is, like the relative standing and stature of the powers, changing all the while.

Is relative stature not just another name for relative influence? Not exactly. For influence is a function not of a country's stature only, but of its connections. The small power with big friends may be bigger in influence than the bigger with few.

Nothing that a state may publicly do can fail to affect its 'image' in the minds of many. Some states, in their manner of life, show less sense of the importance of this consideration than others.

Even those of us who, when Lunik II landed, so publicly, on the moon, might have simulated indifference to the technological achievement, on the vague general ground that wonders notoriously never cease, can hardly have failed to be struck by how scientists had been struck by how the moon had been struck. And certainly no student of diplomatics can but have been impressed by the apparent careful timing of the achievement. And that was only one of the many examples that there recently have been of the virtuosity of Moscow's constant conditioning of that image of the social cosmos which, in the mind of so-called uncommitted peoples, may well be a decisive factor at some day of reckoning not perhaps, as yet, in sight.

Watering the Seeds of Self-reproach

Asked what they would do were they to suffer defeat in the War, Nazis are said to have said that they would at once set about 'organizing sympathy'. They failed of course to allow for their own approaching absence from the scene and consequent inability personally to carry out that programme. But certainly the sort of thing they so envisaged does appear to have been undertaken by some of their predecessors after 1918. It was not long then before the defeated Germans had got in Britain an anti-Versailles movement. And by and by this had its counterpart in France. Frenchmen were found developing doubts on the propriety of their having sought to preserve a settlement designed for the preservation of France. It is, one may suggest, the Achilles heel of democratic self-rule that foreign policy must rest upon the support of those who cannot be expected to understand what at bottom it is all about— the support, that is, not of the sophisticated few, but of the gullible many. 'Don't,' said, in effect, Mr. John Foster Dulles, 'come quoting to me what those people say. I judge by what they do.' With how many of his countrymen will this have improved his standing? Did it not earn him a name for excessive inflexibility? When Wendell Willkie toured the world in the early 'forties his book was in one place reviewed as 'Gullible's Travels'. No one would dream of so referring to the travels of a Mr. K. His, rather, have been travels *among* the gullibles. Or, at least, the lullables. 'Lullaby's Travels' might better in his case have filled the bill.

If with my right hand I can mesmerise my neighbour, I shall with my left hand be able to acquire his purse. Sometimes it is almost as if Mr. K.'s public-relations right hand was not even aware of what his power-avid left hand was about. It is his right hand that he gives to mass opinion in the democracies. The glad hand indeed—and gladly does he give it. For with it he gives nothing except the grip. And what, with his left hand, he may all the while be doing some people do not even pause to consider. With justice was it written that wars had their origin in the minds of men. It is in the minds of men that the moral underproppings of peace may now be in the process of being 'washed' away.

Summer is Icumen In

Mr. K. is not going west just to gaze at the corn on the cob.[1] The visitor will have more than that to see. Will he be disturbed when he finds that, despite their capitalistic fetters, the people of the U.S.A. are happy and content. The happier the better, may he not feel? Notoriously the price of liberty is vigilance. He might well be only too pleased to see them happier yet. Forward the mood-engineer. A job for you.

Writing on 17th September 1959, it is difficult not to animadvert upon tomorrow's prospect of Mr. K. making a new disarmament proposal at the United Nations. Ostensibly he will be addressing the assembled delegations. But not to them the delegates, nor even to them, their governments, will he in reality be appealing: but to them, the peoples of the United Nations, in whose name the Charter was ostensibly drawn up. It was symbolic that so early on his first morning in the U.S.A., the visitor should have been seen without his jacket.

[1] This (cf. the next paragraph) was written in 1959. It has not lost its point.

Like every other great illusionist, he was doubtless anxious to convince his public that he had nothing up his sleeve. One might have guessed that Moscow would on such an occasion run so true to form. Ever since Litvinov disconcerted the Preparatory Commission at Geneva in 19 (was it 27?) with his plan for a total abolition of armaments, that has been a recurring motif in so much that for world consumption has emanated from that selfsame source. As well might Moscow propose immediate agreement on the setting up of a world state, the form of it, whether Stalinist or Jeffersonian, being left over as a mere matter of detail.

Writing with the hindsight of 17th January 1960, there seems no more reason to modify now the wording of that last paragraph than Moscow seems to have seen to revise its proposal of a generation ago. As, in Detroit, Mr. K. so enthusiastically exclaimed, munching his second hot-dog: 'It's excellent! don't change the formula!'

Flies Today, Mice Tomorrow

It used to be said, of the gods, that when bent on destroying a man they would begin by making him mad. As with men, so with societies. For, as John Austin perceived, what gives its essential character to political society is the element of 'habitual obedience'. One thinks of the lighting system of a city. So long as the power keeps on flowing, the globes will continue to glow. Let the current fail and out go the lights. Let 'the habitual obedience of the bulk' be subverted, and no longer does the society conform to the Austinian definition. Austin's concern was not, of course, to explain, but merely to postulate, the obedience. To explain it would have meant moving into social psychology: speaking, that is, of prejudices and predilections, and above all of beliefs. Switch off the basic beliefs, and out go the political, the constitutional, and along with these the legal, lights. In a society, if not equally in the individual, madness might almost be defined as a compound dislocation of basic beliefs. And on them depends unity, that condition for collective self-preservation in the hour of trial.[1]

[1] My respect for Austin, which is unabated, was expressed in *Modern Theories of Law*, W. I. Jennings (ed.) 1933.

The Conditioning of the Image

Whether or not Waterloo will have been won where they say it was, the future of many little children is probably now being predetermined on the field of psychological war. Anyone who doubts that the agents of the Kremlin are playing on the minds of the young folk wherever in the world they can, must presumably himself have been played upon, whether by those agents in person or by others upon whom they have played. Most likely by some of these last. Such people even flatter themselves that their concepts and interpretations are their own.

Any Answer?

If a young man takes an illness, he may not know how he came by it, but, if he comes to see that, but for the bigotry of his parents, he might have had immunity against it, he will hardly acquit them of blame. Why, the young folk yet may ask, when we were so evidently the object of certain processes, was there so little undertaken to protect us from their effects? Are our elders, in their seeming indifference, themselves so cogent a testimonial to the kind of education with which in our turn they seemingly would have us rest content? Might we not have been offered at least the chance to discover whether, by a different method, we might not have become even better equipped? Not perhaps well, but at any rate better, equipped?

What would such an offer have involved? What in this field are the conditions of connoisseurship?

The Connoisseurship of the Middlebrow

It is not strictly necessary, before one can prudently take part in an intelligent interchange of evaluations on, say, a game of cricket, to have made a lifetime's study of cricket history, of the philosophy of captaincy, or even of the mysteries of every movement with the bat. What is however fairly indispensable is a certain amount of personal experience of at least looking on at the game, and a feel for the dramatic tension of each succeeding moment in a particular match.

Similarly, if one is to contribute to the crystallising of public judgment on an industrial conflict, there are certain basic insights that one needs must have into the nature of modern society and into those conditions that make it so seemingly unavoidable that the various interests should from time to time feel it so incumbent upon them to dig their moral toes in and put up a fight.

What now, by comparison, must we say of that equipment for the want of which the layman might well be shy to cross argumentative swords with the veteran in diplomatic affairs? Admittedly it is the right of every citizen, in a free society, freely to speak his mind. Yet prudence, if not a sense of humour, may tend to neutralise the impetuosity of anyone who, though speaking 'as a fool' in such concerns, might be minded to favour the public with some bright new notion of his own on whatever world-shaking political issue may happen to have caught the limelight at a given time. What is that virtue of which in such conditions such a person should be conscious of his lack? Is it simply the difference between being, and not being, well posted on current events? Nothing could be more false than such an idea.

Connoisseurship at a cricket match is not simply the knowledge of what at any moment is the score. Every onlooker, however inexpert, may be assumed to have some interest in the state of the game. And in order to show an interest in the course and the state of the 'game' of international politics, one need not be qualified to shed independent light upon what every new development may imply. But on the other hand, to be competent to shed such light, it is not enough merely to have such an interest. For there is a difference between casual alertness to the course and the state of a particular match, and knowledge of the *kind* of game of which it is merely an instance—knowledge, namely, of its principle, its possibilities, its spirit and traditions, its ethos even—knowledge, in short, of the understandings, the assumptions, the anxieties, the expectations and the hopes, with which, as well as the context and conditions in which, so many specimens of man the player come together on such occasions on such a field. There is in particular a knowledge of the *global* 'game', for want of which no holistic appreciation is possible of even the clearest-looking current issue. And the mistake is to suppose that, because only those themselves experienced in the very playing of it can know the game so to say 'from within', therefore no one not privileged personally to have played it can usefully aspire to any better-than-superficial knowledge of it at all.

By definition, no mother will herself have been a schoolboy. But one ex-schoolboy at any rate can recall the truth of things his mother told him in advance about how it would feel to find himself for the first time at school. And many are those other sorts of strange adventure with respect to which we mortals may well see the sense of learning beforehand, from those who know of it a little more than we do, of how it will be, and look, and feel, 'when the balloon goes up'. We see the sense of this, and it is by no means a matter of being informed, prophetically, of how the battle will go. Comment on current events, as supposedly a medium of education, is something we might be willing to dispense with, did it not make for a familiarity with the setting—that is, the socio-cosmic theatre—which gives to all such events their ultimate significance. What makes such comment so effective for the purpose is partly its relevance to the condition of those concerned, to the felt need, that is, of the students themselves. Men are glad of advance information of 'what it will be like': so much so that they are apt to accept it uncritically from whoever professes to know. How many an anxious soul will not have been grateful to Dante for his circumstantial picturing for them of Paradise, and not of Paradise only. How many will have paused to wonder how he could possibly know, or to note that even ostensibly his was but the story of a dream. There have been well-intentioned teachers of International Relations whose prefigurings of a world just about to be born can have been little better than a dream. There are various visions of paradise in the dreams of new nations today, and more than one Dante to tell them how it will be. Is there nothing to be done, by their teachers, to protect the inexperienced against this traffic in dangerous drugs? What they need is an awareness not just of the current course of the game, but of the nature of the game as such. This, if they continue to seek it, they may progressively acquire; but a taste for it and a notion of where and how to do their seeking could, and surely should, be offered to them in their youth.

Why—Why—Why?

Familiarity with the fabric of the social cosmos, as understood in this essay, has not, at all events in Britain, been typically insisted upon in candidates for either a parliamentary seat or a university degree. Yet for at least two sorts of adult citizen the rudiments, if no more, of such a subject might seem to be something which it was a pity to be without. There are the social science researchers, and, there are, after all, the persons of general education. If of course we assume that for those of general education the subject is strictly unnecessary, we may suspect that the same may be true of the researcher as well. For the economists there is no doubt a recognised ABC, descriptive Economics. And similarly for many other sorts of specialism. Can it be that International Relations, in its fundamentals, is seen by contrast as so readily comprehensible that a command of all of it that matters may be taken as coming incidentally to anyone who reads a paper in the train? Its students, as they proceed with it, will doubtless discover for themselves whether the subject is indeed so self-explanatory as that.

Man is not born politically literate, sophisticated, critically world-aware. But all of these, in his own interest, as well as in society's, the adult may wish he could early have become, even were it at the cost of having a further subject, and that not merely Current Events, in his syllabus as a freshman. The appreciation of present-day problems is of course important enough. But even during the Battle of Britain the Military Academy at Sandhurst will neither have closed down nor been diverted to the discussion of those. As soldiers-in-the-making are steeped systematically in the fundamentals of war, so, one must submit, might citizens in the making be grounded in the fundamentals of peace. The time will come quite soon enough when theirs are the crucial opinions on current events, but the events then in question will not be the events of today. They will by that time be a nasty lot of new ones. But the world-awareness requisite for their understanding: that is something which, with suitable academic arrangements, we might presumably be giving to the young men now.

Survival as a Part-time Job

What proportion of our thinking do, or could, we normally devote to matters of world concern? Can we be expected, for the sake of such things, to neglect matters of personal, parochial, or professional, interest? Should we not be busybodies, rather than responsible citizens, if we did? And what proportion of our thinking time can be given over to thinking in the sense here referred to at all? For there are problems and there are problems. The problem of becoming clearer and more realistic in our conception of global affairs is one sort— a problem of vision. But each day upon our personal and professional plates there arrive a series of problems requiring more than that: requiring indeed that we decide. 'The buck stops here!' 'What does "A" do?' Problems these, of decision. We have so many of this kind: and for so many of them mere snap decisions will scarcely suffice. So much so that unless we do some thinking today in view of possible decisions in possible situations tomorrow we may tomorrow be at a loss to know what then to decide. So, in view of the decisions of tomorrow, we give, if we are responsible persons, some thought to a third category of problems, here and now. Problems these, not of mere vision, or of immediate decision, but of short term and long term pre-vision. Life is not wholly unlike the stock market. All we who have to live it must be studying these three sorts of problem all the time. Vision, decision, prevision. We have plenty of domestic food for thought. We can never be full-time thinkers on world affairs. All the more need then to be equipping ourselves betimes for that part-time thinking on which in the future we may have so largely to depend.

While We Yet Have Time

The ultimate impediment to our salvation, theology tells us, is pride. With our other failings we may come to cope: but pride we must discard before we can. So too for the understanding of the cosmos. Only to the humble in mind can that nursery-talk be acceptable which is requisite for getting straight the fundamentals of their thinking on themes such as we have been touching in this study.

Of the modes of self-indulgence there are few so originally

innocuous as sleep. But even this is to be valued in terms of the where and the when. For sleeping when on duty in a war, a man can be shot. But it might no doubt be admitted in mitigation of sentence if he could claim to have lost his memory—of there being indeed a war. In so far as the young of today may even now be not aware that in effect they are living in a war, and a war, moreover, in which, not their own survival merely, but so much else that they must value, is at stake, they too might perhaps be forgiven if found asleep. But the beginner who perceives that whatever effective service it may by and by be his to offer to the cause of human freedom may depend upon the depth of his awareness of the perils it is in, and having, would he but accept it, the chance to be pursuing that awareness, must, if he forgo that chance, be chargeable with sleeping at his post.

What manner of subject then is this that the freshman might propitiously be permitted and enabled, and encouraged, if not indeed required, to include within his academic purview?

CHAPTER XVI

SOCIAL COSMOLOGY—ITS PROBLEMS, PROCEDURES AND PLACE

The Non-attainability of the Indispensable

More than once already in the course of this essay reliance has been put upon the metaphor of the thinking-cap. One and the same head may be at home in several sorts of world, thinking in several academic languages and manipulating as many different systems of esoteric ideas—provided there be at its disposal the necessary assortment of caps. Even your law-student may need a change of cap when migrating from a case in the King's Bench to one in the Chancery Division of the High Court. As a metaphor, the cap can be even more convenient than is the bag of tools.

To say then of International Law that its study required a special cap was not to say anything very startling. For such is the way with whatever branch of law one may care to name. All of us are accustomed to encountering, if not to wearing, those legal caps. But what of this other one, the cap required for the study of International Relations? Not quite so familiar, this distinctive piece of headgear. And not quite so typical either, of what your specialiser's cap can be. For, unlike so many another specialisation, International Relations is not the study of an 'aspect'. Its business is, as we saw, with life, life in its concrete complexity, its multi-dimensional variety, and, above all and more particularly, in its many-levelled, imagination-taxing, depth.

The Status-seeker States

In the eyes of formal diplomatic theory what occurs internationally happens as among the members of a 'social' category, the category of the sovereign states. And, for seeing what so happens as happening simply so, a certain sort of lenses may be worn. In the sight on the other hand of the social analysis which looks behind the formulas in force to the forces in operation, the picture is less clear-cut. And, for seeing just how other than clear-cut, the need is for another sort of lens. Or, to revert to the earlier metaphor, another shape of thinking-cap. With our study of diplomatic theory we cannot think to dispense. For that theory provides the formal framework within which the world-wide play and cross-play and counter-play of social energies works itself out. But, for the sources of those energies, it is necessary to look, and this through different lenses, elsewhere.

Structure and Sub-structure

The difference should thus be appreciated between the thinking-caps respectively of formal-structure study, and of social dynamics proper. In terms of formal-structure study the social universe is essentially a compresence of sovereign states, equal in their sovereignty and, as some would add, sovereign in their equality. But in terms of social dynamics it is indefinitely more complicated than that. There are so many more social organisms in the human universe than are dreamed of in the philosophy of the student merely of formal structure, the student, that is, of the lily-bedecked surfaces of the ponds. In particular, besides the states, there are the peoples, and the people, and the groups, the organisations, and the associations not yet articulated for effective action. All these go to compose a world whose full complexity it would be difficult to reflect in a helpfully simplified chart.

It is not just a partial, or superficial, but a total view that International Relations, as a subject, has to strive for, of the real-life situations that are its *raison d'être*. Because it is real-life situations that have to be assessed, situations as they actually come about—this is why a deliberate training of the mind for their eventual less inadequate appreciation is so desirable and so difficult to provide. Not of course that any man's capacity for this can ever be fully sufficient. Men have to do what they can with the means, and mental equipment, at their disposal. Even were it to be suggested that Sociology could leave psychology to others, it is certain that Strategics—based on the logistics of the mobility of armies—depends in vital part upon the logistics of the mobility of men. And it is no less certain that Diplomatics, a study indeed of state behaviour, involves study of the behaviour, with its manifold motivations and in its varying contexts, of men. Men, groups, nations, organisations, governments—all must be included in the picture—as intrinsic to the study of what is done, that is, deemed to be done, done, that is, notionally, by states. The question is not just whether a special thinking cap is called for, but whether it is producible—and, if produced, whether there will be anyone found worthy to wear it.

What the novice should be interested to develop, and his friends to see him do so, are (*a*) his familiarity with the milieu in which diplomatic situations occur; (*b*) his synoptic eye for the essentials of the particular situation, state-behaviour in the face of which it will be his concern to observe and understand; and (*c*) his capacities as a connoisseur of world-political gamesmanship. Given these as his desiderata, to what sort of a processing should he as a beginner be exposed?

Keeping Up with the Economists

Consider first what Economics is about. 'Out there': a multiplicity of processes and situations classifiable into types, and inviting analysis with a view to the formulating of 'laws' in the light of which that analysis may the more effectively be further prosecuted with a view to the formulating of further such 'laws'. Economics is a bag of intellectual tools, the employment of which has as a by-product the adding from time to time of further tools to the bag.

Consider next what International Politics, as pioneered in some very important centres, is conceived to be about. 'Out there': once again a multiplicity of situations and processes classifiable, presumably, into types, and inviting analysis. International Politics thus similarly aspires to become a bag of tools, in the use of which new tools may from time to time be added to the bag. Of the social utility of such an academic development there should presumably be no question. It would almost be sufficiently attested by the mere readiness of so many gifted scholars to engage in its pursuit.

Not Keeping Up with Anybody

Consider, however, thirdly, the subject with which we here are avowedly by contrast concerned. 'Out there': the social universe, mankind as a whole conceived of as embryonically a single society and recognised as organisationally one already in certain important theoretical aspects, aspects well understood by many—so well indeed that they might find it difficult to find a common language in which to bring knowledge of it to those still radically uninformed: and, on the other hand, the uninformed who might well wish to be better aware of those background conditions against which any stand they may at some time have to make on social, economic, political, or diplomatic, issues will most propitiously be determined.

Maps and Maps

A map showing the London bus routes and the layout of the underground railway system may be of great value, for certain purposes, to someone whose aim it is to become an authority on London; but not for all the purposes with which he will be exploring his field. (No use to tell him that the tube-map will give him all that he need wish to know.) The tube-map is a simplification, and a salutary one, of what could be a most complicated picture. As a substitute for the picture of London as she really is, it does not suffice. And, were the student of international relations to be presented at the outset with the equivalent of the London tube-map, with the assurance that it will be of help to him, he would need equally to accept this with the appropriate reservations. He should equally be unwilling to spare himself a study of his subject-matter as it really is. What the tube-map in effect tells the visitor is that, for certain purposes, it is *as if* London were as it suggests. And for those purposes he does well enough to proceed as if she really were. But he will not suppose that for other purposes he can safely so proceed. And so the student of society can with advantage proceed, for certain purposes, as if the abstract picture that Economics provides were indeed the full truth of things as they concretely are. But, for the full understanding which he desires of things as actually they are, *can* the student of International Relations expect to be supplied with a serviceable simplification? *Is* there for him any such short cut to an appreciation of reality as it is?

Rocket-borne Researchers and Pedestrian You and Me.

A great deal of high-grade thinking has nevertheless been in recent years directed towards the development of what for the student of International Relations could serve as the same sort of conceptual outfit, apparatus of ideas, or bag of intellectual tools and techniques as Economic Theory does for the practitioner in Economics. And impressive results have already been so achieved. Impressive, and of value. But, of value to whom? To practitioners, shall we infer, in the International Relations workshop? To researchers in particular, it is claimed. And, if by researchers one may understand persons having the purposes and the qualifications that make this true, well, true then it is. But the beginner has neither the qualifications nor the purposes here in question. His qualifications are in principle minimal, and his immediate purpose must rather be to become familiar, as by acquaintance, with the field in which no doubt he may some day be qualified to do fruitful research. And that field is of course the social universe.

Who, for the purpose of becoming familiar by acquaintance with village, or university, or family, life, would ask merely to be provided with a specialised conceptual outfit, apparatus of ideas, or bag of intellectual tools? Who would not rather demand to be told in words of one syllable, and, better, to be shown at first hand, what it was like to be personally a participant in the life that he was anxious to understand?

Meet the Family!

Malinowski it was who set his fellow-anthropologists the example that so many have since been content to follow. To understand his islanders he elected to reside among them for long enough to appreciate their way of life as a whole; and his resulting report was as much descriptive as analytic of the life he had so observed. Let the student of International Relations think then of the international society as Malinowski did of his Trobrianders, and be content with nothing other than whatever may prove to be the nearest practicable approach to a personal participation—in the role, as it were, of a sovereign state—in the life of the international family. One can point to many roles which it might be difficult, in imagination, to assume. What for instance would it feel like to be a prima donna, or a witch-doctor, or a space-man, or a fugitive from justice, or a trout in a stream? Yet all these exercises in empathy would be easy as compared with the veritable impossibility of playing, in imagination, the part of a state. The part, that is, of a member of the society of states. Yet this in a sense is what one had better be trying to do. A far far better thing it is, in this connection, to have tried, and inevitably failed, than never to have tried at all.

Of life as lived in the village, the factory, the college, the family, mankind has had ample experience: yet always the tyro must seek it anew. No set of diagrams will give him a 'knowledge by acquaintance' of, for example, village life. No rule of thumb will furnish solutions ready-made for the problems to be tackled. Yet the fact is that in respect of these, as of all other, aspects of life there is always something that, from those of more experience, those of less experience should be able to learn. There was much that, on his return to what we call 'civilization', Malinowski was able to teach, about the Trobrianders, to those who came to sit at his feet. If they could not all be shown at first hand what it was like to live that island life, they could at least be told in words of one syllable something of what had been revealed to him. The recruit who has not yet been near the battlefront may learn much that, when his own moment comes, will make it the less unintelligible, from the veteran in whom are joined a gift of description and a love of truth. Teaching is the art of the communicable. Great teachers are great artists, as rare as are the great ones in any other branch of art. But the ideal for them to aim at may with some confidence be defined. Whether it be Social Anthropology, and the topic life as lived on a given island, or International Relations with its focus on the life of the family of sovereign states, two elements seem indispensable in one who would convey to others that sort of knowledge-by-vicarious-personal-acquaintance which, until himself sent on active service, is all that the young soldier can aspire to. The teacher must have been at pains to win for

o

himself that kind of appreciation of his subject-matter which is accumulated not rapidly but over the years; and further, he must covet the genius of a Zimmern for making his subject come alive for those still at the gateway into the garden in which he for so long has walked, and watched, and talked and thought. The well-taught beginner is the one who is coming to have that connoisseurship, that 'feel' for his subject, that orientation in his field, which an Alfred Zimmern, or an Ernest Barker, had the power to impart. Great teachers indeed are few. Those who may have in them the makings of great teachers should at least be referred to such examples as these ones from the past. Admittedly neither Barker nor Zimmern had himself been able to sense at first hand the life of ancient Greece. Malinowski had the advantage of them there. Yet, as readers of *The Greek Commonwealth* will testify, it was almost as if Zimmern at any rate had been there himself. And, when Zimmern transferred his interest to the world of his own day, it was in much the same spirit that he furnished himself for his pioneering service in a field whose importance and whose possibilities he was so successfully to show. What fortune for those generations of grateful young men that it seems never to have occurred to him to try to make his subject look like economic theory.

The Disease of Terminological Orthodoxy

The conceptual toolbag of theoretical economics is in principle largely standardised. It is as it were a Queen's English which all aspiring economists must begin by learning to talk, just as all young geometers must acquire the language of triangles and squares. As the virtuoso, for instance a poet, may from time to time enrich mankind by taking idiosyncratic liberties with the language, so will the pioneer economic thinker introduce new concepts into the equipment of the researcher in his field. It is as yet too early to assume that political science, or even sociology, will ever rival economics in the degree of its resemblance to geometry in this regard, even could we take it as selfevidently desirable that it should. And, as for International Relations, the issue here is still as open as the sky. As yet there is nobody whose favourite set of concepts need be accepted as the only 'correct' one. Even when one elects to think about International Relations on the analogy of a game, one has not thereby committed oneself to a single model, pseudo-chess, or pseudo-cricket, or what have you.

When people speak of the chessboard of diplomacy or the diplomatic poker table, one may see the point of their language without assuming that a thorough knowledge of either game would constitute an all-sufficient clue to the dynamics of international conflict. He who speaks of the chessboard says no more than that diplomatics is in interesting respects like chess: and this is a useful insight to impart. Yet it can at the same time, in other respects, be like horse-trading, like poker, like war. Each of these analogies may have its value.

The Perils of Premature Conceptualisation

Indeed the most illuminating thing about the game-analogy is that there are so many games to which in turn one may with benefit point. Cricket, of course, is always with us. Here, as equally in football, the relevant thinking is performed upon the actual field of play: whereas in chess the players are in a sense above the battlefield. Poker again is another perennial standby, particularly in that here a plurality of participants play each for his own hand instead of being aligned in one or the other of two competing camps.

What is particularly suggestive about chess is that, while treating an opponent's king with respectful forbearance, capturing his supporters one by one, the object is to get him at a hopeless disadvantage and then to claim the victory. It would perhaps be hard to think of a game which exemplifies the kaleidoscopic series of temporary groupings that occur among the participants in diplomacy. Some such game may very well exist, however.

Meanwhile, we may notice that at some points diplomacy is primarily 'additional', as is football, each side from time to time adding something to its score; at others, 'attritional', as in draughts, the object being to erode the opponent's patrimonium even though not thereby adding to one's own; at others again, sheerly 'acquisitional', the kind of beggar-my-neighbour process which is officially the communist interpretation of world history; at others it is, as in association football and above all in chess, primarily 'positional', wherein it shows its peculiar affinity also with war. In the present phase of the game the most revealing model must at least include some sort of a jackpot to represent the uncommitted areas of the world.

Acknowledgment of Debt

There thus is room in the thinking of the enterprising observer for all these and other analogies, as well as for any non-game-like models that the newest recruit to the army of the analysts may propose. No one who has not considered the contributions of Snyder, Deutsch, Kaplan, the Sprouts, and not least of Quincy Wright, to this side of the subject can have any just appreciation of its exhilarating possibilities. We all owe much to them already and may live to owe more. And anyhow, for the still impenitent practitioner and defender of the natural-history, idiographic, descriptive, ostensive, portrait-painting treatment, who else might feel threatened by the numbers and the spectacular feats of the conceptualisers, there is after all a certain safety in the very variety of their masterpieces: for no single one of these can possibly be the right one, if that has to mean that all the others must be wrong. Perhaps it will have been after acquainting himself with the prospects of the international relations discipline that the Chinese dictator coined his celebrated metaphor of the garden wherein so rich a diversity of blooms could be permitted to flourish side by side.

Existentialist Diplomatics or Rule of Thumb

Let the free world not think to demonstrate its freedom by emulating the Chinese dictator in his subsequent relapse into the obscurantism of his Kremlin prototype. If there is indeed any single 'correct solution', let that be left to reveal itself under the tests of accumulating experience, as in the natural sciences would surely be the case. And meanwhile let the student keep an open mind, admiring the admirable, availing himself of the useful, and exploring the novel, in all their forms. Let him recollect that no formal listing on the age-height-colour-of-eyes pattern can really do duty for a knowledge-by-acquaintance of a man, and that no conceptual model of the game in question can give the beginner that 'feel' for the distinctive character whether of chess, or bridge, or halma, or poker, which comes to him from the moment of his first involvement in the actual playing of the game. Only the man who has, as it were, savoured diplomacy as from within can appreciate the full validity of the dictum that, in foreign policy, every move is 'a step in the dark' (and a step, one might add, upon a winding path with a minefield or a precipice upon either hand). The historian and cosy commentator can always tell us on which horse a government ought to have placed its bet, once the race has been run. What practitioners have to do is however to assess, on the past form of each of them individually, the chances of an assortment of probable runners in a race only now about to start. Or, changing the model, to make, however agonisingly, a succession of reappraisals of the outlook in the light always of the momentary passing state of the global game. Intimacy with the basic realities of the world situation in its currently evolving condition: this, rather than familiarity with a diagram, is what the statesman, and those who assume to judge him, pre-eminently require.

Before one can hope to understand, at any moment, the world situation, one must first, within the limits, of course, of one's single lifetime, have striven to understand the world: the human world, that is; in short, the single society of all mankind. One must, shall we say, have gone in for quasi-sociology on a global scale.

No Holds Barred

And if mankind is indeed conceived as a single society, and if Sociology is seen as the study of society as such, then the study of mankind comprehensively, the study, that is, of the human universe, admits just about as readily, perhaps, of being described as global Sociology as in any other way. Hardly less well, for instance, than as Social Cosmology, or as Metadiplomatics, or as the Structure of International Society, or as Prolegomena to the Study of World Affairs. Yet each of these designations has something to commend it. More important than our choice of any one such label is our appreciation of the appositeness, in their several ways, of them all. But perhaps Social Cosmology should, after all, be conceded a special 'just-rightness' of its own. For a study of world affairs which was not prepared for by an overall examination of the layout of the social cosmos would be a precarious enterprise. Yet even this assertion could, if preferred, be differently verbalised. A study, that is, of diplomacy not grounded in Diplomatics, or of Diplomatics not founded on that 'meta' subject which, to Diplomatics, is as to Linguistics is 'meta-linguistics', would be like the study of cloud formations unrelated to any knowledge of the physical composition of clouds.

There thus seem to be labels enough to cater for all the tastes. Even Global Social Dynamics is understood to have its friends. And, for this, incidentally, the abbreviation G.S.D. has a mnemonic advantage: for it can remind us, quite seriously, of how the truth to which Marx pointed could be but a half-truth only, since the reality of social coexistence was so much more than a mere matter of L.S.D.! Even the one-sided social dynamics of Marx was in principle, global enough, in the particular sense that it prefigured a future for the workers of all the world. But global in another sense it could not have claimed to be: namely, as according their full importance to the multifarious factors that in social life, as lived and experienced, condition the doings of men.

It is not however sufficient merely to have perceived that the economic factor, even were it the most important of all, would still be only one among many important factors. For one might still be challenged to offer some alternative interpretation, more plausible than was Marx's, for what Marx had been purporting to explain. Global Social Dynamics, with its unidisciplinary blinkers discarded, is global in our second sense as well, namely, in comprehending what are loosely described as the various 'approaches', studies of the several 'facets' that severally expose themselves to those investigating their subject-matter from the several significant angles. But the 'approaches' metaphor, with the companion image of the 'facets', still does less than justice to the nature of that which is to be approached. For, in its planetary dimension, the collective life of social man is not just diamond-like, a thing with facets. It also is pudding-like, a compound of ingredients; not to say skein-like, a tangle of threads; and weather-like, the resolution of a complex of inter-acting forces; and battle-like, the occasion of a matching of nerves and skills with nerves and skills—with the difference however in this last case that of those engaged, whether as brass-hats or as rank and file, some seem not as yet fully awake even to the very existence of a state of war. Who knows if it might not be different had at least the livelier among them been more infected with social cosmology in their cadet-school days? For so might they the better have known what might be coming to them and the more correctly have appraised it when it came.

Academic Affinities

Social Cosmology, as here understood, is, however, simply not in a category, either with applied economics or with policy-science politics or with any other species of applied, or policy-, science. In fact it is not, limitatively, a science at all; but a branch, rather, of humanistic-cum-scientific study. In so far of course as it is indeed in principle scientific, it is a form of 'fundamental' science, the analogue of elementary physics. Its most obvious cousin perhaps is cosmology proper (if we may understand this as scientific and philosophical, not theological, in its viewpoint). Ecology and oceanography are other near relations. But these are still none of them quite so closely akin to it as is that sort of Social Anthropology for which we have here been thanking Malinowski. For, as we saw, the social cosmologist has need to focus on the way of life obtaining in a specific milieu; that, namely, in which the units are the sovereign states. In so doing, it is true that he may incidentally discover new reasons why some suggested remedy for some regretted condition might or might not be likely to succeed. Without, that is, formally presenting itself as a policy science, social cosmology may, in passing, animadvert upon the technical adequacy of given nostrums. At the same time, as already indicated, it will not even aspire to be exclusively scientific. The probing of presuppositions, the evaluating of ends, the weighing of issues, the elucidating of concepts—all philosophical rather than restrictively scientific undertakings —will in principle also have their place within it, though so far only as may appear germane to the student's understanding of the cosmos as it is. Within that cosmos, men, groups, organisations, are everlastingly astir, their activity contributing to the universal movement of events, and this all the time in the light of premises and preconceptions failing an appreciation of which their behaviour can be but imperfectly understood. For the student's concern is essentially with life in its wholeness, and on this science, as such, can have little to say.

Even so, there remains an important difference between the empathy without which the logic of men's behaviour cannot be sensed, and the sympathy which involves the student himself in the situation he is seeking to appraise. Men's behaviour, with their premises and preconceptions, is a part of his subject-matter: his sympathies are privately his. And them he should know to keep under control. The difference, from his insight-seeking standpoint, between the several possibilities, may be suggested by means of the simile of the traveller and the maps. Three would-be tourist-visitors call at some agency abroad. Says the first: What tours in Britain do you recommend? Says the second: Maps, please, of routes to the north. And the third: A good road map, please, of Britain. Which does the student demand? To be told what he should want and work for? To be given the know-how for the promoting of a particular end? Or, to become so apprised of the layout of the country that he may pick out for himself his route to wherever he may choose to make for? So far as space-travel is, for instance, concerned, all that traditional astronomy seems to offer is this last. It neither discusses the relative attractiveness of Venus and of Mars, nor does it say how to get to the Moon. Yet astronomy too has its uses. And so, similarly, has a *wertfrei* Social Cosmology.

Thus, while, where fitting, this subject will seek to be scientific, where appropriate, it will remain frankly philosophical. Linguistic analysis, philosophical anthropology, and, in general, the philosophy of the social sciences—these are all of them lines of intellectual enterprise which the teacher, at least, of Social Cosmology must see as his own. For how without them can he hope to provide the student with the kind of road-map that he requires?

Not by Figures Alone

Will the travel-agency then say nothing whatever about the probable weather? Like the rest of us, the teacher too will have his forebodings and his hopes. But to hope for fine weather is not to foreshadow its coming. In the matter of forecasting, the proof of the product is in the sequel. If, whether in terms of esoterically meteorological concepts or of the notions of the man in the street, and whether or not with a computor for doing the sums, the deliverances of the weather bureau are often enough borne out by the morrow's conditions, then the place will be earning its keep. If, comparably, business forecasting gives degrees of probability that are worth their price, then more scope, we shall say, to its exponents. But even had those gentlemen more to show than yet they have, it would still be appropriate to keep an open mind on the likelihood of there coming to be developed anything analogous for probing the possible future of international affairs. (An open mind: not, that is, a mind prematurely closed against it.) There are, it is true, games and games. But has anyone successfully employed a computor for his operations in the pools? Those at any rate who see the similarities between Diplomatics and, for instance, cricket may need a lot of convincing that the outcome of an impending 'Berlin' showdown ought by scientific methods to be already even only approximately predictable, when the summit season is still only about to begin.

Time for a Break

Some of which may make this new-fangled subject sound not a little alarming—a discipline indeed! And perhaps rather grim. Has then the student to abjure altogether his modicum of reasonable relaxation, to forgo all kindly commerce with those, his friends, whose furrows run in other fields? Not so. A man first, a scientist only incidentally, let him live life at least to the two-thirds full, part humanly social, part, but part only, analytically austere. In situations where, among those otherwise biologically mature, the combustibilities of world politics are being ventilated as in terms of fools and knaves,[1] he may, with good-humoured abandon and mock-irresponsibility, acquiesce, and even share, in the general punt-about, reserving for worthier opportunities such shafts of insight as may have resulted from his broodings on things as they so very much less simply are. His warrant for his so

---

[1] One recalls the air with which, at such a session, someone by no means a nobody dismissed a state of international tension as due simply to the fact of Mr. John Foster Dulles being 'just an awfully stupid man!'

condescending will be his recognition that some topics are too serious for serious treatment in a not sufficiently serious vein. He cannot be the paragon of sobriety all the time. His poise and personality might be the worse of it if he were. But at the proper moments, in the right company, and on suitable issues, he will be only too prompt to expose his whole sociocosmological hand. For so may he hope to elicit the reactions of those who, in other caps and from other angles, can shock him into the further thinking that his interpretations require.

Things to be Thinking About

Further thinking, for that after all is what, on the world's great issues, is, as always, needed today. Given that nine out of ten are by commitment to parochial perspectives precluded from even aspiring to the global vision of affairs, it is all the more incumbent on the social cosmologist, pretentious, on his part, though it may seem, to pursue as if on everyone's behalf his explorings of social outer space. And, since in the nature of things he must do this so largely on his own, he had better be fully aware of just what it is that he is at. In particular he should be mindful of how his inquiries may differ from those of many others. Only a bold man would, as from the outside, assume to say what in detail Political Science must presumably be about; and it will not be attempted here. But, if of, say, economics it can with propriety be stated that it focuses on a particular aspect of life among men, then of International Relations it has by contrast to be insisted that its concern is with something more. As we have seen, its business is with the totality, and not with an aspect merely, of life among the states. And thinking about life in its wholeness, whether the life of states or of men, calls for a multiangular approach not needed for the study of an aspect only, even of the life of men. And the thinking which social cosmology requires is multi-disciplinary too. For it must needs consider, in their respective idioms, questions that variously arise on the several analytically distinguishable aspects of the single subject-matter of its concern. And with respect, moreover, to its different levels.

'*I Tell You, It's Only a Game!*'

The cosmologist must indeed be conscious of the independence and interdependence of the various levels, and relate his thinking to them all. He will be aware too, even within himself, of the disharmonies that declare themselves between man as moralist, as analyst and as politician; and not ask it of anyone that, in his capacity as politician, he be other than partisan. He will know too that, when acting as a functionary or in a ministerial office, man is not the Kierkegaardian individual: but essentially the rolesman, the wheel in an organisational machine; that that machine, the state, exists to serve a purpose, its own survival: that the conditions of its existence, though dubbed the international 'anarchy', are not those typical of the jungle, but rather of a kind of quasi-game; that the prize this is played for is that very survival for the purpose of which the state exists; and that, even if in theory a player might elect to leave the field, he could not at the same time hope to win; nor, while remaining within the game, can he think to play it save as in subjection to the rules. And he will appreciate that, though many may be in a game together in ostensible obedience to the self-same rules, that need not mean that this must be in the light of the same illusions. Nor will he expect it of others that they abjure their particular illusions merely because they are unable in an argument to convince him of their truth. Meanwhile, what of his own?

'. . . *He Remains an English Man!*'

It is neither to be expected nor desired of social cosmology that it dispossess the student of his illusions, or, in particular, of his political 'faith'. Rather may it be hoped that it do not. What however it may well do is reveal to him what sort of thing, when held without humour, a political faith can be. It may, that is, illuminate for him the difference between political, and other kinds of creeds, showing him that, although none of them can in the last analysis be rationally authenticated, politics without their credal foundations would be like a play without a plot. It can help him to adjust his own position to the extent of seeing as itself but a myth the idea that his myths have been anything more than myths. What, for instance, does anyone take to be the logical status of his 'knowledge' that universal suffrage is a good thing? Myth he will see to have the dual function of rendering more prehensible and of making assimilable, an element of dogma less easily internalised in its primal form. The realisation that myth must often have resulted, intendedly, in illusion should not seriously upset him, since it is so largely by some of their illusions that the drabness of men's lives is sometimes in a measure redeemed. For a people collectively to have a good conceit of itself may for instance be of value, however tenuous the basis for its comforting beliefs.

But to concede that an illusion may be beneficent is not to say that it ought not to be shown up. Before the academic débutant can blossom into a demographer he must have overhauled his early understandings on the habits of the stork. Social cosmology, however, will authorise the student to re-accommodate his mere beliefs even after seeing them for what they are—and this (*a*) because this is so expedient, and (*b*) because it is so congenial. For it should reveal to him that myth is of the stuff of life—as indispensable to politics as is water to a shoal of fish. Nevertheless, as necessary to his profounder appreciation of things political, he will have accepted the relative disinflation of his own social image, and the zoological reduction, if one may so put it, of his sacred herd.

Then, however, having so to say domesticated his early vision, let him relapse into living along with what is left of it for such aid as it still may afford him, and with such gusto as he can. For so will he avoid the stultifications of fanaticism on the one hand and of a pale non-alignment on the other. And so incidentally will he vindicate, if only by implication, the virtue, secularly speaking, in an age of evaporating values, of sophisticated realism as an attitude to life.

INDEX

ACCULTURATION, 83 ff.
adolescent scepticism, 56
Afrikaner people, 175
'agitation', see 'propaganda' and 'agitation'
ambivalence, 59, 119, 188
analogies, 151–2, 207
Anthropology, see Social Anthropology
'anti' cults and movements, 93
appreciation, see sociology of appreciation
approaches, 6, 115, 210
Aristotle, 79, 123
assumptions, 9, 30, 32, 108, 135, 160
Atlantic Community, 43, 67
Austin, John, 50, 193, 193 fn.
authority, 141, 143, 147

balance of sympathies, 184, 188–9, 191
Balfour, the Earl of, 64
banks, 23–4, 105
Barker, Sir Ernest, 206
battle fleet, see fighting ships
beliefs, 32, **171** ff., 216
binding force of law, **103**, **133**, 160
binocularity, 190
bluebottle, 119
Borden, Sir Robert, 163 fn.
Boulding, Kenneth, 75, 108, 180
Brierly, J. L., 156
brotherhood, 67, 168–9, 177
Butterfield, Herbert, 82

calculating machine, 48, 150
Camus, Albert, 172
category mistake, 67, 98, 105 ff.
ceremonial, 128
Chamberlain, Neville, 97, 167
Charter of the United Nations, 74, **154** ff.
Christendom, 168
Christianity, 54, 120
Christmas, 29, 67, 134, 153, 158
Churchill, Sir Winston, 99, 157
class
  social, 18, 171
  statistical, 18
clubs, 151, 153
collectivism, 39
Columbus, Christopher, 4
committees, 38, 46–7, 53
communal
  feeling, 70, 77
  mentality, 52, 97
  mode of thought, 82
  mythology, 93
  opinion, **90**, 92, 143, 150, 170, 179, 186
  standpoint, 49, 52, 90, 116, 146
  will to resist, 72
  willing, **46**, 51, **53**, 77

community, 67, 86, **176** ff.
compliance, 112, 193
conformity, 86, 186
conjuring, 29
connoisseurship, **6**, 150, 182, **194–5**, **202** ff.
'consciousness' and 'spontaneity', 154, 187
constellation, 14, 18, 25
constitution, 110, 166
convention, 12, 56, 58, **62**, 107, 128, **134**, 165, 173, 176
convictions, 118, 180
cosmology, see social cosmology
cosmos, see social cosmos
countries, **35**, 54, 73, 76
Covenant of the League of Nations, 154 ff.
Coward, Noel, 70
creeds and matters credal, 44, 135, **171** ff.
Cromwell, Oliver, 125
cultures and sub-cultures, 84 ff., 90, **95**, **98**, **171**, 174–5
curricula, see university curricula

Daniel, 145–6
Dante, 196
Decatur, Stephen, 146
decisions and decision-making, 45–6, 60
definitions, 12, 126
de Gaulle, President, 6, 148
descriptive Economics, see Economics, descriptive
Deutsch, Karl, 208
Devil, the, 13, 17
diplomacy, 120, 168, 187
Diplomatics, 57, 122, **182–3**, 202, 213
diplomatic theory, see theory, diplomatic
disarmament proposals, 192
distinctions, 64, 74, 171
doctrine, **33**, 55, 61–2, 91, **94**, 104 ff., 141, 186
dogma, 32, 110, 152, **173**
doxa, 117
dualisms, 29, 100, 122
Dulles, John Foster, 191, 213 fn.
Dumbarton Oaks Conference, 154

Economics
  descriptive, 197
  and economic theory, 131, 202, 204
educatedness, 86, 194, 197
Eiconics and Eirenics, 75
Eisenhower, President, 68–9, 188
elections and electorate, 50, 60
empathy, 205, 212
England, 118
episteme, 118

INDEX

'Ernie', 149
erosion of sovereignty, *see* sovereignty
essences and essentialism, 32 ff.
ethical issues, 140

faith, 92, 128, 172 ff.
Fascism, 174
federation, 167
fiction, 24, 104
fighting ships, 40
folklore and mythology, 49, **57**, **60–1**, 85, **93**, 127, 135, 162 ff., 174
forecasting, 130
France, 6, 31, 35, 65, 148, 150
friendship, 31

games and quasi-games, 17, 29, 32, 45, 75, **107**, 111–12, 131, 160, **164–5**, 173, 196, 202, 207, 215
Gemeinschaft, 176–7, 179
general will, 91, 173
Germans and Germany, 61, 119, 191
Gesellschaft, 176–7
Global Social Dynamics, 201, 210
global Sociology, 209
government, 21, 52, 182 ff.
Great Bear, the, 18
Greece, 206
group thinking, *see* thinking

Hague Court, 161
Hamlet, 5, 152
historians, 7, 55 ff.
Hitler, Adolf, 82, 91, 97, 112
holism, 38–9, 47, 50
homo ludens, 164
horse, pantomime, *see* pantomime horse
hypostatisation, 8, 36, 165

illiteracy, political, *see* political illiteracy
I.L.O., 152
image, 2, 4, 9, 11, 16, 19, 22, **40**, 57, 75, 93, 108, **148**, 150, 162, 165, 174, 179–80, **189**, 191
impressions and impressionism, 3, 55–6, 74
imputation, **18–19**, 26, 31, 36, 38, 48, 52, 56, 90, 102
'in effect', 15–16, 23
individualism, 38–9
influence, 141, 147, 182, 191
'inner-directedness' and 'other-directedness', 89
'inquisitive' and 'deliberative' questions, 124
International
 Law, 7, 61, **100** ff., 159, 167, 200
 Politics, 202
 Relations, 125, 182, **196–7**, 200 ff., 206, 211, 214
Israel, **40**

Jenks, C. **Wil**fred, 178
Jesuits, 9
judgment, 79, 85, 145, 161
justice, 13, 96

Kaplan, Morton, 208
Khrushchev, Nikita, 69, 92, 188, 192–3

kindergarten of peace, 163
knowledge-by-acquaintance, 196, 205, 208
Kremlin, 194

Lauder, Sir Harry, 189
law, *see* International Law
leaders and leadership, 82, 179, 186–7
leagues of nations, 75, 155–6
Lenin, Vladimir I., 136–7, 170
lenses, 2, 16, 190, 201
levels, 34, 41, 61, 65, 69, 75, 84, 170, 183
Litvinov, Maxim, 193
Lloyd George, David, 126
Lodge, Senator Henry Cabot, Jnr., 92
London, 26, 175, 203
Lunik II, 191

Macmillan, Harold, 69
make-believe, 28, 43, 51, 107
Malinowski, Bronislaw, 204 ff.
maps, 3–4, 203, 212
Marx, Karl, 82, 84, 92, 108, 124, 135, 165, 171, 210
Marxism, 137–8
mentality, 81, **97**, 119, 171
Meta-diplomatics, x, 209
metaphor and the metaphorical, 2, 26, **40**, **43**, 56 ff., 73, 129, **151**
methodological essentialism, *see* essentialism
methodological individualism, *see* individualism
might as opposed to right, 147
Milan, 174
milieu, 27, 183, 202
Mirabeau, 84
mistake, *see* category mistake
Moore, G. E., 58
moral super-state, 142
morals and moral pressure, 140 ff.
Moscow, 187, 191, 193
Mother Hubbard, 30–1
mysticism and mystiques, **53**, 91, 135, 150, 174
myth, **24**, 43, 82, 138, **162**, **174**, 180, 215
mythology, *see* folklore and mythology

names, 77
nation, 11–12, 14 ff.
nationalism, 98, 169, 174
N.A.T.O., 152
Nazis, 93, 191
Nelson, Lord, 57
nominalism, 38, 65
norms, 115, 160
notion of the nation, 13
notional
 behaviour, 6
 bone, 30
 community, 177
 entities, 23, 32, 41, 49, 57
 line, 49
 persons, 8, 22 ff., 35, 142, 177
 responsibility, 64
 society, 30
 world, 27, 33, 41, 166, 177

INDEX

obedience, 114, 193
Oder–Neisse Line, 95
Old Testament, 40
Olivier, Sir Laurence, 29
Omar Khayyam, 8
oneness, *see* unity
opinion, 50, 89, 144
organisations, **23**, 66, 79, **84**, 121, 147, 153, 176
orthodoxy, 24, **110**, 112, 152
'other-directedness', *see* 'inner-directedness' and 'other-directedness'
'oughtness', 114, 126

Palestine, 175
pantomime horse, 51, 73–4
partisanship, 80, 82, 95, **120–1**
party line, 90
Pascal, Blaise, 4
peoples, 7–8, 23, 42, 45, 67, 72, 74, 82
pep-talks, 185
personality and personification, **26**, 39, 42, **58, 102**
persons, 8, **22, 25, 35, 42**, 48, 61–2, **166**
perspectives, 81, 114
Phillimore Committee, 159
philosophical inquiries, 13, 211–12
Plato, 87, 117
plausibilities, 125
political illiteracy, 74, 100, **184**, 187, 191
Political Science, 182, 214
politics, 187
ponds, 34, **80**, 87, 180
'powers', 190
prejudice, *see* race prejudice
pressure, 141–2, 147
pressure groups, 79
prevalence, social, *see* social prevalence
pride, 198
primitive impressionism, *see* impressionism
princes, 81, 168
processes, 22, 45, 47–8, 143, 162
'propaganda' and 'agitation', 187
psychology, *see* Social Psychology
Public Administration, 182
'publics', 84, 92, 170, 188

quasi-games, *see* games and quasi-games
quasi-*Gemeinschaft*, *see Gemeinschaft* and quasi-*Gemeinschaft*
quasi-Sociology, 209
Queen Bess, 126
Quincy Wright, 208

race, 20, 175
race prejudice, 20
realism and sophisticated realism, **31, 35, 46**, 55, 216
reality, 11, 15, 18
reality-thinking, *see* thinking
reductionism, 41, 43, 65
responsibility, 47, 49, 64
right–wrong antithesis, 117, 123, 147
roles and rolesmanship, **5–6**, 69, 95, 115, **120–1**

Sandhurst, Royal Military Academy, 197
San Francisco, 74

Santa Claus, 134–5
Sartre, Jean-Paul, 52
scepticism, *see* adolescent scepticism
science and scientific, 125, 211
scruples, 115, **121–2**, 184
Second Commandment, the, 119
set-ups, 22, 32
Snyder, Richard, 208
social
  anthropology, 205, 211
  control, 146
  cosmology, **1**, 26, 58, **77**, 80, 87, 95, 162, 170, **209, 211–12, 214** ff.
  cosmos, 1, **4, 5, 7**, 9, 14, **78**, 85, **167**, 176, 203
  doctrine, 33, 61
  dogma, 110
  dynamics, *see* Global Social Dynamics
  organisation, 23
  prevalence, 11, **18** ff., 27, 58, 146
  psychology, 85, 92, 133, 180, 193
  technology, 76
  theory, 58
  topography, *see* Topography and Social Topography
  universe, 16, **78**, 166, **201**, 203
  wholes, 13, 15, 22
  worlds, 27, 183
society and international society, 8, **27**, **30, 41** ff., 73, 77, 80, **103**, 106, 113, 157, **165, 168–9, 176**, 205, 209
sociology
  of appreciation, 29, **36**, 61, **79, 81**, 85, 91, 93, 95, 121, 213
  of knowledge, 77, 88
solidarity, 20, 169–70, 176 ff.
sophisticated realism, *see* realism and sophisticated realism
Sorel, Georges, 3
sovereignty, 45, 49, **102**, 143, 161, **166** ff., 190
  erosion of, 167
'spontaneity', *see* 'consciousness' and 'spontaneity'
Sprout, Harold and Margaret, 208
standing, 190
states, 6, 11, **21** ff., **35, 41–2**, 59–60, 69, **75–6**, 82, 147, 165, 190
stature, 141, 190
status, 17, 27, 37, 79, 103, 106, 146, 178, 190
Strategics, 122, 201
structure of society, 70–1, **78, 168, 190**, 209
'stuff', 86, 93
sub-cultures, *see* cultures and sub-cultures
sunrise, 15, 25, 31
super-state, *see* moral super-state
Switzerland, women of, 177, 180
sympathies, *see* balance of sympathies
system, the multi-state, **34**, 120, 168

teaching, 205
team, 13–14, 186
term of art, 12, 67
The Times, 42–3, 172
theory
  and theories, **17–18**, 22, **26, 29**, 31, 42, **55**, 58, 62

theory (*contd.*)
  constitutional, 49
  diplomatic, 15, **42**, **58**, 61, **132**
  official, 29, **31**, 42, 60, 108, 163
  of game, 32
  of the occasion, 29, 51–2
thinking, 85
  collective, 87
  conventional, 56
  economic, 131
  group, 85, 93–4
  legal, 128
  official, 24, 91, 158
  part-time, 198
  reality-, 86, 93, 135–6, 162
  social and socio-cultural, 27, 128, 132–3
  socio-psychological, 133
thinking caps, 32, 35, 55, 70, 83, **200**
tools, 4, 67, 200, 202, 204, 206
Topography and Social Topography, x
Treaty of Versailles, 154 fn.

unity, 16, **18**, 23, 38, 48, 82, 134, 186, 193
universe, *see* social universe
university curricula, 1–2, 30
U.N.O., 50, 65, **142** ff., 153, 192

values, 173 ff.
Vattel, Emmerich, 103

Voegelin, Eric, 79
Volk, the German, 91, 97
Vyshinsky, Andrei, 189

Waltz, Kenneth, 75
Waterloo, battle of, 124, 194
Wells, H. G., 169
will, 26, 45
  of Parliament, 142
  see also general will
willing, *see* communal willing
Willkie, Wendell, 192
Wilson, President Woodrow, 154 ff.
world and worlds, **5**, 25 ff., **33**, **35**, **41**, 98, 109, 114, 177, 200
  of dreams, 27
  of fact, 27, 35
  of fiction, 27, 44, 104
  of law, 27, 35, 179
  of notions, 27
  possible, 181
  social, 183
World Affairs, 209
world-awareness, 197
world community, 176 ff.
world opinion, 50, 144 ff.

Zimmern, Sir Alfred, 206